THE ART OF CENTURIES

STEVE JAMES

BANTAM BOOKS

LONDON • TORONTO • SYDNEY • AUCKLAND • JOHANNESBURG

TRANSWORLD PUBLISHERS
61–63 Uxbridge Road, London W5 5SA
www.penguin.co.uk

Transworld is part of the Penguin Random House group of companies
whose addresses can be found at global.penguinrandomhouse.com

First published in Great Britain in 2015 by Bantam Press
an imprint of Transworld Publishers
Bantam edition published 2016

A CIP catalogue record for this book
is available from the British Library.

ISBN
9780857502421

Typeset in Times New Roman by Falcon Oast Graphic Art Ltd.
Printed and bound by Clays Ltd, Bungay, Suffolk.

Penguin Random House is committed to a sustainable
future for our business, our readers and our planet. This book is made
from Forest Stewardship Council® certified paper.

1 3 5 7 9 10 8 6 4 2

Acclaim for *The Art of Centuries*:

'Combines anecdote and insight drawn from personal experience into a fine book on the art of batsmanship'
Guardian, Books of the Year

'A beguiling insight into the trials, tribulations and triumphs of life as a batsman'
Lawrence Booth, editor of *Wisden*

'I love the way Steve James writes about cricket, his endless curiosity and generosity. *The Art of Centuries* distils a lifetime's wisdom, joy and frustration – a three-figure literary innings'
Gideon Haigh

'Excellent'
Mike Atherton, *The Times*

'A delight . . . It is always fun to read Steve's work. His previous book *The Plan* was a terrific breakdown of how Duncan Fletcher and Andy Flower took England to the top during their time as head coach. This new book has a nice, light, often discursive touch to it, and I like discursive, that delightful pathway into digression where one memory prompts another'
Mike Selvey, *Guardian*

'Leave a copy in the England dressing room'
Weekend Sport

www.penguin.co.uk

Steve James has been writing about cricket and rugby for the *Daily Telegraph* and the *Sunday Telegraph* for more than ten years.

He read Classics at Swansea University before becoming a postgraduate at Cambridge, where his first Blue was in the side captained by Mike Atherton. He played his county cricket with Glamorgan for eighteen years, scoring nearly 16,000 runs at an average of over 40, and captaining them for three seasons, winning a National League trophy in 2002, before retiring due to injury.

In 1997 James helped Glamorgan to win the county championship for the first time in nearly thirty years and was named the Professional Cricketers' Association Player of the Year. He still holds the record for the highest score by a Glamorgan batsman (309 not out against Sussex at Colwyn Bay in 2000) and also won two caps for England.

Also by Steve James

Third Man to Fatty's Leg: An Autobiography

Ashes Regained (*with Duncan Fletcher*)

Behind the Shades (*with Duncan Fletcher*)

The Plan: How Fletcher and
Flower Transformed English Cricket

Refuse to be Denied (*with Sam Warburton*)

Lions Triumphant (*with Sam Warburton*)

The Gloves Are Off (*with Matt Prior*)

To Mum and Dad
I miss you both terribly

Contents

Contents

Acknowledgements

A confession first: this book was not initially my idea, so many
thanks to my publisher, Giles Elliott of Transworld, for providing
that, in such detail too, and also for his unstinting support and
guidance throughout. Thanks also to David Luxton of DLA for
his support of the project and his advice, especially during its
completion.

Thank you too to Adam Sills, Andrew Fifield and everyone
else at the *Telegraph* for allowing me to complete this long project
alongside my main job.

I must make special thanks to Benedict Bermange, Sky Sports'
statistician, whose help was invaluable in a book where statistics
have to have a certain prominence. He is undoubtedly the best in
that business.

Thank you to those people I interviewed: Graham Gooch,
Andy Flower, Mike Atherton, Andrew Strauss, Murray Goodwin,
Matthew Maynard, Nathan Leamon, Kirk Russell, Ian Thomas,
Mike Powell, Adrian Dale and Gareth Rees.

And also to others who have helped in some way or other: Huw
Bevan, Douglas Henderson, Gideon Haigh, Peter Hayter, Ed Smith,
David Parry, Scyld Berry, David Morgan and Peter Mitchell.

Finally, thank you to my family, wife Jane and children Bethan and Rhys, for their patience and love. This is my eighth book and the commitment required never relents. I hope they understand.

Introduction:
The First Century

I'd forgotten my socks. This was important. I'd forgotten the grey marl socks that I'd been told all cricketers had to wear. I had my vest, my Viyella shirt and my cream flannels all packed into my leather bag, but I did not have my socks.

My father was a stalwart club cricketer deeply imbued with the traditions and habits of the game. For many a long year he had already stressed that in order to become what he termed 'a proper cricketer' one had to look like 'a proper cricketer'.

And so the short white socks used for PE lessons? No chance. Normal grey school socks? Sacrilege.

No, this 12-year-old had to get hold of his proper cricket socks if he was to perform on the cricket field that sunny summer afternoon many years ago in 1980.

It was a Saturday, and the usual morning lessons at Monmouth School were taking place. But at breaktime there was sufficient time to slip just outside the school to the phone box (mobile phones were still a very distant thought, of course) to call Peter James Sports in Lydney.

'Hello,' came the answer. In went the coin. 'Dad, it's me,' I said.

'Hello, my son,' he said, as he always would, even if there was some surprise in hearing my voice at this time.

'I've got a problem,' I said. 'I've forgotten my socks.'

'You silly bugger,' he replied. He knew that there was no option here. There was no arguing. He knew that I had to have those socks.

'You're playing at Brightlands, aren't you? I'll meet you there,' he said.

Brightlands School no longer exists, but it was situated in the village of Newnham in Gloucestershire, on the west side of the River Severn. The cricket field is still used by the village team. If you drive from my hometown of Lydney on the A48 towards Gloucester, it is up on the left as the road takes a straight stretch alongside the river into the next village of Broadoak.

Every time I take that road, I think the same thing: 'This is where it all began.' For it was there on that day in 1980 that I scored my first century.

My dad was there at Brightlands when we arrived. He had those socks. He then lingered a while until it was ascertained that we were batting. He decided to stay a bit longer. My mother could tend the shop for a while. I was hardly going to bat all afternoon. I had never done that before.

Well, not before that day anyway. It was a declaration match, and by the time the tea interval was called, I was 97 not out.

There was now a dilemma. It was, of course, usual for the declaration to take place there and then, but in this instance it was decided that we should go back out in order to allow me to score my first century.

I must admit that I was very uneasy about this, even more so when I overheard a few of my opponents' parents complaining about it.

But out I went, hitting the four required and in doing so

changing my life for ever. My father, quite an influence upon my career as you may have already gathered, had always said that any batsman wishing to be recognized at any level had to score hundreds, lots of them, and big ones if possible.

Sadly he passed away in February 2014 before I completed this book, just as my mother had in 2011 before I had finished a previous book, *The Plan*, about the influence of the Zimbabwean coaches, Duncan Fletcher and Andy Flower, upon the England team between 1999 and 2011.

But when beginning this book, I was able to ask my father about this importance of scoring centuries. 'I always told you that,' he said. 'It's bloody true, it always will be.'

My father was actually a bowler, who bowled off-cutters in the style of the great Glamorgan bowler Don Shepherd, and was a specialist No. 11 batsman, who was quite proud of the fact that he once made 25 consecutive ducks, 11 of them being first-ballers. That statistic was recalled, to much laughter, during his funeral service. But he knew his cricket, and he knew what was required of a batsman.

Just for confirmation, let's look at the opinion of a rather more reliable batsman. At the beginning of the 1962 season, Yorkshire's second-team captain, former batsman and future scorer, Ted Lester, gave Geoffrey Boycott some advice. 'If you get the chance, score centuries,' he said.

Simple advice to any batsman, and very obvious. But as Boycott says: 'It coloured my approach to batting. Good scores are valuable but centuries stick in the mind. There are influential people who might not notice a good innings of 60 or 70 but they will react if you get a hundred. The difference between a score in the 90s and a century is often reflected as the difference between failure and success. It may be illogical but in cricket a century has its own magic.'

I had found my first bit of cricketing magic that day in 1980. I had begun a fascination, maybe even an obsession, that held sway from that moment until the end of a nigh-on 20-year career as a professional cricketer in 2003.

As Nathan Leamon, England's team analyst appointed under Flower and a former Cambridge University mathematician, says: 'I've always thought that the number of hundreds scored is probably the best all-round measure of a batsman's career. If you play enough games you will make a large number of runs. Averages don't always tell the whole story, particularly over a short career. The number of hundreds is a good measure of excellence and longevity.'

Every night before he batted, the great Australian batsman Ricky Ponting would make a checklist of what he needed to do the next day in the middle.

'Watch the ball. Play straight. Loud calls. Be patient. Be positive in attack and defence. Bat for a long time,' he would write, and they are all sound pieces of advice for any batsman worth his salt.

Then next he would write: 'Make 100.'

I'm not sure I could ever have written that down as a goal. Even thinking about a century early in an innings was a non-starter for one like me so lacking in confidence, but we shall come to the intricacies of cricket's mind games later.

But there can be no doubt that a century truly is special. It has always had special resonance in all walks of life. It always signifies a mark of tangible achievement.

When you reach 100 years of age, the Queen sends you a telegram; when you reach a century in a cricket match, the crowd applauds you warmly to recognize the milestone. Most of the opposition usually do too. You rarely see such mid-match generosity from the opposition in any other sport. That in itself tells a tale of a century's significance.

Soon after making that first century, I made another, much bigger one, scoring 149 not out for Gloucestershire Under 13s against Herefordshire at Ross-on-Wye. I distinctly recall returning to the cricket club at Lydney and being asked how many I had scored that day. Club legend Rob 'Basher' Brain, who scored over 30,000 runs for Lydney, with at least 30-odd centuries, was there and he said to me: 'That is a seriously big score, you know. Well done.' Chuffed? Too right.

Recently Brain wrote a book, entitled *Rich Wine Untold* (a phrase from Ivor Novello's patriotic song 'Rose of England'), about his cricketing life, and in it he commented: 'Those who say it is no big deal making a century do not know what they are on about and certainly do not appreciate what it means for the player who only does it once and will never forget it.'

It does not matter what the level, the feeling is still the same. As the former England captain Andrew Strauss says: 'Scoring an international century is incredibly hard to do. You are very fortunate if you have 20 days in a career when you go to bed at night with the warm afterglow of scoring an international century.'

Not everyone can be like the Australian Mark Waugh, who nonchalantly returned to the Australian dressing room having made a century on Test debut to say: 'I should have been playing for years!'

I love the stories of those who have only scored one century, of their pride and delight at becoming members of 'the club'.

Without wishing to denigrate the cricketing prowess of those who sit there, some of the best have come from those I have sat with in various press boxes since retirement from playing.

Take Peter 'Reggie' Hayter, the larger-than-life former correspondent for the *Mail on Sunday* and now performing that role for the *Cricket Paper*. He once scored a hundred for the Fleet Street Strollers team at the beautiful Valley of Rocks ground, against Lynton and Lynmouth in North Devon.

Hayter bought every postcard from the local shop so that he could send news of his achievement to all of his many friends. Some time soon afterwards he was at Lord's reporting on a match. He was busy writing some of the postcards when a fellow approached him. It was Geoffrey Boycott.

'What are you up to, Reggie?' enquired the great batsman. Hayter explained, so Boycott took one of the postcards from the pile. On it he wrote: 'Well done, Reggie, only 150 to go!'

For the uninitiated, Boycott made 151 first-class centuries. It is, of course, 150 to go for Hayter, and always will be.

In 2013 Gideon Haigh made his first century. To me Haigh is the greatest living cricket writer. He is also a fanatical club cricketer with his beloved South Yarra side in Melbourne, about whom he once wrote a wholly diverting diary called *Many a Slip*. As his current blog, called 'Cuts and Glances', says in excellent summation: 'Gideon Haigh has been a club cricketer since he was nine and a journalist since he was 18. He is the author of 30 books, 20 of them about cricket.'

Haigh was born in England and raised in Australia, but his first journey into three figures came in England, playing for Old Sawbuttkeane, a wandering team founded by Simon Lister, a radio producer and cricket writer, against his old club, Frieth CC in Buckinghamshire.

I spoke to Haigh about this during the 2013 Ashes in England, and he said he would tell me all about the century. Due to my decreasing amounts of cricket writing that summer, as I gradually became the *Sunday Telegraph*'s rugby union correspondent, we never did get to talk about it at length face-to-face, but, upon arriving back in Australia, Haigh duly kept his promise and emailed me with all the details.

'Anyway, the long and the short is that I made 106 not out off about 90 balls,' he wrote. 'My opening partner Chris also made what turned out to be his first century, which surprised me, because he can actually play, and I can't really.

'The closest I had come before was a 92 I'd made for the Yarras a couple of years ago – first in, last out, batted all day in hellish heat on a huge, slow field. Batting ugly incarnate. It didn't really bother me missing out – I had a slog with number 11 in, and didn't actually know how many I was. But afterwards I did think: "I wonder if that's as close as I will come?" It didn't bug me. In some respects it rather suited my self-perception: huge, unceasing efforts trending towards futility.

'I can't say it was a great century. It was a pretty ordinary attack, and I struggled to adapt to the slow wicket. I was feeling embarrassed by my lack of progress when on about 20 I suddenly nailed an on-drive off their only bowler of any pace. Just a push. Knew it was four. After that it was easy. I was even able to enjoy it. Beautiful day, lovely ground, good partner, peachy bat (given to me by Ed Cowan [the Australia opener with whom Haigh has developed a close friendship, helping Cowan write an excellent diary of a season, *In the Firing Line*, in 2011]), my wife and three-year-old daughter watching. Of course, when I reached the milestone, I turned around to give them a wave, and they were playing knock knock games on the toilet door of the little pavilion.'

Haigh's reflections on that first century were, for me, particularly interesting. He was rather perplexed by the fuss for a start. 'I think it's too late for me to feel particularly blissed out,' he wrote. 'But when word of the innings got back to some Aussie teammates on Twitter I was surprised at how excited they were for me – wanted to know about it, wanted to hear how I reached it, told me I'd always looked like a guy who should get hundreds, and that I'd get more. Really? That's what you thought?'

I was rather like that when I scored my first century. Rather more than that, if the truth be told. I was embarrassed, not least because it was the custom at Monmouth at the time for any centurion to be presented with a new bat.

That would happen at the full school assembly on the Monday morning after the achievement. The thought of walking up to receive this award from the headmaster scared me stiff, a feeling exacerbated by the fact that my day-boys' house, Hereford, sat at the back of the school hall. I had to make my very self-conscious way right from the back of the hall!

On that Monday morning in 1980 I so wished that I had only made 99, or that we had declared at tea when I was on 97. My love for centuries had an uneasy beginning, you see. I knew their importance, of course, but shyness was a much stronger emotion back then.

Of the many people I interviewed for this book, the one who seemed most shocked at the reaction to his first century was Murray Goodwin, the former Zimbabwe Test batsman. He retired in 2014, after two seasons with Glamorgan, and had previously had a hugely successful career with Sussex, as well as playing for Western Australia, having emigrated to Australia from Zimbabwe when he was 13 years old.

At the start of the 2014 season, he had made 71 first-class centuries, more than anyone still playing that form of the game, with the West Indian Shivnarine Chanderpaul next with 69 and Australia's Chris Rogers not far behind him on 66. Unfortunately Goodwin could not add to his tally during the 2014 county season; nor could Chanderpaul, but Rogers did, making three more centuries to equal Chanderpaul with 69.

At the start of the 2014 season the highest England-qualified batsmen were Kent's Rob Key and Somerset's Marcus Trescothick, with 51 each. By the season's end Key had 52 and Trescothick 55.

Goodwin was '10 or 11' when he made his first century, at Groombridge Primary School in Harare. But he had been play-ing organized cricket since the age of seven for the school's Colts side, playing against boys sometimes three years older than himself. And he was also playing cricket in the school holidays in the famous 'Eagles' programme run by his father, George, a journalist and keen sportsman.

'I remember all the kids going "That's amazing,"' Goodwin says. 'But I was always lucky because I had the opportunity of batting up the order, and we were playing 35- and 40-over games at junior school.'

Goodwin's son Jayden also made his first hundred at the age of 10. He made it in a 30-over festival match in Sussex in 2012, when his father was having something of a horror season with the county, resulting in his surprising release after making more than 14,500 first-class runs for them, with 48 centuries.

'He said to me: "Dad, I've scored more runs than you,"' says Goodwin senior. 'I was obviously irritated – that was the start of the downfall of my Sussex career. They ended up releasing me because my son was scoring more runs!'

For Jayden Goodwin the chance to score a century had been the single most important thing. In Australia he had always been forced to retire having faced a certain number of balls. 'It was a massive thing for him to be able to bat and not retire,' says his father. 'It was hugely important for him not just being able to score a hundred but a fifty as well. All the kids are saying: "I wish I could get a fifty."'

Even though we had plenty of time to do so, there never seemed to be too many centuries scored when I was young. Maybe the memory plays tricks. Certainly double centuries were never heard of, not even at school first-eleven level.

So I contacted Douglas Henderson, who now collates the schools cricket records for the *Wisden Cricketers' Almanack*. He confirmed that there had indeed been an increase in the number of centuries scored at schoolboy level.

Henderson suggested a number of reasons, not least the fact that more and more schools cricket is now limited-overs rather than declaration-based. There may be less time, but having to use five bowlers is a handicap. Most school sides do not have five decent enough bowlers.

It is a bit like that in club cricket too. And I know that was a huge gripe of my father's, who said that he would have hated playing in today's leagues because he was only just warming up after 10 overs. He would not have been half the bowler, he reckoned.

There are also England and Wales Cricket Board regulations that permit a bowler under 19 only to bowl seven overs in a spell. Added to that, anecdotal evidence suggests that the pitches have improved across the board.

But the truth is probably that most batsmen can score more quickly these days. The game has changed, and so have the shapes of those playing. Even the schoolboys look like men.

Little wonder that double centuries have become almost commonplace. Looking at the 2008 schools season I see that a certain Jos Buttler once made a score of 227 not out for King's College, Taunton. He has already gone on to do extremely well for Somerset, and for England in Tests and limited-overs cricket, but if evidence was ever required of how batsmanship has altered in recent times, it is surely manifested in Buttler, with his combination of muscularity and invention. Reverse sweeps and scoops over the wicketkeeper were not too prevalent when I was at Monmouth!

Monmouth, though, has had two double centurions. The first double century, in 1992 against Kimbolton, was made by Reuben Spiring, a fine young batsman who went on to play for Worcestershire, but whose career was cruelly cut short by injury. The other was made in 2013 by Jeremy Lawlor, who has played for Glamorgan's second eleven, and whose father, Peter, played one match for Glamorgan against Sri Lanka in 1981.

In fairness, when I was at school, I think the number of centuries was increasing. Without wishing to brag too much, I made four centuries in one particular season and it was soon decided that I should not receive a bat for each of those centuries, as would previously have been the case.

There can be no argument, though, that one's cricket career is never the same once a century has been made.

'I don't know but maybe first hundreds excite us because they're transformational,' says Haigh. 'They change our expectations of ourselves, make us aim a bit higher thereafter. A bit late for me at 47, but maybe I will go into the season at home feeling a little different about my batting.'

Or as Ricky Ponting said after his maiden first-class hundred: 'It wasn't just getting my first hundred, it felt like I had matured as a cricketer and taken my game to another level.'

But there is also the small matter of centuries causing problems, in other words getting in the way of the game. My first had been the classic example, and I remember another similar occasion at Bristol Grammar School, when I had batted far too slowly but was allowed to reach a century I probably did not fully deserve.

On this matter it seemed a good idea to seek the opinion of Mike Atherton, who, of course, as England captain once famously declared in an Ashes Test with Graeme Hick stranded on 98 not out. 'I generally think that the game situation is the most important thing,' Atherton said, rather unsurprisingly. 'Once a hundred is scored and it is secondary to what is trying to be achieved then it should be celebrated. But once a hundred is scored for its own sake, for myself that is giving it undue prominence.'

Atherton cited an example in 2011 when on the final day of a Test against Sri Lanka at Cardiff, England allowed Ian Bell, 98 not out, to reach his 13th Test century before declaring. It had been a rain-affected match, and, with further rain forecast, it looked as if a result was highly improbable. As it was, Bell made his century, and then England bowled out Sri Lanka for just 82, in only 24 overs and four balls, to complete a remarkable victory.

The Hick incident is still much talked about. I have a friend from Lydney called Colin Henderson, who was always a huge Hick fan in his playing days. When I once told him that I had Hick's phone number, I seriously feared for my life when I refused to share it. He still mentions that declaration incident today. Thankfully he's down to doing so only once a week now.

It occurred in the Sydney Test of 1995. And, as it was, the game ended as a draw anyway. But on that fateful fourth afternoon Atherton was looking to push for victory. 'I wanted to have a bowl at them before tea and I wanted to have a bowl at them after tea with the new ball,' he says. 'We all knew where we wanted to be.'

A message had been sent out to Hick, who had joked with its sender, Alec Stewart: 'OK, as long as he [Atherton] doesn't declare on me!'

But that was what Atherton did after Hick had blocked several balls. There was shock and anger. Hick would not speak to Atherton for the rest of the day, and it was a silent, stunned dressing room to which Hick returned. It was little surprise that by the end of the day Australia were 139-0.

'It has been raked over a lot,' says Atherton rather wearily now. 'I regretted the fact that he was obviously upset. But really I delayed it too long. We should have come out earlier.'

Hick, the great underachiever at Test level with just six Test centuries included in his total of 136 first-class hundreds, never did make an Ashes century.

Atherton also mentions another incident, the occasion of Dirk Wellham's only Test century, made against England on debut at the Oval in 1981 (he remains the only Australian to have made centuries on both first-class and Test debuts). Wellham spent 27 anguished minutes on 99, playing and missing regularly and offering a catch to Geoffrey Boycott at mid-off that was dropped.

Captain Kim Hughes was understandably waiting for Wellham to reach his milestone, but in doing so he wasted valuable time on the fourth evening of the Test, as Australia pushed for a declaration and the hope that they might subject England's openers, Boycott and Wayne Larkins, to a testing period of some 30 or 40 minutes' batting before the close.

But as Wellham struggled to his personal landmark – his only century in seven Tests – the light worsened and it was not worth Hughes declaring once he did so, because England's openers would not have had to face a ball. The match was drawn the next day as England survived. And Wellham was dropped for Australia's next Test.

As Atherton says: 'Hundreds are important and should be celebrated in the right context.'

A century at the age of six? That should be celebrated, right? Well, that is how old Hick was when he made his first century. To be precise, he was six years and eight months old when he scored his first century for Banket Primary School in Zimbabwe. 'My dad still has the scorebook,' he wrote in his book *My Early Life* in 1991. 'He tells me I scored twenty-four boundaries out of a total of 102 not out.'

Recently Hick said: 'Don't ask me to remember too much of it. I'm not sure how I managed it, but it really fired my enthusiasm for the game.'

Hick's next century was aged eight, when Trevor Penney, who went on to have a good career with Warwickshire and is now Sri Lanka's fielding coach, was in the opposition. Hick scored 132 not out of a total of 162-0 declared, and one of his drives hit a boundary stone, kicked up and hit Penney's mother, who was doing the scoring, on the shin!

Little wonder then that Hick, who is now Cricket Australia's High Performance Coach at the centre of excellence in Brisbane, is not impressed by the sorts of restrictions faced by Murray Goodwin's son in that country, where retirement after scoring something between 25 and 40 is commonplace. 'I'm very much against that,' he says. 'It's everywhere now.'

But limited opportunities at a young age do not necessarily mean that a batsman cannot progress eventually. Take Graham Gooch, who made 128 first-class centuries, and in first-class cricket made a total of 44,846 runs. He also scored 22,211 runs in List A cricket (any limited-overs cricket apart from Twenty20, which was not played during Gooch's playing career), meaning that no one has ever made more runs in top-flight cricket.

He made his first century aged 'about 14 or 15' for Ilford Colts. 'It was at Brentwood, the old county ground,' he says. 'It was a 20-over game – it was all there was then, after school. I made 120-odd. It was a big thing. At that age getting 30 or 40 was to be quite successful. Getting a hundred was huge.'

Some cricketers develop more quickly than others, but often that is because of the opportunities granted to them at a young age. I know that I was very fortunate that my parents made significant sacrifices to send me to public school at Monmouth, where I encountered excellent facilities both for practice and for playing, a superb fixture list of mostly all-day declaration cricket and top-rate coaching, firstly from 'Sonny' Avery, the former Essex batsman, who scored over 14,000 runs for the county, and then from Graham Burgess, the former all-rounder, who was an integral part of the very successful Somerset side in the 1970s, playing alongside the likes of Ian Botham, Viv Richards and Joel Garner.

One of the bats presented to me at Monmouth School was a cast-off of Richards'. How lucky was I to have that? As lucky as I was that I eventually became a team-mate of Richards' when he finished his career by playing at Glamorgan, and at Canterbury in 1993 famously helping us secure a first ever one-day trophy and the county's first title since 1969.

Mind you, I was not exactly short of cricket kit as a youngster, with my father owning a sports shop. By the time I was showing some sort of promise at the game, it was fairly simple for him to talk nicely to one of the various cricket equipment representatives who came to his shop to ask if they might 'sponsor' me for some items of kit.

I look back now and realize how fortunate I was. I played a lot of cricket in Zimbabwe during my professional career, wintering there regularly, and the battle their young cricketers faced to garner decent equipment did reinforce that point starkly. And that was not just among the cruelly impoverished black lads with whom I was playing. The affluent white cricketers struggled on that front too, with import duties high and availability low.

I came to know the Flower brothers, Andy and Grant, well from my time there and they, like most of the other young and aspiring cricketers there, were always keen to know if I, the county pro with all the free gear, could spare any kit. As it was, I gave Andy Flower a pair of Reebok half-spiked, half-rubber boots to wear in the 1992 World Cup in Australia and New Zealand. He promptly scored a hundred at New Plymouth against Sri Lanka in the first game on what was his one-day international debut.

I spoke to Flower for the purposes of this book and asked him if he could remember his first century. He was one of the few who could not recall it. I found that strange, because, as you have seen, I can remember mine in such detail.

But some of us are greater cricketing tragics than others. It will probably come as no surprise to anyone that Jonathan Trott, a man whose obsession with batting and cricket got the better of him during the winter of 2013/14, when he sadly had to return home from England's tour of Australia with what was described as 'a stress-related illness' at the time, can recall the minute details of his first hundred.

He was nine years old, and playing for Rondebosch School Under 11s in Cape Town, where he was born and brought up. It was against Western Province Preparatory School. 'I got 108 not out, with seven sixes and 12 fours,' he has said.

I can remember that I hit 17 fours in my first hundred, but no sixes, that is for certain. At that age I do not think I could have done so if I had tried. Skinny forearms have always been a problem.

It is interesting that Trott hit so many sixes in that first century, because, as at the hiatus in his Test career in 2014 (though he returned to county cricket with Warwickshire in 2014 and was selected in England's touring Lions squad that October), he tops the list for most Test runs (3,763) without a six; followed by India's Vijay Manjrekar (3,208), New Zealand's Glenn Turner (2,991) and Pakistan's Sadiq Mohammad (2,579).

What Flower does remember is an early near-miss of a century and the lesson it taught him. He was playing for Mashonaland Under 12s in a trial match at Highlands School in Harare, and his coach was Peter Carlstein, the former South African Test cricketer.

'I got 90-odd and slogged one up in the air,' says Flower. 'And Carlstein came to me and he gave me a stern talking to about giving my wicket away in the nineties. It stayed with me, that lesson. I still remember it very clearly now – it was at a school called Highlands in Harare – and I don't think I ever got into the nineties in Test cricket without getting to a 100. I remembered those words and made sure I kept it nice and simple whenever I was getting close to the landmark.'

Flower did actually get out in the nineties once in Test cricket, when making 92 against India in Delhi in 2002, but the point is still most valid.

You wonder whether Flower, in his role as England's team director, ever made this point so forcibly to Kevin Pietersen, with whom he never enjoyed a particularly harmonious relationship in the England set-up.

Pietersen did, after all, call for Flower's removal, as well as that of head coach Peter Moores when Flower was an assistant coach in 2009. Flower went on to become the main man, however, even if both he and Pietersen were not involved with the full England side again after the Ashes debacle Down Under in the winter of 2013/14 (Flower kept a job with the England and Wales Cricket Board and was Lions coach in 2014).

But, interestingly, only one of Pietersen's five nineties in Test cricket came under Flower's full tenure, his 99 against Bangladesh in Chittagong in 2010.

Anyway, penury does not always prove the ultimate road block. Jack Hobbs, or Sir John Berry Hobbs, to give him his full name, was called 'the Master', and in terms of this book he is indeed the grand master.

He has scored more first-class centuries than anyone. That is 197 according to *Wisden*, or 199 according to the website Cricinfo, which counts the two he made playing for Maharaj Kumar of Vizianagram's XI in India and what was then Ceylon in 1930/31, but, whatever it is, it is still a figure way beyond the next on the list, Patsy Hendren, the Middlesex and England batsman, who played from 1907 to 1937, with 170. And Hobbs' is a record that will never be beaten.

But he was born the eldest of 12 children into poverty in Cambridge, so it should come as no surprise to learn that he did not score his first century at any level until he was 18.

He was, of course, fortunate that his father, John Cooper Hobbs, was the cricket professional at the university ground, Fenner's, where John senior would umpire and bowl at the undergraduates in the nets. He later took up a better post at Jesus College, where he was groundsman. So at least young Jack was well versed in the arts of the game at which he would eventually become a giant.

Hobbs played in an era when middle age was still very much the age to be playing top-level cricket. Indeed he made 98 first-class centuries after the age of 40, and at 46 remains the oldest Test centurion.

But his first century in any cricket was in 1901 in a match between two sides in Cambridge whom he represented: Ainsworth, a team connected to his bible class, and Cambridge Liberals, for whose football team Hobbs also played. Hobbs did not know which side to play for in this match and eventually a coin was tossed to decide. It came down on Ainsworth's side and Hobbs, batting at No. 4, duly made his first century. He was to make a few more!

The late Lord Cowdrey, who in 1997 became the first English cricketer to be given a peerage, and who was previously known as Michael Cowdrey (his first name and thus the initials MCC), Colin Cowdrey and then Sir Colin Cowdrey (he was knighted in 1992 before becoming a life peer, as Lord Cowdrey of Tonbridge), scored 107 first-class centuries, but he could hardly be said to have had a poor upbringing, although he was separated from his parents for seven years.

Born in Bangalore in India he was playing cricket from the age of four with one of the family servants, as well as his father, who was a tea planter. At the age of five he was sent to England, where he went to Homefield Preparatory School at Sutton in Surrey.

At the age of seven Cowdrey thought that he had scored his first century. It was in an Under 11s match, and having made what he thought was his hundred, he gave his wicket away, only to discover later that he had only made 93. No matter, Cowdrey still received a Jack Hobbs bat and a congratulatory letter from 'the Master'. Cowdrey framed the letter and put it on the wall of his bedroom for inspiration.

The current England Test captain, Alastair Cook, was 11 when he made his first century for London Schools against Berkshire at Ascot. But he made a more famous hundred when aged 14. At the time Cook had been disappointed not to have been picked in the Bedford School first eleven by the master in charge of cricket, Jeremy Farrell.

I once knew Farrell well. He was a contemporary of mine at Cambridge University, known to all and sundry as 'Boris'. He did possess ginger hair, after all, and there was a rather famous flame-haired German tennis player around at the time, called Boris Becker.

Farrell was decent at both rugby and cricket, a hooker who appeared occasionally for the LX Club (the university second fifteen) and an off-spinner who also played for the Crusaders (again the university second team).

Anyway, one day Cook was enduring a double physics lesson at Bedford when Farrell appeared at the classroom door, asking him: 'Do you want to play for the MCC against the school?'

Did he ever. Cook rushed off, grabbed his kit, and ran to the ground, where the game had already commenced.

He was batting at No. 3 and, once he reached the crease, he was immediately sledged by his own school side. 'Send him back to nursery school,' they said, but he went on to make a hundred.

And when Farrell congratulated him afterwards, Cook, unusually given his placid character, muttered 'Told you so' under his breath. He did not miss another first-team game for the school for the next four years.

'He was minute at that age,' says Farrell, who went to Cook's wedding, just to show that Cook bore no grudges on that particular matter.

Mike Atherton was also at Cambridge at the same time as Farrell and myself, and when Cook announced himself with a hundred on Test debut in 2006, Atherton phoned Farrell to ask about the lad Farrell has always called 'the prodigy'.

'He just gets hundreds for fun,' said Farrell. 'He will be a good bet to score more hundreds than any other England batsman.'

Good old 'Boris' was right. In December 2012, aged just 27, Cook made his 23rd Test century, overtaking Lord Cowdrey, Wally Hammond, Geoffrey Boycott and Kevin Pietersen (who was on 22 at the time). Pietersen finished his Test career with 23. Cook has, as of the end of 2014, a total of 25.

And by a quirky coincidence Bedford School has a connection with Jack Hobbs. Although he was not educated at Bedford School, Hobbs did work there briefly as the assistant professional in 1902.

Having had their importance inculcated by my father, I

assumed that every young cricketer also knew the significance of scoring centuries as a batsman. Apparently it is not so.

For Matthew Maynard soon disabused me of that notion when we spoke for the purposes of this book. I played alongside Maynard for all of my career at Glamorgan, and I have no hesitation in stating that he was among the most natural stroke-makers I saw in my team or the opposition in that time. That he only received four Test caps was mystifying.

Maynard hit a century on his first-class debut aged just 19. He reached it by hitting three consecutive sixes off Yorkshire's left-arm spinner Phil Carrick. The cliché is that reaching a century with a six is described as being done 'in the grand manner'. Well, this was the grand, grand and grand manner.

There is the exuberance of youth and all that, but surely only a young man unencumbered with a hundred's worth and weight could have done such a thing.

The match was at the St Helen's ground in Swansea in 1985 and rain had affected proceedings, so that Glamorgan's first innings had lasted just 16 overs before they declared at 27-1 in order for a game to be set up. Maynard had not batted in that first innings.

Glamorgan were chasing 272 to win on a turning pitch on which they had played three spinners, in captain Rodney Ontong, left-arm spinner Mark Price and a debutant, another left-arm spinner, Phil North. Yorkshire had Carrick and the off spin of Ian Swallow to call upon.

The ninth wicket had gone down at 185, so Maynard decided to chance his arm.

'I'd been consistent for the seconds but not got a hundred,' he told me. 'My highest score for the second team in three-day cricket that season had been 83. So when I got to 84 it was like "Fuck it, that's my best score of the season. That's quite a good start to my first-class career!"

'We were nine wickets down. Phil Carrick came on. I blocked the first couple of balls, but one turned quite sharply. So I just came down the pitch and went bang, bang, bang, to the next three balls. Both men [long-off and long-on] were back. The first one I hit dead straight, the second one just cleared long-on towards the pavilion. As soon as I had mishit that second one, I thought he would throw the next up, as he would not think I would come down the pitch again. So I went down to the third one as well!'

It is a wonderful story. You would think Maynard might have recognized its significance when none other than Geoffrey Boycott, who had made 64 in Yorkshire's only innings, came to congratulate him. 'I remember Boycott came in,' says Maynard. 'He didn't knock, walked over to me in the corner by the window and said: "Well played, lad" and walked out.'

But no. 'That milestone wasn't much to me,' Maynard says. 'It had never been impressed upon me to score three figures.'

Maynard had scored his first century aged 12 at Ysgol David Hughes, Menai Bridge. It was made on a concrete strip with a mat rolled over the top. 'We only played about four school matches a year,' he says. 'The day before, I had got 63 against Bangor Normal College in a 40-over match. The old man said: "Shame, because had you got a hundred I would have bought you your first bat." The next day I got 147 in a 20-over match. Dad bought me a Gray Nicolls scoop, then later in the year the school gave me a bat for that hundred.'

Maynard's father had instead impressed upon him the need to play attractive cricket. 'The old man said to me: "Cricket is an entertainment sport,"' he says. 'I didn't get as many hundreds as others my age but I scored quicker than them. No one impressed on me the importance of hundreds. It was like if you got 80 you had done well. It didn't help me in the early part of my career. Only later did I realize their importance.'

Indeed, Glamorgan's very next first-class match after his Swansea heroics was away at Nottinghamshire. Maynard travelled with the captain, Ontong.

'Andy Pick got me out for 58,' he says. 'Rodney got 130 and 13 wickets in the match. We won by an innings. I was travelling with him and he talked about the need for hundreds. It was the first time it had been really impressed on me. "Could I have done more to stop that ball and continued that partnership with Rodney?" I asked myself afterwards.'

Maynard certainly worked it out. He ended up with 54 first-class centuries for Glamorgan. No one has scored more for the county. Alan Jones and Hugh Morris both made 52. Some chap called James is next on the list with 41. Maynard always very kindly told me that I would have broken his record had my career not been cut short by a knee injury.

I am not one who is filled with undue confidence; indeed I have very little confidence at all, and am certainly no braggart. But I think he might have been right.

Working out how to score centuries regularly is an art. There is no one-method-fits-all solution. Every century is different. But also every one is special.

Whether batting for a living or batting just for fun, there are so many disappointments to endure. Centuries bring light to those dark times. They bring weary content to the end of a long day.

This is a book about them. It is not a text book and it is not an exhaustive piece of technical advice or historical research. It will hopefully bring both of those to bear, while combining my own experiences with those of many other players, some great, some very good and some good. My experiences more often than not may seem like the 'what not to do' guide, but cautionary tales can be of value too.

The aim, though, is to ensure that, whether you have not made a century or have made many, you will be able to understand the mental and physical efforts required to reach those magical three figures.

Bowlers might not agree, but there really is no better feeling in cricket.

1

Fear of the Duck

The old Irish joke tells of a tourist in the country asking a local for directions. 'Well, sir, I wouldn't be starting from here,' is the much-quoted, hilarious reply.

But it is a bit like that with centuries. Everyone starts from the same place, walking out to the middle without a run to their name and with all the attendant worries of such a situation. But no one wants to start from there. It is a horrible place. No one wants to be on nought. No one wants to make a duck.

And for a professional cricketer that fear becomes doubled. A club cricketer can make a duck in a weekend match, maybe even make another one the following day. But at least they are separate, unconnected ducks. A pro can make two ducks in one match, the dreaded pair. For many it can be a terrifying prospect.

It worried even the great Sir Jack Hobbs. He once told Wally Hammond of his fear of a pair, even if it never came to pass, and towards the end of his career he was ever more mindful of getting off the mark. That was well known around the

23

cricketing circuit at the time. 'I always like to make my first run quickly,' Hobbs said.

Even a batsman as outwardly confident as Kevin Pietersen wants to get off the mark as quickly as possible: hence his famous 'Red Bull run', usually a scampered single hit just wide of mid-on, fuelled apparently by a can of the caffeine-filled drink before going out to bat. To bat with Pietersen when first at the crease is to be on full alert. At the time of writing, Pietersen had not made a pair, though, and is unlikely to, given that his future career looks destined to be filled mainly with Twenty20 rather than first-class cricket.

Talk of a pair leads me to only one ground. Luton. Bloody Luton. Wardown Park, Luton. Its mere mention still makes me shudder now. It was not the scene of the first pair of ducks in my first-class career. That initial ignominy had come two years previously at Edgbaston, when I had recorded two ducks batting at No. 3 for Glamorgan.

But Luton was the scene of my only pair in a day. Yes, that's right, I got a duck in the morning, and then, when we followed on after lunch, I got another duck in the afternoon. Two innings and not a run to show from either.

No matter that the great West Indian fast bowler Curtly Ambrose was in the opposition on a pitch offering his considerable height even more bounce than usual, and indeed he dismissed me in the second innings after the England left-armer Paul Taylor had done so in the first innings.

That is still one seriously bad day at the office. And it was made worse by the fact that I had to act as a runner for our injured captain, Alan Butcher, who made a gallant 59 not out batting down the order as we lost by an innings and 184 runs. But that was only part of my agony. I also ran out Steve Barwick for nought, so that he completed a pair in the match too.

I felt a little like Kim Hughes, who, having finished his Test career in 1984 with a pair, went as captain of the rebel Australian side to South Africa in 1985/86 and recorded a king pair (out first ball in both innings) and then acted as runner for Rodney Hogg, and was promptly run out first ball.

By then, in 1992, I already knew that first-class cricket could be harsh in its treatment of any player, whatever his reputation, but this was the day on which it revealed its most cruel streak. It left me utterly devastated.

Mind you, it wasn't quite as bad as the pair endured by another Glamorgan player, No. 11 Peter Judge. In 1946, at Cardiff Arms Park against the touring Indians, he was out first ball to complete Glamorgan's first innings.

The Indians asked the home side to follow on, and with captain Johnny Clay still at the crease, he decided that he and Judge should open the second innings. The usual 10 minutes between innings was also waived, and then Judge was out to the first ball of the second innings, the fastest pair in history and a record that cannot be broken. You simply cannot make a swifter pair.

'You can't say that you have played the game until you have made a pair,' my old school coach Graham Burgess always used to tell me.

A pair? I sense some may be asking about its origins. Well, that would be a pair of spectacles. Cricket loves its terms to describe these failures. It even has a verb especially used for a pair – 'to bag'. So then that becomes the noun 'baggage'.

When Marcus Trescothick bagged his first pair in 2013, he tweeted, as you do these days, of course: 'Today I joined the illustrious group of players that have got a pair, it took me 21 years to achieve it. I thank you #baggage.'

And his Somerset team-mate Craig Kieswetter then tweeted a picture of some airport baggage. It was quickly deleted, possibly because it was considered a little too insensitive, but that was probably because it was so public.

For cricketers have long mocked colleagues about ducks. I have known colleagues place a pear in the bag of a batsman who has scored a first-innings duck and is about to bat again. And what about what team-mates of the Australian Matthew Hayden did after his first and only pair, in the 1994/95 season for Queensland against South Australia?

When he returned to his room that evening Hayden found a parcel. It was wrapped in brown paper and in it were some ornamental ducks, as well as a message written by colleagues Jimmy Maher and Allan Border. 'Welcome to our exclusive duck club. Bring a partner,' it said. 'Come as a pair. On the menu we have Peking duck, double duck burger. You'll find us at the corner of Zero Street and Duck Terrace.'

Apparently Maher, a real character, whom I got to know well when he spent time playing for Glamorgan, considered buying two live ducks to put in Hayden's room, but thankfully thought better of it.

I know that I would not have seen the funny side of any of that. Cricket dressing rooms can be cruel places, with the humour cutting and personal. Interestingly, when Trescothick was first selected by England he made it plain that he did not approve of some of the humour in that vein.

As Nasser Hussain was to write in 2006: 'Marcus is the ultimate team man; he does everything for the team. He changed the dressing-room culture of mickey-taking which tends to go on in any team. He felt strongly from early on that players should not take the mickey out of each other and he often made this point at team management meetings. I wonder if it was because, as a chubby lad in his youth, he had been victim of a lot of it.'

But Trescothick does not mind taking the mickey out of himself. It is well known now, of course, that he suffers from stress and depression, an illness that ended his international career after he had to leave the 2006/07 Ashes tour before the first Test. But the next season he was seen sporting a baseball cap with the word 'Fish' written on it. By himself. As in 'mad as a fish'.

And when Trescothick did make that pair mentioned earlier,

he rather bizarrely raised his bat as he walked off. It was a lovely piece of self-deprecation, but it was actually interpreted very differently, mainly because Trescothick had just made two ducks in Twenty20 cricket too (and he very nearly made a fifth – he was perilously close to being lbw to Glamorgan's Jim Allenby but the appeal was rejected). It was his *valete*, it was assumed.

'When I held my bat aloft to the Taunton crowd to acknowledge the first "pair" of my 21-year career as a professional cricketer on Tuesday afternoon, I little knew what a reaction it would provoke,' he wrote afterwards. 'Soon there were suggestions on social media that it was a gesture of farewell and I was about to call time on my spell as Somerset captain or even my playing career. Apparently, there was also a rumour going round the ground that my eyesight was failing.

'Professionals in our game are fond of using the expression "Mother Cricket" for the unknown force that watches over us and seems to govern our fortunes. At the moment, she is not on my side.

'Only last Sunday night I was driving home, dwelling on getting two noughts in the T20 games with Gloucestershire and Northants, but consoling myself that at least I had never bagged a pair in the same game.

'What happened next? I was given out mistakenly in the first innings against Sussex when the ball hit my arm, rather than the bat, and then got a jaffa from James Anyon in the second innings to edge a catch behind.

'I always told myself that if I did get two ducks in the same game I would make some sort of acknowledgement of it as I walked off. So when I passed incoming batsman Alviro Petersen I removed my helmet and raised my bat, not for a moment realising how it would be interpreted.'

I'm pretty sure that when playing I suffered from anatidaephobia, the fictional fear created by the American cartoonist Gary Larson in his 'Far Side' series. It is the fear that somewhere, somehow, a duck is always watching you. Or, to place it into cricketing context, that somewhere a duck is always waiting to be placed alongside your name on the scorecard.

Why is it called a duck anyway? Well, that began in the 1850s apparently, when the shape of the figure 0 was first likened to a duck's egg. That became shortened to a duck, and that was that. We batsmen have been afraid of them ever since.

A golden duck is, of course, a first-ball dismissal, and, as already mentioned, two golden ducks mean a king pair. I never got one of those, even if, in addition to my two pairs, I was out for 0 and 1 three times. Not much difference? A world of difference, in truth.

New Zealand's Chris Martin holds the record for most pairs in Test cricket with seven, but he was the proverbial batting ferret. He went in after the rabbits.

King pairs can happen to some very good players. The aforementioned Hughes wasn't bad, but not as good as India's Virender Sehwag, who bagged a king pair at Birmingham in 2011, or Australia's Adam Gilchrist, who suffered the same ignominy in Kolkata in 2001.

There is also what is called a diamond duck, whose meaning is disputed. It can be used to describe being out to the first ball of a team's innings, or it can refer to being run out without facing a ball.

If it is the former, I think I had two diamonds in first-class cricket. I usually took first ball because my partner at Glamorgan, Hugh Morris, preferred to be at the non-striker's end initially. So in first-class cricket, of my 27 ducks I can only recall two of them being diamond; first ball of the match, by Devon Malcolm against Northamptonshire at Cardiff in 1999, and first ball of my second innings against Worcestershire at Swansea, by Glenn McGrath, in 2000.

If diamond means being run out without facing, that never happened to me, but I was at Adelaide in 2010 as a journalist when it happened to Australia's Simon Katich, run out by Jonathan Trott from square leg. Ricky Ponting was out next ball for a golden duck and later in the match their team-mate Ryan Harris recorded a king pair!

There were two diamond ducks of this sort recorded in the 1932 Australia versus South Africa Test at Adelaide. Australia's Alan Kippax and tail-ender and debutant Hugh 'Pud' Thurlow were both run out for nought without facing a ball. Donald Bradman made 299 not out in that innings.

Kippax was run out when Bradman was on 99, and Thurlow when he was on 299. Apparently Bert Oldfield should have been run out when the Don was on 199 too.

But are all players as scared of ducks as I was? I doubt it. 'I was never scared of getting a duck,' says Andy Flower. 'I didn't get a pair. It never entered my mind. The logic I would use, whether I was on nought or on six, was that it was still the start of my innings, and watching the ball, moving my feet, making a good decision dependent on what ball was bowled would not be different on nought, one or two.'

My fear of failure and a duck was perhaps never more evident than in a match I played against Flower – Glamorgan versus Essex in 2002 – when we had dismissed Essex just at the end of day one, so close to the end of the day's play in fact that there was just one over remaining in the day.

As I said earlier, I usually faced the first ball. But not in this instance. I decided as captain that I would stand at the non-striker's end for the over, while sending nightwatchman Dean Cosker in as the striker, which meant that the young opener Dan Cherry had to drop down to No. 3.

I did not even put a thigh pad on. What made matters worse was that Cosker clipped a ball off his legs to the huge leg-side boundary away from the pavilion at Chelmsford, but the ball did not quite make the fence. It was the longest and easiest three in cricket history. We ran two.

The abuse from Flower, who was keeping wicket, and Essex captain Ronnie Irani was frightful. They said I was scared. And they were right. I was not scared of the bowler, Joe Grant, but I was scared of getting out that evening in that one over.

I actually scored 249 in that innings. Once I got going I was OK.

'I've heard others are scared of ducks,' says Flower with a playful look at me. 'I don't understand logically why. I never ever felt that way.'

Murray Goodwin admits that he was a poor starter, and 45 first-class ducks is evidence of that. 'Historically I haven't been a great starter,' he says. 'I find that between nought and 20 I get out quite often. It is something I have really worked on in the last 5–10 years.'

But he never bagged a pair and feels that he learnt to cope with the pressure of not scoring. 'I am trying to keep a level head when I first walk in to bat,' he said before retiring from first-class cricket in 2014. 'I am trying to get off the mark, then playing the ball as I see it, keeping in the present.

'A lot of guys feel under pressure if they are not scoring, that their name is on one ball. I go the other way. I back myself, I can handle that even if the bowler is bowling maidens at me.

'There was one game that stood out for me in grade cricket on a wicket that was doing a bit, and it was against Bruce Reid [former Australian left-arm fast bowler] – he was a sensational left-arm bowler, up there with the best I have faced. I played eight maidens in a row off him, and I was trying to score. Sure, the outfield was lush and slow – so cut shots dug into the turf – but not once did I feel he was going to get me out. I had a simple game plan. I ended up getting a hundred. That was a huge turning of the corner for me. I did the same sort of thing for Western Australia about a week later.'

Goodwin recalls a game for Glamorgan against Kent in 2013 on a spicy pitch where run-scoring was extremely difficult. He was batting with a junior partner, who, when Goodwin said to him: 'I know this is hard work, but we've got to get through to lunch here,' merely replied: 'I don't know where to score here.' The tyro didn't last long. He felt his name was on one ball and played in a manner that suggested that.

Mike Atherton made 20 Test ducks. And when you look at the list of most ducks made in Test cricket, headed by West Indies' Courtney Walsh with 43, only Steve Waugh and Sri Lanka's Marvan Atapattu, both with 22, stand above Atherton as specialist batsmen. Waugh and Atherton, eh? Two of cricket's finest examples of mentally strong batsmen?

Atherton made 46 ducks in first-class cricket in total. 'I just think there were times when my technique was dodgy,' he explains. 'It makes you more of a bad starter, especially in Test cricket, where the bowlers are particularly at you. If your technique isn't solid, it makes you more vulnerable and there were times when it wasn't particularly solid.

'I think technique is a bit like intelligence. There is a threshold beyond which you have to be competent. Once you are beyond the threshold you will get runs as long as all the bits are in working order. If you are below the threshold it makes you more vulnerable. I don't think I was an unduly nervy starter, just occasionally a bad starter.'

He made two Test pairs (as well as one for Lancashire against Sussex in 1987), against Australia in Melbourne in 1998 and the following year against South Africa in Johannesburg. 'The one in Jo'burg I just got a couple of fantastic deliveries from [Allan] Donald in the first innings and [Shaun] Pollock in the second,' he says. 'I don't think that I could have done much. Melbourne was where I was playing poorly and was below the threshold of technical competence. They were obviously both away Test matches, and I remember feeling a bit tentative in the next innings after Jo'burg.'

But he did make 108 in that match at Port Elizabeth. I opened with Atherton on my Test debut at Lord's against South Africa in 1998. We hadn't actually opened together that much while at Cambridge University because Atherton had preferred to bat at No. 3. With Graeme Fowler and Gehan Mendis a settled opening partnership at Lancashire at the time, he wisely felt that first drop was his best route into his county side.

So when we opened at Lord's he asked if I wanted to take first ball. 'Yes,' I replied instantly. There was no way I wanted to be hanging around at the non-striker's end waiting for my first ball in Test cricket. Mark Butcher, whom I replaced at Lord's because he had broken a thumb, had taken first ball in the first Test at Edgbaston anyway.

I got off the mark in Test cricket with a single from Allan Donald off my forearm protector (many thanks to umpire Darrell Hair!), before succumbing caught down the leg side by the flying Mark Boucher off Donald for 10. But Atherton did not make it off the mark, caught at slip off Pollock.

The following day we collapsed to 110 all out in response to South Africa's 360. As our innings was coming to an end, I happened to meet Atherton in the toilets at the back of the Lord's changing rooms. 'Is it OK if I take first ball?' he asked, 'I'm on 'em!'

He was indeed on a pair. I asked him about that incident at Lord's. 'You don't want to wait,' he laughs. 'You just want to get on with it!'

He cites the example of England wicketkeeper Matt Prior, who bagged a pair against New Zealand at Lord's in 2013, his first in Test cricket, indeed his first in all first-class cricket. But he spurned the offer of an easy single in the second innings before being dismissed. 'It was bizarre,' says Atherton. 'It was an easy single he turned down. I find that curious.'

Prior wrote afterwards: 'Whether it is a pair, one and one or five and five, it makes no difference to me. A fail is a fail. Good bits of bowling happen. Everyone is very vulnerable first ball.

'I had a chance to get off the mark in the second innings. I did not take it but what difference would it have made to the game if I got one? Not much. People go on about pairs but I am not interested. I am not a stat watcher.'

Fair enough, even if it was the beginning of a horrible slide in form for Prior that led to him being dropped the following winter Down Under during a calamitous 5-0 series defeat for England, but it is a view endorsed by Graham Gooch, who famously began his Test career with a pair against Australia at Edgbaston in 1975. He also made a pair in his second first-class match, against Gloucestershire in 1974.

'Pairs?' Gooch asks rhetorically. 'Worried? No, not really. It just happens, doesn't it? I don't remember having any big issues with the situation. I did get six noughts on the trot in 1987 but my game had fallen into disrepair.'

I'm not sure he did get six on the trot actually. More like three on the trot and six in 10 innings, still pretty rotten stuff, a bit like Greg Chappell's seven ducks in 15 innings for Australia during the 1981/82 season.

But it is nothing compared with getting five on the trot in Test cricket, a fate to befall three players so far – Australia's Bob Holland in 1985, Pakistan's Mohammad Asif in 2006 and India's Ajit Agarkar in 1999/2000.

Agarkar earned the nickname 'Bombay duck' for his troubles. Others who achieve five ducks on the trot are credited with having achieved 'the Olympic rings'.

Those who make four in succession are called 'Audi', after the car-maker's four-circle logo, as Mark Waugh's colleagues in the Australia side called him after he made two consecutive pairs in Sri Lanka in 1992. He is hardly alone in making four on the bounce in Test cricket, though. Twenty-two others have done it, with West Indies' Merv Dillon having the distinction, or otherwise, of having done it twice.

Gooch is not in a club of his own having bagged a pair on Test debut either: 37 others have done so, beginning with G. F. Grace against Australia in 1880 and the latest being South Africa's Dean Elgar in November 2012.

Chris Tremlett did so against India at Lord's in 2007, but the only England player to manage this in between Gooch and Tremlett was poor old Gavin Hamilton, the Scottish all-rounder who played just one Test, against South Africa in Johannesburg in 1999, when, as stated already, Mike Atherton also bagged them. He did not take a wicket, either.

I remember observing the start of Marvan Atapattu's Test career between 1990 and 1994 and sharing his agony. He began with scores of 0 and 0, 0 and 1, and 0 and 0.

And they reckon the one run he got might have been a leg bye! It showed remarkable resilience for Atapattu to recover from such mental torture. He did play 90 Tests and score 16 Test centuries, after all.

And it must have been a mental problem as much as anything else. 'It takes a big man to come back from a pair with a century,' said my then Glamorgan team-mate, the great Vivian Richards, to me when I made 105 against Surrey at Neath in my next first-class innings after my pair-in-a-day experience at Luton.

I'm not sure about that – me being a big man, that is – but if Richards was impressed, then that made me very proud, not least because he had taken enough notice to realize what had happened to me in my previous first-class match.

But really it should not be that surprising. Batsmen know about the ducks as much as they do the centuries, whether their own or those of their colleagues.

THE ART OF CENTURIES

2

Preparation

So how do you get yourself in the right frame of mind to avoid getting a duck? How do you prepare yourself to bat in order to make a century? Sometimes ducks are unavoidable. Every batsman is at his most vulnerable early on, when nerves are at their most rampant and the bowler is at his most bloodthirsty.

Preparation is everything, both mental and physical. Let's start with the physical. Batting is an art of repetition. Long hours of repeated practice are vital to the creation of a technique that can provide a batsman with the runs he desires.

And it is always said that net practice should replicate what happens in the middle as closely as possible. In other words a batsman should play as if he were batting in the middle, and take care of his wicket just as he would in a match. Which is fair enough, and the reason why when I was playing for Glamorgan Colts, our then coach, the former Glamorgan all-rounder Jim Pressdee, used to order you out of the nets when you were dismissed.

It was a harsh school. At that time we were playing as a side in the South Wales League, and often we would have nets on a

Saturday morning before playing in the afternoon. I was still at Swansea University, so with the nets taking place in Neath, it was not a long journey on a Saturday morning.

But for the slightly older players, there had often been a long journey on a Friday evening back from a county second-eleven match.

On one occasion one of those second-eleven matches had been in Leeds, and our left-arm spinner, Phil North, had made a tortuously long journey on the Friday night, getting back home to Newport in the early hours before rising and travelling to Neath on the Saturday morning. Sure enough, when it was his turn to bat, he was out first ball. Pressdee had no hesitation. 'Out you come,' he shouted, to North's consternation.

These nets were being conducted in the Neath indoor school, so Pressdee followed North out to the back of the hall to console him. The next batsman in was a chap called Michael Cann, a real joker, who, before taking guard, decided to rattle the metal stumps as if he too had been bowled. 'Right, next man again then!' shouted Pressdee, and Cann never even got to face a ball!

The message was, and it always is, that nets are not for horseplay, especially at professional level. I do have to say, though, that the standard of net practice was my biggest bugbear in all of my near 20-year professional career.

The quality of the outdoor net surfaces was nothing short of a disgrace. There was so little attention given to them that it was embarrassing. Only Leicestershire, where at Grace Road they used to put a separate groundsman in charge of the nets, which were away from the main playing arena, could really escape censure from experiences during my playing days.

When I was captain of Glamorgan and pre-season tours abroad were being discussed, I would normally ask only one question: 'What are the nets like?' For me pre-season was all about long hours in the nets, grooving body and mind, and ensuring that a long-established technique was working smoothly.

But I can recall only two instances where that was really possible, coinciding incidentally with my two most successful seasons, when I scored over 1,700 first-class runs in each.

First was a pre-season to Pretoria in South Africa in 1996, where the nets at Centurion Park were quite magnificent. We stayed at a hotel near to the ground, and were able to spend as long as we wanted in those nets. It was a joyous trip, even if Matthew Maynard still talks about the leg-cutter with which he bowled me in those nets. And it was also during one of the matches at the ground against Northern Transvaal that I faced probably the fastest spell of bowling in my career, from a short, stocky bowler named Rudi Bryson, who terrorized me for six overs with short-pitched stuff, while my partner, Hugh Morris, gleefully played rather well at the other end.

Morris, by the way, was one of the worst net players I have ever seen. He was a mighty fine player, of course, who made 53 first-class centuries in all, with the aforementioned 52 for Glamorgan, and he might have made many more had his first stab at county captaincy not been made at the tender age of 23. He undoubtedly should have won more than three Test caps.

But in the nets he used to get out for fun, edging balls, getting bowled, the lot. I remember my first season at Cambridge University in 1989, when our first match was against Glamorgan. Captain Mike Atherton conducted a meeting about the opposition, and obviously leant on me heavily for input. 'Morris looks in shocking nick,' I said of my net experiences down at Glamorgan. 'He looks really vulnerable outside off stump at the moment.' He duly scored a century. Oops.

The second occasion on which I prepared properly for a season was 1997, when we won the county championship. This time it was at home in Cardiff, where the weather was unusually clement and the arrival of a new coach called Duncan Fletcher ensured that the nets were in decent order. We practised morning and afternoon for two weeks. It was wonderful.

Off-season is the time to make technical changes, if required. Malcolm Gladwell, in his book *Outliers*, reckons that it takes 10,000 hours to master an art, so, whether you entirely agree with that or not, it does give an idea of the time required to alter any part of a batting technique.

But there are some who have liked to spend many hours in the nets even if not working on a particular area of technique. It should come as little surprise that Geoffrey Boycott was one of them. 'I usually tried to stay in the net for 45 minutes, half an hour longer than most batsmen would stick at the county nets,' he once said. 'There was a reason for this so-called gluttony for practice: it was a conscious effort to make myself concentrate for long periods of time in circumstances as close to the real thing as I could make them. Concentration does begin to wander in the nets after 15 minutes or so – batsmen get sloppy and begin to play shots that would be fatal in the middle. I wanted to push my mental capacity that little bit further.'

That was, though, nothing compared to what the Australian Mike Hussey used to do. A good story is told by his team-mate at Western Australia, Ryan Campbell. It tells of a weekend when his Perth club side, Wanneroo, had a weekend off, and so Hussey asked the coach if he could go to the nets.

So he went there in the morning and batted against the bowling machine for two hours. Then he had some lunch. Then he batted for another two hours. Then he had some tea. And finally he batted for another two hours.

'How can I bat all day if I haven't done it before?' asked Hussey later. It is indeed a very valid point, but it is often impossible to conduct such lengthy practice. I once batted for over 12 hours in a match. You can hardly replicate that in practice.

As I said, it is always the mantra of net practice: to make it as close as possible to being in the middle. But that is usually nonsense. Sightscreens are often not provided, bowlers often bowl no-balls and bowl in fours rather than completing an over themselves. And as the session goes on, the intensity usually drops significantly, so that it finishes with batsmen who are part-time bowlers bowling at the bowlers. Much is done these days to prevent those things happening, but in general that is still the reality.

But that is not to say that net practice cannot help. For instance, when Steve Waugh was dropped from the Australian Test side in 1991, he decided that his approach to net practice had to alter. 'The biggest change I made was in the way I conducted my net practice sessions,' he said. 'I wanted to simulate match conditions every time I walked in. I had probable field placements in my mind depending on who was bowling to me and what type of pitch I was on, and I played each ball on its merits rather than premeditating. Every imaginary innings was built up as if I was in a real contest. I tried not to get out, I wanted to get into the habit of winning the one-on-one battles, and rehearse concentrating when the stakes weren't that high.'

But even Hussey's practice was not that realistic. Bowling machines are very useful, but they are not like facing a real bowler, even if they have advanced significantly with the advent of Merlyn, the spin-bowling machine, and more recently ProBatter, where a video screen is used so that the batsman can watch the bowler running in and time his movements accordingly before the ball appears from a hole in the screen. Proper cricket balls are used for that too.

But even that has its problems. Batsmen have said that facing bouncers while using it is very difficult.

I used bowling machines a lot. In fact I used one of them too much one winter when my pick-up became just like Graham Gooch's, with the bat raised. That in itself is not necessarily a bad thing, as Gooch proved rather well, but my problem was that my head starting moving around, as I tried to keep the rest of my body still. I had to go back to the traditional tapping of the bat on the ground after that.

For that is one of the bowling machine's greatest disadvantages, in that timing one's movements is almost impossible when a ball suddenly fires out of a hole, notwithstanding the feeder's command of 'bat up' as he lifts the ball in the air before placing it into the machine.

Their best use is for grooving shots, especially when working on a particular technical deficiency, and for speeding up reactions. But you need to be careful, especially when using them regularly on indoor surfaces, where it is far too easy to stand there and drive on the 'up', in other words drive through the line of the ball when the ball is not quite a half-volley. You can usually do that with impunity inside. Do it in the first game of the season outside, and you could easily either edge behind or find the ball looping to mid-off.

But Hussey's work ethic in transforming himself from a scrawny blocker to an international batsman mentioned in the same breath as Sir Donald Bradman became legendary in the game, not least when he spent time playing for Northamptonshire in the county championship, where he would practise against the left-arm spin of Monty Panesar for hour after hour.

'That's why I'll play a couple of games for Australia, and he'll play a hundred,' Ryan Campbell said. Hussey did not quite play 100 Tests but he did play 79, averaging over 51 with 19 centuries. In first-class cricket the left-hander averaged over 52 with 61 hundreds.

Hussey strikes me as one of those players who did not mind what the quality of a net surface was like. He would just get on with it. Matthew Maynard was a bit like that, even if there was a chance of physical danger. I know that impressed coach Duncan Fletcher.

And Michael Vaughan did the same with England. Fletcher once told me about a net session in Sri Lanka where no one else wanted to bat. Vaughan went into the net and batted bravely and skilfully.

I was never so sure about this. Surely net heroics mean nothing. 'I wouldn't have nets if the ball was jagging about,' says Graham Gooch. 'I'm not looking to show how brave I am. I am looking to hone my game. Whatever you do in the nets you will take to the middle. When you come out of practice you must feel good about yourself. You must not come out of a net feeling shit.'

When I spoke to him during the 2013 season, Murray Goodwin had not netted for years. 'I haven't had a net basically since I left Zimbabwe,' he said. 'I just don't net. In Zimbabwe we used to have terrible nets at Harare Sports Club. They were green and the boys had new balls. It wasn't fun. So I did a lot of work with Grant and Andy Flower having bowl-downs at 15 yards or throwing with new balls. I found that prepared me better than anything. When I was at Sussex, I faced spin in the nets but never had a net against the quicker bowlers. I would use the machine a lot to keep my triggers, balance and all my processes going.'

But that is not, of course, to say that you cannot challenge yourself in net practice. Nick Compton, the Somerset and England batsman, has spoken publicly about the practice he did with his mentor, Neil Burns, prior to being picked for England. During winter sessions indoors, the bowling machine would often be set to 99 mph for sessions that might last two hours.

'The aim is to make conditions as uncomfortable as possible and see how long I can maintain concentration,' Compton said. 'There is a fear factor, and it's often very cold too. You get hit and there are times when you just want to walk away, but I figure if I can handle that, nothing in games is going to intimidate me. I smile sometimes when I see people practise. They tend to practise attacking the ball. They practise in perfect conditions and they like to express their talent and hit the ball. But how much help is that when you play on a pitch where the ball nips around?'

I found that at least as you became older and more established, you could pick and choose whether you wanted to bat when conditions were not good, especially before and during a game.

Throw-downs are an integral part of any batsman's preparation. But I'll be honest and say that so many are just done for cosmetic purposes, especially those conducted on the outfield before play. Basically they are a waste of time, with the bounce often uneven and sometimes not even a front pad worn by the batsman to protect his leg. Maybe a couple of balls are hit in the middle of the bat, and that might engender a small sliver of confidence, but is it really of any benefit?

Although it does have to be said that Brian Lara reckons he used throw-downs to good effect during his world record highest score in first-class cricket of 501 not out for Warwickshire against Durham in 1994.

He just did not feel right early in his innings. 'The period before tea was one of the sketchiest at the crease in my first year with Warwickshire,' he said. 'My feet simply wouldn't go to the right places. Having quick feet is essential to a top-class batsman but like a dancer they have to be in time to the music, or, in this case, the bowling.'

So at tea on the first day of his innings (at the end of which he finished 111 not out), he called his team-mate, the wicketkeeper Keith Piper, to go out onto the outfield to have some throw-downs. Then they went to the indoor school for some more. 'I believe I can put things right with some co-ordinated practice and it works,' said Lara. 'Bob Woolmer [Warwickshire's coach] believed videos were the answer. That's not a method I prefer. After 10 minutes' work with Piper I felt happier.'

In my view, you need to be in a net with a good thrower for throw-downs to be of proper benefit, as Lara probably found when going inside. And, having already mentioned the standard of net surfaces, finding such a thrower can also be difficult. Maybe Piper was good. Again, let's be frank and say that team-mates don't really give a toss about throwing to each other. It is a bind when you would rather be thinking about your own game.

My former team-mate at Glamorgan, David Hemp, is a dear friend but he was a shocker when it came to throw-downs. He just wanted too many. We used to play rock, paper, scissors (best of three!) to determine who would bat first, but, if I lost, my heart would sink.

Hemp was an elegant left-hander and one of the finest strikers of a cricket ball I have seen, but, boy, did he like to do a lot of striking. Ball after ball he would hit, all with greater timing and power than I could ever dream of, but he was never satisfied.

'I've got to finish on a good one,' he would say, which is a fair enough theory; as Steve Waugh says of his throw-down sessions: 'I always made sure I finished with a couple hit out of the middle of the bat, so I could walk away with a positive note as my last memory.'

But Hemp's idea of 'good' was rather different from mine. He would berate himself for shots that I would stand and admire. But maybe that was his problem. Often we would bat together in the middle and he would hammer shots like that straight to fielders. I would be at the non-striker's end thinking: 'I would want some runs for that!' Ball-striking and batting are two very different matters.

I am not sure that I was a particularly good thrower anyway, with a poor throwing action that meant I undercut the ball, giving it the impression of being an off-spinner. If the length was wrong, it could be frustrating for the batsman, as my old school coach Graham Burgess once articulated to me very clearly when we were playing together at Southampton in a match for the Three Counties League. 'For fuck's sake, stop bowling spinners! I want some seamers!' He still got a hundred anyway. I didn't.

The best thrower I ever encountered was Duncan Fletcher. His arm was strong, and his throwing fast and accurate. If the ball was newer, he could swing it too. He tells a great story of throwing to his protégé Jacques Kallis, to whom he gave a debut when he was coach at Western Province and in whose class was Fletcher's son, Michael, at Wynberg Boys' High School in Cape Town.

Fletcher was coach of the South Africa A side that toured England in 1996, and during a match against MCC at Shenley, Fletcher and Kallis went to the nets armed with six new balls. Fletcher wanted to throw away swingers and the first four he threw all swung away from Kallis. The last two, rather surprisingly, swung in, even though Fletcher had done nothing different. They marked those two balls and, lo and behold, they kept swinging in for the whole session. Ah, the unfathomableness of swing and reverse swing!

Steve Waugh has no hesitation in nominating his ideal thrower. 'Tom Moody was the best giver of throw-downs in the business,' he says. 'Often I wouldn't have a full-on practice net session before or during a game, preferring a team-mate to toss me 20 or so balls. Obviously, the quality of throwing was key. Bad throwing could be frustrating and lead to scrappy shots, rendering the exercise useless.'

Nowadays at the top level, there seem to be so many coaches that there are enough to go round. And there has also been the emergence of the 'dog ball thrower', or 'Sidearm' as it is known more officially, which allows the thrower to generate much more speed and can save his shoulder from damage. Although it can also damage the batsman, as Lancashire's Stephen Parry discovered during 2013, when his coach, Peter Moores, hit him flush on the arm with an intended yorker, breaking it and meaning that a plate had to be inserted.

Gooch has helped advertise the 'Sidearm', but at the end of his playing days he had his own answer to his desire for perfect practice. He employed his own personal coach, just to give him throw-downs.

So his former Essex team-mate Alan Lilley was to be seen

throwing to him for hour after hour. 'The reason I took him to Tests was that I wanted someone there for me,' says Gooch. 'I wasn't unhappy with the practice we were getting, I wanted to go one step further. If I was playing now, I would have my own coach, like a tennis player or golfer.

'Asking a team-mate to do it is leaving it to chance. At the top level why would you do that? It might be a problem if you had 11 personal coaches but we didn't do it during team time. We would do it at the front or back end of team practices. The one thing that you need to do in professional sport is be absolutely confident that when you walk over that white line you've done everything you possibly can to be ready to do your job.'

For Gooch preparation was, always has been and always will be everything. It must be done even if you are captain and have other matters to concern you.

'I always liked to practise early, especially when I was captain,' says Gooch. 'I have said this to Alastair Cook. "You mustn't take short cuts on your own batting, your main job is to score runs. Forget the captaincy, your job is to score runs. You've got to prepare yourself and give yourself time, so come in early and get it out of the way without compromise."'

And Gooch averaged 58.72 as England captain, compared to 42.58 overall. He certainly did not let the captaincy affect his run-getting.

While Gooch would have throw-downs on the morning of a game rather than a proper net, I actually forced myself to have a net whenever I could, even if the surfaces were not ideal and it was just, say, fast bowler Steve Watkin bowling off a few paces, because I felt this would better train my eyes and feet for the day ahead. For me the easy option was throw-downs, so I had to force myself to don all my protective kit and net, even if only for five minutes. I rarely scored centuries after just throw-downs.

'I preferred someone throwing at me,' counters Gooch. 'The morning of a game you want to do what suits you. I would go for throw-downs – testing ones – because on the morning you are not trying to change technique, you are not coaching anyone. What you are trying to do is warm up the things you need when you get to the crease, so you can be the master of the crease. And those are footwork, head position and eye line.

'It's not about the shots – I know I can cover drive, clip through mid-wicket, cut or whatever. I am getting myself in the right frame of mind. People call it the zone or focus, but I just call it my own little world. One of my better skills later in my career was the ability to shut everything out.'

There is definitely no point in putting in 'showy' practice after the event. So many players head straight for the nets after falling for a low score. It is too late then. I remember playing at Cambridge University against Leicestershire when Mike Atherton had been out cheaply, and he immediately retired to the nets at Fenner's to do some work.

I was still batting and for all the time Atherton was in the nets, the Leicestershire side, which was full of gnarled old pros like David Gower, Jonathan Agnew, Peter Willey, Les Taylor, Nigel Briers and Gordon Parsons, were giving Atherton grief from a distance. 'Too late now, sonny,' they were saying. 'You don't get gentle half-volleys like that out here.'

I had had a similar experience myself. Playing for my club side, Lydney, I had made a duck away at Trowbridge. I immediately went to the nets. But the opposition were even less subtle than the Leicestershire team had been. Not only did they make it clear that it was a waste of time, I think they also intimated that my intentions to become a professional might be similarly productive. I never did that again.

As Gooch says: 'As a general principle, when you are feeling good and scoring runs, that is when you practise hard. When your game leaves you a bit, you do what you have to do, but you don't over-practise.

'I don't have a lot of time, and I know [Andy] Flower [who

was then England's team director with Gooch as his batting coach] doesn't, for people who get out and then want to go to the nets and exorcize the demons. Go and work beforehand – that's what you should do! They want to put things right straight away but that is not the issue here – get your preparation right beforehand.'

And that includes the moments before you bat too, even though some of the greatest players in the game have had some very strange methods of dealing with that. Indeed many of them have slept while waiting to go into bat. Being an opener, that was never an option for me, although I did bat in the middle order in one-day cricket quite a bit later in my career. It was certainly not something I could ever have done.

But Viv Richards did. So too Majid Khan, and David Gower. As Richards says: 'One of the great things about going to sleep before I batted was that I had a picture in my mind of what the opposition could do, and only the outgoing batsman could further influence me. What could be unnerving would be watching a turning ball or a fast bowler going past the bat; from the pavilion it could look ten times as quick or be turning far too much. That's when it starts playing tricks with your mind. It was never as hard out in the middle as it looked in the pavilion.'

And that is very true. Pavilions that are situated side-on to the pitch can be very misleading for waiting batsmen. As Richards says, the bowling does look so much faster. It can play tricks with your mind. It is sometimes enough to drive you to drink.

Which is the path Gower once took. For on one occasion he popped into The Cricketers pub outside Grace Road in Leicester to have a whisky before play. It was in 1976, when Leicestershire were playing the then ferocious West Indies, so you could hardly blame him. And he did make 89 not out!

I was once rather surprised to find Matthew Maynard having a glass of port and some raw eggs at breakfast one morning in

Derby, but then his father had been a professional boxer and in days gone by it was not unusual for them to break their fast in such a manner.

In his most recent autobiography Gower tells of how he often used to do a crossword while waiting to bat – 'a handy way to calm myself down,' he says – but he also tells the story of the last home Test of 1990 against India, at the Oval, and how a prolonged nap helped him prepare for a vital innings.

He desperately needed a score to gain a place on the winter tour to Australia. It was the fourth afternoon and Graham Gooch and Mike Atherton opened the innings as England followed on. Gower had made just eight in the first innings.

When Gooch was out 40 minutes before the close Gower had been dozing for some time – 'not a hundred per cent asleep exactly but in that alpha state where you are largely resting,' he says.

'I heard the crowd respond to the fall of a wicket and got myself up. I had no idea what had been happening, how Gooch had got out, who was bowling. But by the time I'd put on my gloves and looked out at the light, I was completely switched on.'

The next day he batted all day, making 157 not out, and he secured a place on the tour.

It was little surprise then that he and Gooch did not always see eye to eye when Gooch was captain of England. Their approaches to training and preparation could not have been more different.

'I'm an organized and tidy person,' says Gooch. 'I don't like mess. I'm a big believer in getting into habits. For instance, if you go to the gym and have a routine it makes you want to go to the gym. The system evolved. In my early days I was talented, but lacked structure. I practised but not with a lot of purpose. Nowadays I don't like the in-tray on my desk.

'I see a lot of players these days who are next but one in to bat and they have done next to no preparation to go in. They are walking around in their tracksuit, suddenly they are next in and they've got to get ready. I just don't get that.

'I had a slight issue on my last tour to Australia, where Athers [Mike Atherton] and Stewie [Alec Stewart] were opening the batting. I was to bat at five and I was not used to it. It was quite difficult to know what to do, sit still and relax, or pace up and down?'

It is slightly strange to think that such a great batsman could have difficulties with as mundane a matter as waiting to go into bat, but that is batting for you. It is mental, in both the formal and the colloquial meanings of the word – of the mind and insane at the same time.

My best innings began in my mind about a week before they took place. Sadly that is not always possible in county cricket's overcrowded schedule. But what I mean is that the mental process of dealing with all the negatives that are part of a batsman's life are fully put to bed, as the ground that you are playing on, its pitch, the opposition and other factors are considered.

For most of my career I thought I was different. I thought that I was the only one suffering such doubts, fearing failure, praying for rain and trying to put off the moment of truth when I took guard.

But the truth is that all players suffer those insecurities. Not all will admit as much, of course, but, with all its inevitable failures, batting lends itself so easily to that sense of negativity. It only takes one ball to end all the hard work. One ball.

You only have to read what Ricky Ponting, a truly great player and second only to Sir Don Bradman among Australian batsmen, has to say on the matter for evidence.

His career was definitely wearing an autumnal cloak when he was in bad form in South Africa in 2011, but in Johannesburg he was plumb lbw to Dale Steyn first ball. 'I can recall pretty clearly what I was thinking about as Steyn bowled that ball,' he has written. 'I had a whole range of things buzzing around in my brain: "watch the ball" was one of them; "don't listen to them", "don't get out lbw", "don't push too far forward", "you don't want your career to end here", "you can still play" were others. Most of all, I think I was looking for the ball that was going to hit me on the pad.

'I had heard sports psychologists talk about the "little voice" that sits on athletes' shoulders as they compete. It's a negative voice, one that says you're no good, that you can't win, that it's not worth it, that you should give up. The great athletes are able to ignore that little voice, or tell it to go away. I never heard that little voice during my best batting days, but I couldn't get rid of the little bastard at the end, not when I was trying to bat in a Test match. The line I heard loudest as the bowler was approaching the wicket was "You're one game away from being dropped."'

Gooch concurs. 'It is so easy to be negative,' he told me in September 2013 as he prepared to go to Australia on his last tour as England's batting coach. 'It is totally normal. Mark Bawden [the England team psychologist] has done a lot of work with our batsmen on this issue, about the little chimp in your mind telling you negative things. The skill is to think this is normal. The trick is to put it at the back of your mind and not at the front.'

As well as working for the England and Wales Cricket Board, Bawden is lead psychologist for the English Institute of Sport. He has already been part of five Olympic Games. 'The art of sports psychology is to simplify people's thinking to its absolute minimum,' he says. 'Get all the noise out of their heads so that they can stay in the present moment, non-judgementally. We call it "staying in the bubble".'

The Chimp Paradox is, of course, the title of a book by Dr Steve Peters, who is one of the more famous sports psychologists of our time and was recruited by the England football team ahead of the 2014 World Cup. He was already well known for his work with the British cyclists who achieved extraordinary success at the 2012 London Olympics.

Sports psychologists are an interesting topic. They were starting to come into cricket when I was playing (I played my last game in 2003), but there was a lot of scepticism about their role.

There still is. Take Sir Ian Botham, for example. 'Sports psychology, what's that all about?' he has said. 'It's the biggest con of all time, people making a lot of money talking bullshit.'

And I must admit that as a county cricketer I was very much of the same opinion. I did not see their value, mainly because those employed came in and tried to talk to the team as a whole. Because they were not cricket people, I did not have the courage to seek out their help as an individual. I just railed at their attempts to talk, for example, about goal setting for the season ahead, while trying to explain that I could not see beyond the first ball of the season, which in one particular case meant facing Allan Donald of Warwickshire. That was enough for me to worry about, thank you very much.

Warren Gatland, the Wales rugby union coach, had it right in 2009 when he first started using the services of psychologist Andy McCann. 'The use of a psychologist is a personal thing,' he said. 'Andy will not be involved in any team stuff, but he is there if players want to talk on an individual basis.'

One of McCann's most frequent visitors was, and still is, Sam Warburton, the brilliant young flanker who captained the British and Irish Lions on their successful tour of Australia in 2013.

Fortune has decreed that I have got to know Warburton reasonably well, firstly by ghosting his regular column for the *Daily Telegraph*, and then when he very kindly asked me to ghost two books for him, both diary-type tomes, the first detailing Wales' Grand Slam of 2012 and the preceding Rugby World Cup, during which Warburton was cruelly sent off in his side's semi-final against France, and the second telling the story of that 2013 Lions tour.

I can say without hesitation that I have not met a finer person in sport than Warburton. He is definitely up there as a human being with the former Australian fast bowler Michael Kasprowicz, whom I played alongside at Glamorgan for a while.

But I will also say that at first I was surprised, and maybe a little worried, about the reliance Warburton seemed to place on his relationship with McCann.

They first met at the post-match dinner of a Wales versus Scotland match in 2010. They immediately hit it off. 'One of the most interesting people I've ever met in my life,' said Warburton.

McCann was once a teacher who competed internationally at karate, but at the age of 37 suffered a stroke while taking a martial arts class. He now runs his own corporate training and consultancy company, and has written an excellent, well-received book called *Stroke Survivor*.

Read any of Warburton's stuff, whether books, columns or interviews, and you will realize how close he is to McCann. He has no compunction in mentioning him and the work he does with him.

And it is not just Warburton. Among others, George North and Leigh Halfpenny, two other bright young starlets of Welsh rugby, use McCann a lot. Indeed when Warburton and North were sharing a room before Wales' match against England at Twickenham in 2012, they both spoke to McCann by telephone on the morning of the match, continuing their usual 15 minutes of what they call one-to-one 'mental priming'.

McCann clearly gives Warburton huge confidence. The two of them have put together a book (not to be published, of course) called 'Warby's Winning Ways', which is a collection of morale-boosting cuttings and quotes, and includes the personal identity statement 'I am the world's best 7'.

That could easily sound arrogant, especially as most will obviously say that it is not true because of the presence of New Zealand's remarkable Richie McCaw, but anyone who knows Warburton will know that arrogance is not an accusation that can be laid at his door. It is simply his way of filling his mind with positivity. And he certainly is among the top five openside flankers in the world, so it is hardly a fanciful notion.

Goodness, I could have done with some of that sort of positivity during my cricket career. Indeed I think a good sports psychologist could have really helped my game.

But as David Gower says: 'The best players are their own psychologists. What others have to learn about self-belief, they possess instinctively.'

And it is true that players can work out their own mental methods over time. That is what I did through trial and error. But would I have ever thought about seeing a sports psychologist personally? Not a chance!

As England captain Alastair Cook, who has worked regularly and successfully with Mark Bawden, once said: 'There was always a bit of a stigma seeing the guy we call the "head doc", but the mental side of cricket is so powerful.'

Surprising then to discover that Gower himself once used a sports psychologist. It was in 1991, when he was going through a terrible time with the bat, and he saw a chap called Brian Mason, who had been recommended to him by Bob Woolmer, then coach of Warwickshire.

Mason was an interesting character, a former squadron leader in the education branch of the Royal Air Force and a tutor at the Police Staff College in Hook, Hampshire. He became what he called a 'motivational guru', and once, bizarrely, was accused of sending threatening letters to David Graveney, then chairman of the England selectors, complaining about his selection policies.

The profession of sports psychologists was probably not helped in its early days by the presence of such men. Some of those professing to work in the field were strange and not entirely trustworthy characters. We had a chap at Glamorgan who claimed to have done work with a top-flight football club, and it turned out that nobody there had heard of him. That, for instance, did not help me in my attitude towards them.

Jeremy Snape, the former Northamptonshire, Leicestershire, Gloucestershire and England cricketer, became a sports psychologist after playing and I think his work has been instrumental in helping an understanding of the role.

The modern professional sportsperson is refreshingly honest and open-minded about these matters now, mocking the antiquated, Botham-like attitudes. The training of the mind is as important as the training of the body. They know that, and they know that it is not a sign of weakness to admit as much.

Other sports have long acknowledged the benefits of sports psychology. Take golf, and the work, say, Dr Bob Rotella has done with Padraig Harrington. But rugby, cricket and indeed football have been slower on the uptake. The work of Steve Black and Dave Alred with Jonny Wilkinson was often viewed with suspicion.

When Bawden went to Australia for the 2010/11 Ashes tour, he was immediately pronounced the 'yips doctor', there apparently just to prevent a repeat of Steve Harmison's famously wild first ball (ending up in the hands of his captain, Andrew Flintoff, at second slip) of the previous tour in 2006/07.

Bawden is actually well qualified to talk about the 'yips', that horrible affliction suffered by, for example, golfers when they shake or twitch while putting, or in cricket where bowlers suddenly cannot let go of the ball. Previously simple actions become impossible. It has affected golfers like Bernhard Langer, darts player Eric Bristow and many cricketers like Leicestershire's Scott Boswell and Yorkshire's Gavin Hamilton.

As a young cricketer Bawden was afflicted by them and by the age of 16 his career as a bowler was over. So he undertook a career in sports psychology, doing a PhD on the 'yips'. 'We've found out that it happens in multiple sports and that it's an emotional problem, unrelated to sport, that manifests as a physical thing when you're under pressure in sport,' he says. 'It is reversible if you catch it early, using so-called less-conscious techniques. Some people try to get those affected to think their way out of it, but it's not possible.'

But batting is different. You have to think your way through it. If you were like me, it was a constant battle within the mind. By the end of my career, I knew that if I could get my mind right before a match, there was a very good chance that I would score runs. But getting myself into that state of mind was exhausting. I officially retired in 2004 with a knee injury that by then had required seven operations, having played just one first-class match in 2003. I probably had another couple of years left in me, but part of me knew that the mental battle was becoming harder and harder.

It was a battle that I was always going to lose in the end. In so many ways I was very similar to New Zealand's Martin Crowe, who in 2014 wrote: 'The mindwork I did proved exhausting – having to disguise a contaminated flow of thoughts. Not surprisingly, the lack of natural positive thinking, of authenticity, got me in the end. Ten years of "performed" mind control was my limit.'

Authenticity is an interesting word to use regarding this, but it is apposite, because discovering confidence and a positive mental attitude is often all about conning the mind. As Crowe says: 'Faking it until I made it into the zone.'

As I said, mental.

Crowe's career, in which he revealed himself as one of the most classical batsmen of his time with an average of over 45 in 77 Tests with 17 centuries, was over by 1996, but he used sports psychologists even though they were still relatively new to the game.

'My mind was often filled with thoughts, coupled with under-developed emotions,' he wrote. 'It wasn't a great mix in which to take on the art of batting at the top level. My footwork was sure and a priority, yet I quickly realized that footwork and mindwork go hand in glove. I needed some mental crutches and so I sought out the new phenomenon of sports psychology to deal with an overflow of desultory musing.

'I learnt techniques of visualization, of playing the future out in the mind first, using pictures. I learnt concentration – turning on and off to conserve energy, and encouraging a fierce focus for each ball for five-second periods. I tried removing negatives with Bruce Lee tips, imagined screwing an imaginary piece of paper up with my hand, tried to stay in the now by activating one of the five senses in between balls.

'Most of all, I learnt to repeat affirmations one after the other ("Head still, head still, watch the ball, watch the ball"), slowly and deliberately, to block out any unforeseen random thought ("What if I get out?") that might jump into my head and trip me up again. Yet using these techniques was akin to a lost man trying to find his way to safety.'

Or was Crowe just demonstrating exactly what mental strength is? Steve Waugh has said – and the definition was given to him by the great Australian rugby league coach Wayne Bennett – that mental strength is just the ability not to give in to oneself. 'In other words, do not take the short cuts or easy options,' Waugh says.

Isn't that what Crowe was doing? It was what Waugh was doing earlier when he talked of his renewed purpose at net practice. 'In a way I was acquiring mental toughness because I was not giving in to myself or taking the easy option,' he said of those net sessions. 'Top-level cricket is a game that is won between the ears and not necessarily by the most aesthetically pleasing techniques. To me, peer-group pressure and ego are the two greatest dangers to a professional sportsperson, because they take you away from being yourself and playing in the present.'

For David Gower that would mean playing in a certain manner, the carefree method that became his signature from the moment he pulled his first ball in Test cricket for four. 'To me, concentration was the ability to keep the inner voice quiet – an inner voice that nagged at me to do the extravagant thing, to take the big risks, play the eye-catching shot,' he has written. 'I had some lively exchanges with this mischievous little voice, which would whisper in my ear, "Next time the ball is anywhere near off stump it's going for four through cover."'

In the early 2000s Mike Hussey's career was not going the way he intended, and certainly nothing like the way it eventually went with such outstanding success. He had just failed in a Sheffield Shield match for Western Australia against Queensland.

He felt that he had simply not been mentally strong enough to cope with the pressure from the Queenslanders, who had stopped him scoring, as well as 'sledging' him relentlessly.

So he had an idea. He grabbed a pen and a piece of paper, and sat down to write a letter.

'Steve Waugh,' he wrote. 'I know you are a very busy man. But it would be hugely appreciated if you could put pen to paper to help me out with just a few words.

'How do I become more "mentally tough"? What is mental toughness? Playing in a game recently at the Gabba, the Queensland bowlers were chirpy and bowling very tight. I really wanted to get through the tough situation. I went through my same routine each ball, had a clear focus and was readily accepting the pressure.

'I'm very big on hard work and preparation. I am a tight player, quite technically correct and like to build up an innings. I'm patient early, watch the ball, work the singles and play straight.

'But Queensland seemed to build the pressure up on me by cutting down my scoring options, bowling patiently, giving me hardly any balls to hit,' he continued. 'They really chirped in my ear (which is really hard not to listen to). It got to the stage where I didn't know where my next run was coming from.

'I really wanted to do well and I wanted to be tough and enjoy the challenge, but deep down I had this fear of failure or doubt in my mind. How can I approach similar situations? What can I do to prepare myself and believe that I can become a more mentally tough player?'

Hussey never sent that letter, but he reproduced it in full in his excellent book *Mr Cricket*. The reason he did not send it? A combination of cold feet and the fact that, as he wrote it, he wondered what advice Waugh might have given and he found that he was answering his own questions. He had given in to himself, and he had given in to the Queenslanders' chirping. He resolved to be stronger mentally, and he certainly did that.

It is not a shock to discover that Hussey used a sports psychologist to help him. He had already been doing so before this, and had been focusing especially on preparation, something that would have impressed Graham Gooch.

Professor Sandy Gordon of the University of Western Australia was the psychologist who talked to Hussey about a player's ideal performance state (IPS).

'Sandy wanted to get people thinking about the game beyond just hitting balls,' says Hussey. 'He would hand out these sheets that you had to fill out about your performance. He wanted you to think of a time when you performed well and consider everything you did leading into that good performance, even those things you thought were irrelevant.

'Pretty soon I was writing everything down – what I ate, how I slept, what I did the night before, the week before. Sandy felt that if you did that each time you performed well, eventually you would see patterns and from there you could work out your IPS, the point from which you could give yourself the best possible chance at being able to re-create that good performance on each occasion.'

I can relate to that entirely. Over time I developed a method of preparation with which I was comfortable and which I felt worked, from always having nine hours' sleep the night before to having poached eggs on brown toast for breakfast, and even to the series of stretching and fast-feet movements I would do just before going out to bat. It was my century-making formula.

It takes time to work this out, though, even for the very best players. Take Steve Waugh and his reaction to getting out to John Emburey for 71 in an Ashes Test in 1986/87. And it should be remembered that this was before Waugh had made a Test century.

'"What a bloody waste you imbecile" was all I could mutter to myself as I walked off,' he wrote. 'I was livid at the dismissal, which came from a cocktail of poor concentration, lack of respect and absence of routine. I had faced up without being quite ready but then again the way I faced up was different every time I came out to bat. I didn't have a method that automatically made me switch on, as I know now the consistent players do.'

Waugh had had concentration problems on his Test debut against India in 1985. He got off the mark with a single off Kapil Dev into the covers. 'There's no reason why you can't start off with a century, it isn't so hard after all,' he said to himself.

He was out for just 13. And later he wrote: 'Concentration is about thinking only one thought at a time and staying in the present. Here I was ahead of myself, thinking of possible outcomes and I fell for the ultimate sin: not giving the bowler enough respect.'

As for batting itself, I think Hussey had one of the best ways of approaching it. 'Think about batting at the end of a kitchen table,' he once said. 'Clear away all the plates, knives, forks, other distractions and just bat on a clean, shiny table.'

That is batting and century-scoring in a nutshell. The absolute key to it is watching the ball. That is so obvious but it is also so difficult to achieve. I reckon I batted professionally for about six years without actually watching the ball properly. It took my team-mate Adrian Dale to mention it to me one day at nets. 'Are you watching the ball?' he asked.

'Of course I am,' I replied.

'No, really watching the ball,' he said. 'Really focusing on it without thinking about anything else.'

The answer to that was an emphatic no. There had always been things whirring in my mind, mostly technical matters.

But I was later to discover that I was hardly alone in this regard. In his thought-provoking book, *Seeing the Sunrise*, Justin Langer tells the story of playing a match for Scarborough, his club side in Perth, and batting very scratchily.

After being out, he walked over to the viewing area, where he found two friends, Victor Smith, a psychologist, and Neil 'Noddy' Holder, a renowned batting coach who has worked with a host of Australian and English players.

Smith asked Langer what he had been thinking about when batting. Langer replied that he had been working for some weeks on his trigger movements, especially the position of his front foot.

'That explains it all,' said Smith. 'If you are thinking about your feet, how can you possibly have your mind on the only thing that really matters: the ball? You have to give the ball 100% of your attention as the bowler is about to let go of the ball, not 90, 80 or 50%, but 100%. That is what concentration is about.'

That is so right. If you look closely, you will see players on television mouthing 'Watch the ball' to themselves as the bowler is running in. I had never done that before, but I started doing it after Dale's prompting. There might often be an expletive inserted too, and sometimes when I was really struggling for concentration, I would say to myself 'Do it for Peter James!'

I was always batting for my dad. I wanted to make him proud. As I said at the start of this book, I wanted to make big scores, big centuries, for him. This was my way of reminding myself of that fact. But I was also making sure that I was trying as hard as I could to watch the ball.

As long as a bowler's action was good, I found that I could actually watch the seam. That in turn helped give me cues as to which way the ball might be swinging or spinning. It meant, for example, that I could pick the variations of the Pakistani leg-spinner Mushtaq Ahmed through the air, just by watching the seam.

Mind you, for some reason I could never pick the googly of Ian Salisbury, the England leg-spinner who played for Sussex, Surrey and Warwickshire. I never truly worked out why that was, although back in those days we did not have the extensive video analysis players have today. If that had been the case, I am pretty sure that I would have scoured the footage for clues that might have helped me.

Sometimes watching the seam is useless. Facing the great Sri Lanka spinner Muttiah Muralitharan is an example, because all his deliveries arrived with a scrambled seam. There was nothing in the flight to suggest which way the ball was going to go. With his, shall we say, curious action and the fizzing revolutions of the ball, it was probably little surprise that Australia's Allan Border mistook him for a leg-spinner upon first sighting in 1992.

I was actually lucky in that I only faced Muralitharan before he had fully developed his 'doosra'. But he still had a top-spinner that was pretty effective, and so when I faced him in my second – and final – Test match, at the Oval in 1998, I mistook the ball I was trying to drive to mid-on for an off-spinner. It was no such thing. It was the top-spinner, and it duly landed back in Muralitharan's hands for a simple caught-and-bowled.

Whether a batsman can watch the ball from a bowler's hand onto the bat is another matter. There has been some evidence to suggest that it is not actually possible.

In 2000, Michael Land, a professor at Sussex University, and Peter McLeod, an experimental psychologist at Oxford University, concluded just that from a study: that batsmen do not watch the ball throughout its trajectory from hand to bat, and that once the ball has left the bowler's hand the eyes are moved swiftly to the part of the pitch where the ball is expected to land, where the trajectory is picked up again.

'We found that the time of the delivery, the time of the bounce and the position of the bounce provides enough information for a batting response,' Professor Land said.

Then the question is whether the ball can actually be seen at the moment of impact on the bat. When photographed, most batsmen seem to have their eyes closed at that moment of impact. I'm pretty sure that I could not watch the ball onto the bat, relying instead on anticipation and muscle memory. But other batsmen have averred that they can, especially when playing back.

'I think I am right in saying that you should always play back if you can because you can watch the ball right onto the bat,' said Sir Jack Hobbs. 'When you play forward, there must be a split second when you lose sight of the ball. If I was in trouble I had a tendency to play back. I would rather have a man play all back than all forward and I do not mind how many coaches of the old school shake their heads at that remark.'

Hobbs' comments are certainly a contrast to the common maxim of 'when in doubt, push out!' and are not much use to a player like Kevin Pietersen, who never plays back at all, always using his height to get forward and even pull off the front foot. A modern player like Joe Root, though, is very much of the Hobbs way of thinking. He plays back whenever he can.

What I do know is that the eyes are a much-neglected part of the training required for a batsman. They are absolutely vital, their muscles every bit as important as – maybe more important than – the other muscles in the body.

But I did not receive any specific eye training until an Australian coach, Jeff Hammond, arrived at Glamorgan in 2000. The only problem with Hammond was that he did not really know what he was doing in terms of the exercises he gave us, but, as with much of his other coaching that was not wholly successful at Glamorgan, his intentions were good.

In 1994 Mike Selvey, the former England bowler and esteemed cricket correspondent of the *Guardian*, conducted a fascinating interview with Ken West, an eye specialist, or 'sports visual consultant', as he termed himself.

'Just one person in 30,000 has a perfect visual system with perfect focusing skills and perfect line-up skills,' West said. 'Eighty per cent of bad habits in, say, cricket technique involve trying to compensate for error in visual input. The muscles in the eye are neglected, unlike any others, but in reality they have to be as high-performance as any skeletal muscle, and they can be improved.

'This doesn't necessarily translate directly to improved performance – some don't know how to employ an improved system – but we have found that once they are aware of the way to look, where to look and how to look, they can gain more consistency, more power and more accuracy as a result.'

West once worked with South African batsman Daryll Cullinan. 'When I started work with Daryll, he was a talented young player who had been discarded and was on the verge of quitting the game,' said West. 'He had been to the top coaches and psychologists and no one could help him.

'In fact we discovered that he had a vision tracking problem – his eyes didn't turn in properly, so he was always looking fractionally behind where the ball actually was.

'We worked on his visual system to enable him to line up on where the ball actually was and then the mechanics started to work together, he began to learn again, came back to the sport and now is a top player.'

Indeed he was, even if Shane Warne got him out so regularly that Cullinan became his 'bunny'. And, happy to report, cricketers now do more training on their eyes, with England having used the former South African hockey player Sherylle Calder during their 2004/05 tour to the country.

Calder describes herself on Twitter these days as 'the Eye Lady' and she worked with the England rugby union side before their 2003 Rugby World Cup triumph, as well as the New Zealand rugby squad and the South African cricket team.

Anyway, back to the 'watch the ball' mantra. It is done as much to focus the mind as begin any optical process. It is the moment at which you are telling your brain that it is time to switch on properly.

This is Andrew Strauss in his recent autobiography describing in detail his Test debut against New Zealand. '"Two please," I call out to the umpire, with my bat held upright in front of middle and leg stump,' he writes. 'I look down at the ground and tap my bat on the crease. I am solely concentrating on the process now. There are no more thoughts. I bring my eyes up to see Chris Martin, a tall, gangly swing bowler who can get them down there quite quickly, starting his run-up. "Watch the ball," I whisper to myself. "Watch the f------ ball."'

Some batsmen, of course, can watch the ball intently without having to remind themselves to do so. Mike Atherton was one of them. 'If I was playing really well, I would say absolutely nothing to myself,' he says. 'My mind would be a blank, not thinking of anything, not telling myself anything. If you are playing badly, then everything – your head, hands, bat, all that kind of thing creep in. The more you can blank your mind and trust your instincts the better. But that's a hard thing to do. Jonathan Trott always says "Watch the ball" to himself, but I would be watching the ball – I actually used to focus very hard on the ball – but I would do it naturally, and not tell myself to do it.'

Interestingly, after a while Mike Hussey changed his cues. 'Routines take you forward, habits take you back,' he said in a series of notes to himself. 'My cue is: watch the ball, see the ball. But after two years of saying the same thing, it isn't as meaningful. Try changing my cues for a while to make it more meaningful: "See the seam".'

Fair enough, but the message and the rationale remain. I think I needed that moment when I said 'Watch the ball' in order to differentiate between the different levels of awareness required for batting.

Because the truth is that you cannot concentrate fiercely for six hours in a day, and, as an opening batsman, that is the length of time you are aiming to achieve at the crease. 'Bat for six hours and you will have scored a century,' Alan Jones always told me at Glamorgan.

I wanted to be in full eyeballs-out warrior mode all the time. But it is simply not possible.

Greg Chappell, the great Australian batsman, once wrote a book called *Fierce Focus*. In it he described the three levels of concentration he had for his batting. The first was 'Awareness'.

It was, he said, like a car being in neutral. He used this when waiting to go in to bat, between balls and between overs. It is the state of being aware of what is happening around you but not focusing on one thing in particular.

The second was 'Fine Focus'. This was the car's first gear. This was for when the bowler began his run-up. Chappell would first count the number of fielders as a cue and then he would watch the bowler's face for clues about his state of mind.

And the third was 'Fierce Focus'. This was for when the bowler was about to deliver the ball.

That for me is a superb way of detailing the states of mind required. At one stage in my career I wanted to be in 'Fierce Focus' from the moment the captain won the toss and decided to bat, or, if we were in the field, when the opposition lost their eighth wicket. No wonder I was a late developer in the game.

But at least I had the capacity and the willingness to take my mental state to full arousal. The problem with a good deal of players is that they do not have the ability or desire to do that.

As even the great Steve Waugh admitted in the earlier stage of his career: 'Switching on is a key element to batting, but unless you realise your method isn't working to its full potential, you'll keep making the same mistakes,' he said. 'My focus wasn't as sharp as it could have been or as clear as I'd imagined. The need for total and utter devotion to each and every ball wasn't being met. I was being hampered by a lack of attention to detail. The lights were on, but the dimmer switch needed to be turned up.'

Unsurprisingly, Graham Gooch thinks along similar lines. 'At the non-striker's end you switch off from technique, instead you think about the score, and other things,' he says. 'It's your mini down-time as a batsman. The way I describe it is as turning the volume down. You don't switch off completely, but you just drop it down. It's like waiting at a set of lights. I learnt over my career that when you step out in between balls, that is almost as important as facing the ball. It is about how you reset. You draw a line under the last ball. The only thing that is important is the next ball, whether you have played a great shot or have played and missed. It is a one-ball game.

'I used to mark my line, something I had watched Barry Richards – one of my heroes as a player – do. That is my message, to draw a line under the last ball. Step back in, reinforce my message, I am ready for the next ball.'

As Matthew Maynard, now a successful coach, says: 'I think that in the first part of your career you don't develop your cues. That's one thing that I try to work on with the younger lads now as much as possible. Try to get your cues and a routine. That routine might change and adapt, but at the start of my career all I was thinking about was hitting the ball. I didn't think about my guard or say: "Watch the ball." I think I was quite a chilled player, I wasn't that intense.

'People used to talk about watching the wrist, say, of Malcolm Marshall to see if he was going to bowl the inswinger but if I was doing that I must have only been doing it subconsciously. Googlies and stuff – how can I watch the wrist when I am trying to watch the seam of the ball? I would try to pick the spin in the air.'

And here is Waugh again: 'The bowler beginning his run-up was the signal for me to move into "semi-awareness" mode, watching but not being absorbed by the action,' he says. 'At the precise moment the bowler took his last stride before delivery, my switch was flicked and the senses aroused to full capacity. If I struggled to reach the level I desired or felt distracted, I would revert to an old technique of talking to myself, saying things like "Watch the ball!" "Concentrate!" Or my favourite "Now!" I really enjoyed the task of lifting into a state of total absorption and then letting go two seconds later. If I did this correctly, I could bat all day long but only had to concentrate intensely for around 20 minutes. In doing so, I could stay relatively fresh.'

Waugh is right. Discovering how to concentrate is almost as enjoyable as the act of concentrating itself. But no major innings, and certainly no century, can be achieved without it.

3
Luck

Sometime during the season of 2013, I spoke to Ed Smith about my plans for this book. Smith is the former Kent, Middlesex and England batsman, who is now a very successful author, journalist and broadcaster.

I like him. I happened to be among the opposition when he made a century on his first-class debut, for Cambridge University against Glamorgan in 1996.

'How do you score a century, Ed?' I asked.

'You play and miss a bit, hit a few, then play and miss a bit more . . .' he laughed. He was being deliberately flippant but his point was clear. Invariably you require some luck to make a century.

And he should know. He's written a whole book about the subject, with the simple title *Luck*. Not just about luck in cricket, of course, but in sport and in life in general.

His mention of the play-and-miss is illuminating, though. It is something that happens regularly, especially early on in an innings, and is often disregarded by commentators with a breezy 'Good ball there from Bloggs that beats the bat.'

Only a matter of inches will have saved the batsman from cricketing death. And it pays not to give this reality too much thought. I remember talking to my coach Graham Burgess at school about how to play the moving ball. If the ball was swinging in the air, he said that the key was not to move too early. And he was right, as he was about all things cricket. 'Go back in your crease and then come into the ball late,' he said.

'But what about the seaming ball?' I asked. The reply really did make me think. The gist of it was that there is often not much you can do about a seaming ball. The deviation occurs too late for proper adjustment. 'Hold the line of your shot,' he said. In other words, hope that you play and miss.

Or, put another way, you hope that you make a greater mistake than if you were out edging the ball. Understand? The idea is to hit the ball in the middle of the bat. Miss doing that by, say, a foot, then you will be OK. Miss it by half the width of the bat, and you are gone, caught behind off the edge. No wonder batting frazzles the mind.

Some players seem to play and miss very well. During England's tour of India in 2012/13, captain Alastair Cook did astoundingly well, scoring centuries in the first three of the four Tests – 176 in Ahmedabad, 122 in Mumbai and 190 in Kolkata – in a series that England won 2-1 to take their first series victory there for 28 years. But he exasperated the Indians with his ability to play and miss without the ball finding the edge. 'It is as if he has invented a new shot that no one has mastered quite as well,' one of them told me.

Maybe it is a left-handed thing. And there was once something in the county game called the 'Kent leave', used by left-handers like Mark Benson from the county, whereby they would push forward and then slide their bat sideways away from the ball as if it was on a curtain rail.

It was difficult to know whether they were playing at the ball or not. Somerset's Marcus Trescothick uses this minimalist method too, as does Michael Carberry, who did play for Kent, as well as Surrey and Hampshire, and who showed this style of batting during the Ashes series Down Under in 2013/14.

On the same subject, Ken Barrington, who played 82 Tests for England and was a hugely popular assistant manager who died suddenly on the West Indies tour of 1981, once said of John Edrich, his Surrey and England colleague, who played 77 Tests and made 310 not out (England's fifth-highest Test score) against New Zealand at Headingley in 1965: 'He is a wonderfully consistent little left-hander, yet in a way an enigma. He seems to have a fantastic knack of playing and missing without getting a touch. I have seen him play and miss several times without disaster when thoroughly well set and presumably seeing it like a football.'

But the upshot of that is that you need some luck. 'You don't see too many chanceless innings,' says Graham Gooch. 'As [former England wicketkeeper] Alan Knott always used to say to me: "It's better to have arse than class."'

Gooch knows all about luck. When he made his 333 against India at Lord's in 1990, the third-highest Test score by an Englishman, behind Len Hutton's 364 against Australia at the Oval in 1938 and Wally Hammond's 336 not out against New Zealand in Auckland in 1933, he was dropped on 36 by wicketkeeper Kiran More.

And then Gooch made his quite brilliant 154 not out against the fearsome West Indies at Headingley in 1991. This, incidentally, was the best century I have watched as it happened live on television, but not the best I have seen live at a ground – that would be Graeme Smith's match-winning 154 not out for South Africa against England at Edgbaston in 2008.

Gooch drove the first ball he faced, a loosener from Patrick Patterson, in the air just wide of Malcolm Marshall at mid-off. 'Sometimes you just get luck,' he says.

Famous instances of luck abound before players went on

to make centuries and, often, many runs more. Take Andrew Strauss on Test debut against New Zealand at Lord's in 2004. He is on 91 and facing Chris Martin. He drives at the ball and inside edges it down to the fine leg boundary for four. He hears one noise as the ball catches the inside edge, but then immediately another.

'What was the noise?' he asks himself. There is no immediate answer, so he continues on his merry way to a debut century, but television replays later show him that the ball had actually clipped the off stump but had not dislodged the bails. Lucky.

What about when Brian Lara, in April 1994 at the St John's Recreation Ground in Antigua, broke Sir Garfield Sobers' Test record 365 with 375? When he pulled Chris Lewis through mid-wicket for four to go past Sobers, his right pad touched the stumps. There is a picture of him looking back very guiltily and very anxiously. The bail moved slightly in its groove, but then returned to its rightful position. But what a death that would have been on 365. Hit wicket with the ball having been crashed away for four.

I was out hit wicket in that way, once, actually. I wasn't on 365, mind, 38 in fact, and it wasn't in a Test match, but it was the only occasion I was out hit wicket, and it happened to come against my county, Glamorgan, in my first match for Cambridge University in 1989. I pulled a short ball from my old mate Steve Watkin through mid-wicket for four, only to touch the leg stump with my left boot as I swivelled around. As you can imagine, the story has been embellished over the years. Done for pace, and all that.

There is another Lara story involving luck, of course, and that involves the record 501 not out mentioned previously. From the first ball he faced in that epic innings, Lara was very nearly caught-and-bowled by Anderson Cummins, a fellow West Indian, who was the overseas player for Durham. Then when he had made 10 he was actually bowled by the same bowler, but it was called a no-ball. 'Luck went my way,' Lara admitted.

On 18, however, came the biggest slice of fortune, and a moment Durham's wicketkeeper, Chris Scott, will never forget. The catch off left-armer Simon Brown's bowling was simple, but Scott put it down. 'I suppose he'll get a hundred now,' lamented Scott.

Lara did make a century, his seventh century in eight first-class innings, a run that had begun with that Test match 375 and had continued with 147 against Glamorgan at Edgbaston, an astonishing innings that I am quite proud to say I witnessed from the covers.

But Lara also did a little more. Indeed he did so much that Scott's drop cost 483 runs. That is shopping-at-Harrods expensive.

What's more, Lara reckons that Scott could have run him out. 'Thinking I was out,' he said, 'I walked a couple of steps towards the pavilion only to realize that Scott had dropped it. If he had been quick thinking he might have been able to run me out.'

Poor Scott, a lovely chap, who had begun his career with Nottinghamshire, where I had often played against him in the second team. He now coaches at Cambridge University.

A month after that 'drop' he joyfully scored his maiden first-class century, 13 long years after his debut, but as he says: 'I know I'll always be the Man Who Dropped Lara.'

It was an unusual set of circumstances that allowed Lara to make such a huge score. They had to be. Such opportunities do not come along every week.

Durham had scored 556-8 on an Edgbaston pitch that the umpires Trevor Jesty and Peter Wight described as being just too good. Warwickshire had reached 210-2 with Lara 111 not out by the end of day two, and then the third day was washed out.

No deal could be done between the captains on the last day, so by lunch Lara was already past 250. It was then that he revealed his plans. Gladstone Small, his team-mate, remembers it well.

'We were sitting in the dressing room at lunch . . . me, Brian and Keith Piper,' he says. 'Brian said, "I'm going for the record." I asked, "What the 375?" He said, "No. Hanif Mohammad's 499." I asked him, "Are you serious? You're still 250 runs away." He said, "You watch me."'

Lara had more luck. He had also been dropped on 238, and then on 413 he was again reprieved, this time by Warwickshire's Michael Burns, who was fielding for the depleted visitors. And then the part-timer John Morris was bowling some filthy seamers in what was always going to be the last over of the day. But Lara, on 497, did not know that. So he was rather lucky that from the fourth ball of the over, Morris hit him flush on the head. Then his partner Piper could come down the pitch, and advise him of the scenario. Lara duly hit the next ball for four, and that was that.

Afterwards Lara's phone rang. It was Hanif. 'I am not sad at losing my record. It is good for cricket,' he said.

As I write this, Kevin Pietersen is very much in the news. Following England's calamitous 5-0 Test series defeat Down Under in 2013/14, it was decided that Pietersen's services were no longer required.

He had made 8,181 Test runs with 23 centuries. But let's go back to the first of those 23 centuries at the Oval in 2005, and consider the luck required, not just for Pietersen to announce himself as a remarkable talent, but also for England to secure the draw that gave them the Ashes in probably the greatest Test series ever played.

Pietersen arrived at the crease with the dismissal of Ian Bell, out first ball to Glenn McGrath for a dreaded pair.

The first ball was short, and was deflected to slip. It had actually come off Pietersen's shoulder, but it could easily have touched glove along the way. The appeal, as you can imagine, was deafening and demanding.

Remember that these were the days before the Decision Review

System. Pietersen mouthed 'no' to McGrath. And thankfully for him and for England, umpire Billy Bowden said not out. It was a brilliant decision. But I think so many umpires might have made a different one.

Five balls later, still without a run to his name, Pietersen could have been out to Shane Warne. Had the ball that Pietersen edged not hit wicketkeeper Adam Gilchrist on the way, then Matthew Hayden would surely have been presented with a simple catch at slip.

Soon afterwards Pietersen was on 15 when he drove hard at Brett Lee. The ball went quickly at throat height to first slip, where Warne, inexplicably, dropped it. He parried it, and tried to claim the rebound, but could not do so.

Pietersen went on to make 158. A star was born, the Ashes were regained. Lucky, lucky Pietersen; lucky, lucky England.

All cricketers require some luck, as Kerry Packer, the late Australian media tycoon who brought the revolutionary World Series Cricket to the game, once hilariously expressed to Justin Langer.

The scene was a dinner at Packer's house in Sydney in 2005, and among the guests were Langer, Steve Waugh, Matthew Hayden, Brett Lee and Shane Watson. The topic of conversation came around to luck. 'You see, men, luck plays a huge part in a man's success or failure,' said Packer. 'Some people are lucky, some are just plain unlucky. I've been plain bloody lucky.'

Packer then looked at Langer. 'As for you, young fella, you've had plenty of luck, haven't you?'

'Yes,' said Langer.

'You're lucky,' replied Packer. 'You're lucky they invented helmets, son, or you'd be dead!'

And Packer was right, because Langer did get hit on the head very often, most notably from only his second ball in Test cricket, bowled by the West Indian Ian Bishop at Adelaide in 1993, and then from the first ball of his 100th Test against

LUCK

South Africa in Johannesburg in 2006. Makhaya Ntini was
the bowler then and Langer, the bravest of batsmen, was badly
concussed. This is, of course, a story given horrible relevance by
the sad death of Phillip Hughes, so tragically killed when hit
by a bouncer in 2014.

Luck can be a dirty word. Describe someone as lucky sometimes, and it is as if you are accusing him or her of treason. I
once wrote a column, for the 'Final Whistle' section of the
Daily Telegraph, about how I thought the Wales rugby team had
had some luck in defeating England at Twickenham in 2012,
when a last-minute 'try' from England wing David Strettle was
disallowed.

Even with the benefit of television referral, there was
insufficient evidence to show that he had grounded the ball, even
if he swears to this day, as do some of the players around him
at that moment, that the try was scored. A difficult conversion
would have ensued to draw the match for England, but the point
I was making was that there was an element of luck involved.
As the Wales captain Sam Warburton, man of the match in that
encounter, said to me afterwards when we wrote his column: 'We
were so lucky there!'

But, boy, the reaction! I got slated. It seems that there are
a lot of people out there who do not believe in luck. They seem
to quite like the Geoffrey Boycott approach to it. As he said:
'Dennis Amiss [his sometime opening partner] used to say,
"Good luck" to me. I used to reply, "It's not luck but ability
that counts."'

I remember once saying 'Bad luck' to Grant Flower after he
had been out when we were playing for Mashonaland together in
Zimbabwe. 'It's nothing to do with luck,' he said quite forcibly,
with maybe the odd expletive thrown in.

David Boon, the rather rotund but seriously good Australian
batsman, obviously did not believe in luck. He once said that
in his first-class career, 350 matches, in which he made 68

75

centuries, only one ball – a leg-cutter from the West Indian Curtly Ambrose – had been unplayable. All the rest of his dismissals were his fault.

These are not rare opinions. I know that if my friend Gareth Rees, the Glamorgan batsman who retired at the end of the 2014 season, has got this far into this tome, he will now be screaming at what he has read. Indeed he might even be calling me right now.

You see, he does not believe in luck. Not one bit. He considers it a refuge for those unhappy about events that they cannot control. 'It is just a perception,' he says. 'With greater skill and knowledge, it would never be considered. It is a spurious imagination.'

He is a mathematician, after all. The view that luck is just 'probability taken personally' is a widely held one.

And I will admit that when I was playing, I was more inclined to that point of view than I am now. As a player you do not want to admit that chance and luck might be playing a major part in your career. You simply want to work harder and become better so that you think you are leaving as little to chance as possible. And that is a wholly admirable policy, probably the only policy.

But retirement offers a detached contemplation that allows you to realize that there are indeed a whole host of events and circumstances which are beyond your control.

It is a subject, of course, that you could write a whole book upon, as Ed Smith has done. And you can become highly intellectual and mathematical about it, talking about randomness and probability theories.

But I am happy to assume that luck does exist and that it does matter. Having made a triple century after being dropped – an absolute sitter – on 15, then I'm pretty sure that luck exists.

Bad luck too, because on my Test debut against South Africa at Lord's in 1998 I was caught behind down the leg side by wicketkeeper Mark Boucher off Allan Donald. It was not just that I was caught down the leg side – always known as an unlucky manner in which to be dismissed for any batsman – but the fact that Boucher took a leaping catch, high to his left. He was not a very good keeper at that early stage of his career, and indeed soon afterwards he dropped Alec Stewart from a much, much simpler chance. I was on 10 at the time. A hundred surely beckoned. OK, maybe not, but you get my gist.

I am not trying to claim that I was more or less lucky than any other cricketer, just pointing out that, in what turned out to be the two most important innings of my career, there were two instances of luck being hugely influential. The examples I've given for Cook, Gooch, Strauss, Lara and Pietersen surely prove that there must be other instances at lower levels in every game.

In fact I will go a bit further about luck in cricket. You know the cliché that form is temporary and class is permanent. What if I said that I thought that form is non-existent, that instead batting is more about luck than form? If I said that batsmen do not go through patches of form, they go through patches of luck?

Yes, there might be periods when a batsman's technical competency dips considerably and therefore he doesn't score many runs, but that is a different matter. Yes, there is also a lot of skill required to score runs. But so too a large amount of luck.

That Lady always walks with you to the crease. As I once wrote: 'Batsmen go through periods when the Lady eagerly holding their armguard is beautiful, kind and generous; others when she is a horrible, cruel bitch.'

What is form? It is just a run of good scores, with every score engendering a little more confidence. Just because a player endures a run of low scores, it does not necessarily mean that he is out of form. It probably just means that he has not had the luck needed to overcome the initial, always difficult, stages of an innings.

Take this quote from Ken Barrington. He was rather famous for mixing up his words and his metaphors, but I understand entirely what he is saying here.

He had just had four single-figure scores, with two ducks among them, when he was approached by a Surrey fan sympathizing with him over his 'poor form'.

'How d'you know I'm out of form?' replied Barrington. 'I've only had nine balls all week!'

Exactly. You hear of cricketers talking about bad form and how awful they feel at the crease. Take David Gower. 'It usually didn't take long to get an idea about how things would go,' he says. 'All being well, by the time you'd reached the crease you'd responded positively to the applause of the crowd and the sense of occasion, and felt uplifted. You would be feeling fully switched on and alert. When that happened, it was a great feeling.

'On other days, though, the tension just would not lift. It stayed in your chest, and was sometimes so pronounced you could really feel it physically. I could take guard in the normal place but my stance might feel just wrong, awkward. I could suddenly and worryingly realise that I was not watching the bowler's hand or the ball properly. I might be lunging rather than moving. Nothing was quite in sync and I'd be churning inside. On the worst days it was genuinely as though I had forgotten how to bat.'

Indeed there is a funny tale about Matthew Hayden as regards this. He was once asked to give a presentation at the Australian Academy, and the question asked was what it was like to feel out of form. 'Like holding another man's old fella in your hands,' Hayden said, to much astonishment, as well as hilarity.

Yes, there are times when the bat just does not feel right in your hands. But that can happen at the start of any innings, whether you are on a run of low scores or not. There is always tension at the beginning of an innings, as we discussed with regards to ducks. A run of scores will give you some confidence that will help alleviate that, but the truth is that you will probably require some luck to make a significant score, a century even.

There is a saying in cricket – 'Never mess with good form' – and it is very true in that you should never take a good run of scores for granted. It is too easy to do that, to forget Graham Gooch's eternal verity that 'You have never got enough'.

But it really should read: 'Never mess with good luck'. That, for instance, is what Alastair Cook was making sure that he did not do when so prolific in India. He probably knew at the back of his mind that all that playing and missing could not continue for ever. I remember talking to him during his record-breaking Ashes series Down Under in 2010/11 when he scored 766 runs at an average of 127.66.

'You've always got that nagging doubt as a batter,' he said. '"What if I don't score any more runs?" You're always thinking: "What about the next innings?"'

In other words, he was worried his luck would run out. It always does at some stage, as Cook discovered during the series Down Under in 2013/14. Yes, Australia bowled very well and very accurately at him, but he started attracting some very good deliveries there, and then started to make some uncharacteristically poor decisions as a result of that bad luck.

His run of low scores continued long into the 2014 season, until, lo and behold, he had some luck. In the third Test against India at Southampton, he was dropped at slip – an absolute dolly – on 15. He went on to make 95. His batting worries were eased, as were growing concerns about his Test captaincy as England won the Test and went on to win the series having been 1-0 down after losing the second Test at Lord's.

We will talk about Jonathan Trott later and his lack of runs that so preyed on his mind and eventually forced him to leave the 2013/14 Ashes early, but just check this quote from him when he later talked for the first time about what he called his 'burn-out' that winter. He is talking about the first Test of the previous summer against Australia at Trent Bridge (remember that there were back-to-back Ashes series in 2013/14).

'I chopped on in the first innings at Trent Bridge and then was given out incorrectly in the second,' he said. 'And, all of a sudden, I was questioning myself. I was going into games anxious. I wasn't as patient as I had been in the past. I was chasing the game a bit; looking for shots that maybe weren't there. I was putting myself under pressure and getting a bit desperate.'

Why? Because some bad luck had begun it all. Trott didn't deal with that very well, and a downward spiral began. Yes, there were obviously a lot of other factors, but luck, or its bad brother, played its part.

It did not help that Trott had set unrealistically high standards. 'The more people said "Oh, you'll be great against Australia" the worse it was,' he said. 'I averaged 90 against them so, in my head, I needed to score 180 runs a game to sustain that. And that meant, if I made 100, I was still left thinking, "Oh no, I need to score another 80 in the second innings just to break even." I had set myself unsustainable standards.'

But it is also key that you do not blame bad luck entirely for a run of low scores. It can get to the stage where you return to the dressing room after another failure craving confirmation from your colleagues of your ill fortune. 'Bad luck, you got the best ball of the day there,' you want them to say.

Worse still, it can even adversely affect your personality. Ed Smith tells a good story of a team-mate to whom this happened. 'I played with one batsman who, if he was already out, would take every subsequent play-and-miss by a team-mate as a personal affront,' he says. '"Look at him, playing and missing," he would mutter, "I must have used up all the bad luck earlier on." Even though his batting was no longer relevant to the innings, he was unable to separate his own narrow struggle for runs from the wider experience of watching someone else bat. His own scarcity of runs was so prominent at the front of his mind that he couldn't see around it.'

Believe me, that is not unusual in professional cricket.

It all boils down to what you do with your luck. When I was younger, I could not cope with luck. If I was dropped early in an innings, it ruined things. It was never going to be a perfect innings, and people were always going to say that I had been lucky, so I immediately played very differently, more skittishly usually, and often got out.

It is fair to say that I never wholly came to terms with it. When dropped early on in that triple century, I convinced myself that it had been a 'bump' ball, that I had hit the ball into the ground before it went to gully, to Sussex's Richard Montgomerie, a delightful fellow by the way, and not just because he dropped that catch.

There was some doubt about it, so it was not just some wild delusion, but throughout that innings I had to convince myself that it had not been a catch. It was just too easy a chance to over-look in my mind.

It was not a 'bump' ball. I'll admit that now. But admitting it then was nigh on impossible.

It was little surprise, then, that I was a walker. To be given not out when you are out is clearly the largest slice of luck any bats-man can receive.

But can you then deal with the consequences? I couldn't. It is even harder to deal with than a dropped chance, because, usually, you are constantly reminded of it. Fielders do not normally sledge you about your luck in having survived a dropped chance or otherwise.

Indeed I can only remember that happening once to me. It was against Somerset in 2001 at Taunton. I had made 77 but was enduring a torrid time on a bouncy pitch from Andy Caddick.

Yet another short ball hit me on the glove and dropped just short of gully. The chirp from Marcus Trescothick, who by the way is a top man and I am not having a go at him, rang out loud and clear: 'Come on, boys, this bloke is having so much luck that it will end soon.'

I wanted to chuckle, but I was in too much pain. The ball from Caddick had actually broken my hand. Trescothick was right. My luck had ended. I faced one more ball (God knows why) and then walked off, pausing only briefly to remove my kit before heading to Taunton Hospital and having my hand and lower arm covered in plaster of Paris.

But the reaction of the fielding side when you have not walked?

Goodness, they tear in with the abuse. I say I was a walker, but there was one occasion during a second-team match for Glamorgan against Lancashire at Old Trafford when I did not walk. It was an awful decision by the umpire as I had gloved a turning ball from the off-spinner to leg slip.

But the resultant abuse was relentless. At one stage a Lancashire bowler shoulder-barged me as I took a single. I simply could not cope with it, and vowed never to do it again.

There were, of course, occasions during my career when bowlers and fielders felt that I had not walked, but I can honestly say that on none of those occasions did I definitely know that I had hit the ball.

For there are occasions when you are uncertain, especially if you hit your bat against your pad, something I did regularly. Get an edge at the same instant as you hit your pad, and there can be a great deal of uncertainty.

OK, there was an incident in a one-day match against the Combined Universities when I gloved a ball down the leg side and nobody, and I mean nobody, appealed, but I hope you will forgive me for that.

Walking is a most contentious issue, as was proved in the summer of 2013 when, in an Ashes Test at Trent Bridge, Stuart Broad did not walk for an edge that ended up in slip's hands via the wicketkeeper.

Therein lay the great problem with that incident. It quickly became the accepted wisdom that Broad had edged to slip. He hadn't, but his actions – or lack of them, because he didn't actually do anything – gave rise to some ridiculously sanctimonious views on the Spirit of Cricket.

What I did not understand was what made Broad's stand so different from any of the other hundreds, indeed thousands, of occasions on which a batsman has not walked. It seemed to be because this was more blatant.

Well, that is tosh. An edge is an edge.

Of course, I would prefer it if all batsmen walked, but the reality is that they don't. Unless everyone walks, it just won't work. Professional sports people will do what they can to win, although I thought that usually stopped at 'Mankad-ing' a batsman (running out the non-striker before letting the ball go), until the summer of 2014, when Sri Lanka did that very thing to England's Jos Buttler. I never once saw a 'Mankad' during my career in the professional game, not even a warning, because I believe that if a batsman is backing up properly, he could be 'Mankad-ed' nearly every ball.

Anyway, by walking I did not feel that I was serving for the morality police. I never forced my opinions upon others, and in fairness no one forced theirs upon me, even when I walked in two of my four innings for England.

And I am not so misty-eyed as to think that everyone will walk.

There was a time when that did happen to a certain extent, a time when the morals of, for example, the amateur golfer Bob Jones were alive and well.

The United States Golf Association has an award for sportsmanship named after Jones. This is why. Playing in the 1925 US Open, Jones found himself in the rough just off the fairway. As he set himself to play his shot, his iron gently touched the ball. No one saw a thing, but Jones summoned the marshals and called a two-stroke penalty upon himself. He lost the tournament by a stroke. When lauded widely for his sportsmanship afterwards he replied: 'You may as well praise a man for not robbing a bank.'

Most modern professional sportspeople simply do not think like that. By standing, batsmen think they are merely asking the umpires to do the job they are paid to do.

That has always been Mike Atherton's view, which is hardly surprising given that he stood having gloved Allan Donald behind at Trent Bridge in 1998, precipitating one of the most famous periods of play in Test match history, as an enraged Donald bombarded him with short balls, and Atherton played with great courage. And no one rebuked Atherton as they did Broad in 2013!

'If everyone walked, if everyone appealed only when they knew it was out, if everyone was 100 per cent honest then it would be a better game,' Atherton once wrote. 'Umpires would become mere bean counters, and judges of lbws, and the game would become a self-governing idyll. Just as I typed those words I looked up and saw a couple of pigs flying above.

'The reality is that sportsmen are not like that, never have been,' continued Atherton. 'In life very few things are black and white, leaving only shades of grey: we might regard ourselves as decent law-abiding citizens even though we routinely break the speed limit. So it is in sport, where different games demand a different adherence to the rules or laws. For myself, I was a confirmed non-walker and could easily live with the fact that I was asking an umpire to perform a job he is paid to do. I didn't, and still don't, regard that as cheating.'

But what about players who deliberately go out of their way to con the umpire? I've seen batsmen rub their shoulder when the ball has obviously hit bat or glove on the way through to the wicketkeeper.

And I have heard of top-class batsmen practising their

non-walking, making sure that they look as innocent as possible. Steve Waugh is not actually accusing Dean Jones of that here, but you can see what he is getting at when he says: 'Dean Jones was the best non-walker I have seen because his reaction never gave any inkling as to his guilt. He just scratched centre, adjusted his pads and carried on in a "business as usual" fashion.'

What confuses me is the distinction between not walking, which is not considered cheating by so many, and, say, claiming a catch on the half-volley, which is definitely considered cheating by all. To me that is double standards.

Walking is not easy to fathom, apparently. When Australia's Adam Gilchrist decided to walk in the 2003 World Cup semi-final against Sri Lanka, his team-mates were not impressed. After he returned to the dressing room, there was a stunned silence. 'The rule of these big moments in life is always that you don't know how big it is until you see others react. And it wasn't good,' he later wrote.

And opponents had their say too. After there had been a heated altercation between Gilchrist and New Zealand's Craig McMillan in 2004/05, the Kiwi skipper, Stephen Fleming, said pointedly: 'We're not all on a righteous crusade like Gilly.'

Gilchrist had actually been walking long before that, even if he had not been entirely clear about his motives. As a 17-year-old playing for Richmond (in London, that is) he had written home to his parents after being dismissed for 93 in a Sunday non-league match: 'For some reason I just walked without looking at the umpire,' he wrote. 'In the dressing room later on, the umpire asked "Did you hit that?" Ahhhh! Oh well, at least I was honest!?!???'

To some, technology has further muddied those waters.

But as an advocate of the Decision Review System, I am of the hope that, as technology improves, honesty might improve with it. Eventually batsmen might realize that they will definitely be shown up by technology like Hot Spot or the Snickometer. At the moment there is still a chance they will get away with it. And that is a chance most professionals will eagerly take.

I needed to be more like Steve Waugh. 'Quality players profit from let-offs, while unlucky ones don't make the most of their opportunities,' he says. 'People never describe a guy who scores 20 after being dropped on 10 as lucky, but if the same batsman goes on to get 120, he is seen as fortunate.'

So too Graham Gooch. 'If someone dropped me, I just thought: "Cash in,"' he says before quoting, with a smile, Randy Pausch, the American professor: 'Luck is when "Quality preparation meets the moment of opportunity."'

4

Superstition

To those who say that luck does not exist, I ask one question: why on earth do so many batsmen rely on superstition then?

The answer is that they are looking for a crutch.

Batting offers failure much more frequently than it does success. Sometimes those failures are a result of uncontrollable factors: lost tosses, poor pitches and wretched umpiring decisions, to name but a few. So it is little surprise that negativity and sometimes fatalism crave for attention in a batsman's mind. Superstitions are ways of easing those fears.

They don't work, of course, but for a time the correlation between the superstition and the scoring of runs is just too tempting to ignore. If you have gone through a series of actions and encountered a certain set of circumstances that have coincided with the scoring of a century, it is very difficult to untangle the whole sequence of events. They can become a package. Centuries are so rare that it is not as surprising, or indeed as silly, as it can look much later with the aid of sober reflection.

The most obvious and probably well-known example of this is the South African Neil McKenzie.

At various times during his career he indulged in a variety of superstitions: from his fear of treading on white lines (tricky when there are quite a few on a cricket pitch and that included the crease line!), to his insistence on putting down all the lavatory seats in the changing room before going out to bat, to always looking over his left shoulder just before facing the bowler and, finally, most bizarre and famous of all, his habit of taping his bat to the ceiling before batting.

The last mentioned happened because one day his colleagues did just that – taped his bat to the ceiling – as a practical joke. The problem – if you can call it that – was that McKenzie then proceeded to score a century.

That was it. McKenzie had to do that before every innings.

Former South Africa wicketkeeper Mark Boucher tells another story to illustrate McKenzie's obsession with these sorts of things. He recalls McKenzie hauling his kit-bag up several flights of stairs to a dressing room, where Boucher opened it up and picked up one of his bats. That was a no-no for McKenzie, who would not allow anyone to touch his bats before he had. So he packed the bag up, took it downstairs, put it back on the bus and then began the whole process again.

I made the same mistake as Boucher, but with my Glamorgan team-mate Matthew Maynard, picking up his bat once while he was waiting to bat at Headingley. He frowned at me, and walked over to his bag to pick up another one.

Compare that with Brian Lara, who on the third morning of the Antigua Test against England in 2004 allowed Sky Sports to have his bat for their programme introduction. He was 313 not out at the time, and of course went on to make his record 400 not out, but it was still rather strange to see David Gower holding the bat while talking to Ian Botham about whether Lara might indeed break the record that day.

'I am not superstitious,' said Lara, and apparently Gower was one of his boyhood heroes anyway, along with Roy Fredericks and Allan Border.

When Maynard explained what I had done, I was surprised. Maynard never seemed the superstitious kind. It was John Steele's fault apparently, though. Steele is the brother of David, 'the bank clerk who went to war' when batting for England against Australia and then West Indies in 1975/76, standing up courageously to their fastest bowlers.

John was an equally brave – and very stodgy! – batsman, who also bowled some left-arm spin. He spent most of his career at Leicestershire but then came to Glamorgan in his latter playing days before joining the coaching team. He was Glamorgan's second-team coach for a good part of my early professional days.

Anyway, he was a great theorist about the game, and he could never help picking up a cricket bat while explaining his latest idea. And that was a problem for Maynard.

I ask Maynard about it now and he first talks about the four personality types into which most sportspeople are characterized these days. There are the feelers, the thinkers, the enforcers and the mosquitos.

'I am a mosquito,' he says. 'I didn't like to think too much about what the bowler was doing. I used to like to go out, see ball, hit ball.'

He didn't want his mind cluttered with too many thoughts before batting. 'Steely was theoried up,' he says. 'It was in 1987, when he had finished playing and was coaching. I was batting at number four then. He was always picking bats up to explain stories, and he was saying things like: "This guy is not the worst bowler" and then he would go through the whole repertoire about every single bowler.

'For me it was not what I needed. On one occasion while I was waiting to go in, he had filled my head with the idea of changing my grip to play the short ball. I was thinking: "I've got a decent grip." I didn't get many that day and in the second innings the same thing happened. That was it. I asked him to stop touching my bat. And that was it for the rest of my career. If someone did touch my bat, I would go and get my number two bat out.'

Earlier in the book I mentioned about how Maynard did not know of the importance of centuries early in his career. Well, by 2000 he did. We were playing a match against Essex at Cardiff. Maynard was in the nineties when he drove a ball from the left-arm spinner Paul Grayson hard down the ground.

Unfortunately, because it was hit so hard, the non-striker, our wicketkeeper Adrian Shaw, could not get out of the way. It was four all the way until it hit Shaw. So then it was nothing.

Maynard went mad. Soon afterwards he was out to the bowling of Danny Law for 98. This was taking luck a bit further. This was contemplating fate. After that piece of bad luck, Maynard considered it his fate not to score a century that day.

'It was a downfall of mine of thinking too much about why something might have happened when batting,' he concedes. 'But that might have been a good thing for being a captain. For instance, if something happened, like some lazy running between the wickets that meant a pair only got one run instead of two and we might get an opportunity to get at the other batsman, then I would immediately be thinking how I could take advantage as captain.'

And he would do that. I can recall a number of times when he would make that point to the batsmen concerned, telling them that they had made a mistake in not taking an extra run and that fate would now deal them a harsh hand.

Going back to superstition, with cricket being such a game of numbers, it is little surprise that so many superstitions surround them. Thirteen is the obvious one, but for Sir Jack Hobbs the number nine was unlucky too.

So when in 1925 he went with the Surrey team to Taunton in an attempt to equal W. G. Grace's record of 126 first-class centuries he was distraught to be allocated room number 39 in the team hotel. Not only was there a nine in the number, but 39 is also three times 13, of course. He asked to swap with team-mate Andy Sandham.

Hobbs also had with him a four-leaf clover that had been given to him by a lady Surrey member. He carried it in his cricket flannels throughout the game. And so he duly made two centuries in the match, equalling and then beating Grace's record.

The number 111 and multiples thereof are considered unlucky in cricket and are known as Nelson because the admiral by that name had one eye, one arm and one leg. No matter that he actually had two legs, the name has stuck. And it gave rise to the famous hopping on one leg of the late David Shepherd, the Falstaffian former Gloucestershire batsman who became such a well-respected umpire, whenever the Nelson score was showing on the scoreboard.

The Australians do things differently, of course, and their dreaded number is instead 87. That is 13 short of 100, but it is also said that the fixation with the number may have come from Keith Miller, the late, great Australian all-rounder, who reckoned he saw Donald Bradman out for 87 once in a state match in 1929 and from then on was transfixed by the 'Devil's Number', as it became known. It later transpired that the scoreboard at the Melbourne Cricket Ground had actually been slow that day, and Bradman had in fact been dismissed for 89, but the superstition has remained.

I had, and still have, a strange aversion to odd numbers, for instance having to make sure that the volume on my car radio was, and is, always on an even number.

Or at least I thought it was strange until I read that Alastair Cook does the same thing. It is all too easy to infer that superstitions are the recourse of the weak-minded. Cook is hardly that.

And neither was Steve Waugh, widely recognized as

possessing one of the steeliest cricketing minds ever. He used a red rag to wipe away some sweat during a Test match against England at Headingley in 1993. He went on to score a hundred and so he kept the red rag in his pocket when batting for the rest of his career.

Unusually it had been a very hot day in Leeds, and Waugh was sweating so profusely that the perspiration had soaked the foam inserts in his helmet. It was continually dripping from them into his face, affecting his vision. Thus the call to the twelfth man for a cloth of some sort. What arrived was a small piece of cloth cut from one of the red towels given to the players for their after-play showers.

'It would accompany me to the crease for the next 10 and a half years, becoming a security blanket and somehow easing my mind whenever I pulled it out to wipe my brow,' said Waugh. 'At times it became a cloak to conceal my worries because it gave me a few seconds' grace to gather my composure. Occasionally I'd see strands of it littered around the crease line and think: "That's a good sign – I've marked my turf."'

The West Indies batsman Marlon Samuels recognized the significance of the rag, and he always used to say to Waugh: 'Hey, man, give me some of your red rag, I need some luck.'

Waugh eventually relented and gave him a tiny piece of the cloth. When Samuels made a brilliant one-day century against India in 2002, he held the piece of rag aloft.

When Graham Gooch passed a milestone he would instantly enact one of his superstitions. Every time he passed 50 and multiples thereof, he had to change his left-hand batting glove. Only his left-hand one. 'I usually had eight left-hand gloves in my bag,' he says. 'They were all numbered so that the 12th man knew which one to bring out next. I had just two right-hand gloves.'

One of Mark Ramprakash's superstitions involved chewing gum. In 2006, when he had scored 2,278 first-class runs, he was asked about the reasons why. 'Maybe,' he said, 'it is because, when I am not out overnight, I take the chewing gum I am using and stick it to my bat handle, ready for me to continue using it when I resume the next morning.' It sounds disgusting.

As a one-time Classics scholar, one of my favourite superstition stories involves Ken Barrington and some Latin. Before every Test his wife would send him a telegram.

'Good luck darling all my love – Ann' it would read.

He had already made eight Test centuries but all of them had been made away from home. So in his desperate search for a home century he asked Ann to send him a different telegram.

So before the fourth Ashes Test, at Old Trafford, in 1964, she sent this: 'Vincit qui patitur' – Ann.'

Barrington had no idea what it meant. 'They didn't exactly coach us in Latin at Wilson Central or Katesgrove, the schools I attended in Reading,' he said.

But he got his century. In fact he got 256. When he returned home his wife told him what it meant. 'He who endures, conquers.'

Other sportsmen are superstitious, of course – take the tennis player Goran Ivanisevic, whose adherence to always replicating the exact circumstances of an early tournament win led to his watching *Teletubbies* every morning at Wimbledon one year.

There was once a coach of the Detroit Lions American football team called Buddy Parker, who threw away a suit every time his side lost a game. Once on an away trip to Green Bay he was given room 94 in a hotel, and instantly sacked his assistant because the two digits added up to unlucky 13.

But cricketers, and in particular batsmen, seem especially obsessed. There are very few cricketers who do not pursue some sort of ritual, even if it is just putting their left pad on first. If a century has been made under a certain set of circumstances, you desperately want to replicate them.

Me? Unless it was ridiculously hot I had to wear a long-sleeved shirt (to cover up some of the skinniest and also hairiest forearms the game has ever seen!) and a sleeveless sweater in which to bat.

Ricky Ponting liked wearing a sleeveless sweater too, or 'woolly vest' as they call it in Australia. He made his third Test century wearing his in Barbados in 1999 in the classic Test won by West Indies by one wicket thanks to Brian Lara's sublime 153 not out, even though the heat was stifling.

'The night before the game I was lying in bed thinking: "I've scored two Test hundreds and both times I wore my vest throughout, so I'm going to do that again this time, whatever the conditions,"' he said. 'After a while I was thinking: "Jeez, it's sticky out here." But there was no way I was taking it off. Afterwards I wondered if I was the first person to play a long innings in Barbados wearing a woollen vest. No one else would have been that silly.'

It is not that silly, really. Players wearing the same kit for superstition is extremely common.

Shane Warne had a pair of lucky pants he always bowled in.

They reckon that the Kent batsman Neil Taylor once wore the same shirt to bat in for eight years. And during his 375 against England in Antigua in 1994, Brian Lara used the same shirt, same socks, same jockstrap and same trousers for all of the 766 minutes that he was at the crease. 'I must have been very smelly!' he said.

But just as keeping the same kit on is perceived to keep the luck, so changing your kit for a change of luck is perceived in the same way. Even the very best do it.

When Frank Worrell was out first ball for a duck against Australia in 1951, he changed every piece of clothing he had been wearing. 'He walked to the wicket hoping that by discarding his old clothes he would change his luck,' wrote Sir Learie Constantine in his obituary of Worrell (who was knighted in 1964) on Cricinfo. 'Not a bit of it! He was out for another first baller!'

Being too attached to certain items of clothing can get you into trouble, however. My long-sleeved-shirt devotion did just that when I returned one winter to Zimbabwe, where I spent many a joyous off-season during the early 1990s, to find that my club side, Universals, were now going to wear green short-sleeved shirts for all matches.

Universals were an Asian side (they may still exist, but so much has changed in Zimbabwean cricket for the worse that they probably don't – the last I heard they were only fielding a friendly side), so being the only white man in the side, when I was also the only player in our side to wear white in the first match of that season, there were all sorts of accusations and taunts flying around. I wore the green short-sleever from there on.

For a time during his career David Gower liked wearing colourful socks, walking socks in fact bought from a mate's shop in Leicester, but that did not sit well with the England management, and one day manager Micky Stewart sternly told him not to wear his blue socks when playing for England.

Then there was, of course, the case of former Gloucestershire and England wicketkeeper Jack Russell and his beloved hat. Russell was famous for his eccentricity in general. For instance, he was always a very private man and did not want any of his team-mates knowing where he lived, so he would blindfold them if they had to go to his house. Mind you, Russell reckons that fewer than five cricketers went to his house during his playing days.

'I didn't want them to have the burden of the press trying to find out where I lived,' he says. 'So it was just easier to blindfold them so they didn't know.'

Obvious, of course!

Russell would drink cups of tea continuously throughout the day, reusing the same teabag again and again, hanging it on a peg in between uses. 'I like my tea weak and sweet, so it was fine,' he says.

At lunch when playing he would eat Weetabix that had been soaked in milk for a specific length of time. That exact length of time has become confused over the years, but it seems that anything between 12 and 15 minutes was about right.

'There wasn't time to get all my gear off and sit down for lunch,' he says. 'I had to have something quick, with energy and carbs. I used to have Weetabix with honey. I don't like Weetabix crunchy, so I would ask the 12th man to put the milk in a quarter of an hour before lunch. That's why the 12th men were so relieved when I retired! I don't see that as eccentric, that was logical.

'Back then I was fuelling myself up. I couldn't dive around on potatoes and meat and Shepherd's Pie. I think I was the first person to have a banana on the field during the drinks break when I needed a bit of fuel. Why are these things eccentric? They are logical to me. On one tour I had buffalo steak burnt and chips every night for 29 nights because I didn't want to get ill. Alec Stewart used to have chicken and chips, but I didn't trust the chicken.'

Goodness me. The title of his autobiography is *Unleashed*. At the bottom of the cover, it does ask the question 'Barking?' though. You make up your own mind.

It was his hat that got him into trouble with the England management, however. The hat was a standard Gloucestershire floppy sun hat that he had used from near the beginning of his first-class career in 1981.

'It's comfortable and provides great vision,' Russell once said. 'When you're bouncing up and down 600 times a day you need a hat that works with you.'

But years of sweating can take its toll. It needed much work. 'The only person allowed to work on it is my wife, she does all the maintenance work,' said Russell. 'It's been repaired so often that there is very little of the original left. After it is washed it is dried on a tea cosy that sits on a biscuit tin. That keeps its shape since the tin/tea cosy combination is exactly the same size as my head.'

Once on tour in the West Indies Russell was drying it out on top of an oven when it caught fire, but it was Russell who was fuming when Lord MacLaurin took over as England and Wales Cricket Board chairman and insisted that there was total uniformity in the wearing of kit. He wanted Russell to wear his blue England cap rather than his battered old white hat.

'There was a hell of a row and I was forced to back down,' says Russell. 'I wore the blue one and didn't play at all well. If the hat were not with me, I would get a panic attack and nothing else in the world would matter.'

I would never wear a long-sleeved sweater to bat. That was because my father had said not to. 'Any batsman coming out in a long-sleeved sweater does not intend staying long,' he would always say.

When interviewing Matthew Maynard for this book, he reminded me that I had once told him that. I think he still wore one occasionally, but he understood the logic.

And a friend of mine from Monmouth School, James Dobson, wrote me a lovely letter when my father died, citing the same advice about the long-sleeved sweater that my father had given him when he was playing in the same school side as me.

It is right. You do not see too many batsmen score a century in a long-sleeved sweater. OK, Ian Botham did while making his famous 149 not out against Australia at Headingley in 1981, but that almost proves the point. The way he played suggested that he did not intend staying long. It was just one of those days.

I never tasted duck meat until I retired. My daughter Bethan was not allowed plastic ducks in her bath until I had finished my playing career. My son Rhys was born after I had finished playing, so he has been OK on that front. I've told him about Bethan being deprived, and he doesn't understand. I don't blame him.

I also developed a curious habit of having to kick any dirt away from around the crease when I was batting. I had never really seen anyone else do that until I watched a Sky Sports programme in 2014 about Ricky Ponting, and he confessed to doing it too. 'I wanted the pitch to look right: it was going to be mine for the day,' he said.

At the end of every over I tapped my bat in the crease as if preparing to face a ball. That could cause problems if, say, the ball went for four and my partner and I were in the middle of the pitch when the over was called. That would mean a hurried scamper down to the crease, to do my stuff and then back to my partner. Madness.

Although, in researching for this book I found this in an article from Ed Smith: 'I grounded my bat in the batting crease at the end of every over – even if there had been a boundary.'

That is spooky. In that article Smith talks of his first-class debut, a match against Glamorgan mentioned earlier. Apparently on the way to the ground to play against us, he bought a can of Lucozade and a copy of *The Times* newspaper – the latter a poor choice if you ask me. But as he scored a century, that was his routine settled. He did everything he had done that day for the rest of his career.

'What I didn't know, on that very first morning of my career, was that my footsteps – so utterly humdrum and banal – would become fixed in stone by my own chronic addiction to superstition,' he wrote. 'I got a hundred against Glamorgan in that first innings, a blessing in many ways. But I was so superstitious that I couldn't change the routine I had stumbled upon entirely by accident – the Lucozade, the *Times*, the same corner of the dressing room, the left pad on first, the velcro straps adjusted just the right number of times, the bats lined up on the table, bat faces staring out into the room.'

Smith also had a habit of asking the umpire how many balls were left in an over. Apparently early in his career it was after the fourth ball, but by the time I could recall his doing it the habit had changed to after the third ball. It naturally caused much mirth among the opposition, and I remember a game at

Maidstone where the Glamorgan lads were particularly amused by this until the heat became a little too much and one of them pronounced: 'This bloke went to Cambridge University, can't he fuckin' count?'

Smith also had a long, precise routine before every ball was bowled. First he would wipe his head with the thumb of his glove, then he would touch the peak of his helmet, next he would secure the Velcro on each batting glove and then finally he would adjust his thigh pad.

What a palaver. Mind you, Smith was hardly alone in this lengthy preparation. Sri Lanka's Sanath Jayasuriya would hit his pads before each ball, England's Alec Stewart would look behind square leg before each ball and South Africa's Graeme Smith would meticulously check his grip.

In days past there was also the 'Mead shuffle'. Philip Mead of Hampshire was the first left-hander to score 100 hundreds and made 153 in all. And he had some interesting, seemingly non-negotiable habits before a ball was bowled. He would pull his cap four times, tap his bat on the ground four times, then take four shuffling steps.

But I think only Jonathan Trott has had a lengthier ritual. He will arrive at the crease, take guard from the umpire, twice that is. He will make a mark inside his crease, then one outside, and he will join the two with a line made by his studs.

That part is understandable, even if the scratching of the mark is done so relentlessly that the line can become almost dangerously deep ('Watch you don't fall down that canyon you're digging,' remarked Ricky Ponting on Trott's Test debut in 2009 at the Oval), and he has even been known to do it after a match has been won. I can certainly remember him doing that after a Test victory at Lord's against Bangladesh in 2010.

Batting outside of your crease is a wise tactic on English (and Welsh!) pitches, especially against medium pacers or medium-fast bowlers. As long as the wicketkeeper does not stand up to the stumps, of course, you can disrupt the bowler's length, as well as going some way to taking lbw out of the equation.

'It's a little bit abnormal but sometimes in county cricket, if it's a slow wicket, you bat outside your crease, so that's why I mark a long line,' Trott has said. 'I'd find that, on early season wickets, I'd be batting on middle stump when I should have been on leg or middle and leg, and I needed to be sure of my guard. I find too that the scratching helps me clear my mind. It helps keep me ticking.'

But less understandable is Trott's habit of undoing, then retightening all three straps on each of his pads, as if he had rushed out of the dressing room and had not been able to secure them properly. He is fortunate that the straps are made of Velcro these days, and not leather, with metal buckles, as they used to be when I first started playing. That would have taken him some time to do.

You have to be careful that habits and rituals do not become compulsions and obsessions. For instance, you do wonder how much of a part Trott's rituals played in his troubles that became manifest during the 2013/14 Ashes in Australia.

Batting had become thoroughly exhausting for him. He admitted that scoring 40 was 'the same as it used to feel when I reached 100'.

The words of Matthew Hayden are interesting here, talking about Neil McKenzie: 'I subscribe to the widely held view that his energy-sapping superstitions made him run out of mental energy,' Hayden says. 'Everyone's limit is different but you've only got so much fuel each day. It got to the stage where McKenzie couldn't go to bed if the sheets had a crease in them. Everything had to be perfect. It probably says a lot about the true worth of superstitions that towards the end of his career McKenzie gave them all up, feeling that they were too much of a burden.'

And it is something McKenzie has admitted himself now. 'It was a disease,' he has said. 'It was not just cricket, it was life in general. You've got numbers that you like, things that you like. It's a ritual, trying to control what you can't control. I've never had superstitions about ladders or black cats. It was OCD [Obsessive Compulsive Disorder]. I've cut it out now. I've got a wife and child now and don't have much time to worry about toilet seats and taping bats to the ceiling.

'I think there are quite a few sportsmen out there who've got their rituals. I see Sanath Jayasuriya hitting his pads before every ball and I know exactly what he's up to. I know Rafael Nadal has got certain things he does (he once refused to meet the Queen because he had not done so the day before when things had gone well). Habits and rituals can make you more consistent but OCD is something else.'

For me these superstitions are just comforting allies (Steve Waugh's 'security blanket') in the fight against the nasty impostors batting provides.

They usually pass. And even McKenzie has mellowed in his fixations.

The key then? As in life, moderation. Have your habits, rituals and superstitions, especially if you are a batsman who lacks organization and routine, but you must still recognize that there is so much about batting that you cannot control. A century involves a long journey, remember. It requires a lot of energy as it is. Don't waste too much else besides.

There are going to be tough times, sometimes horribly cruel times, but the better players remain on as even a keel as they can. As Murray Goodwin said to me about battling through a tough period in an innings: 'Things always get easier.'

And they do.

5
Love and Hate

To score runs heavily and consistently, in other words to score a lot of centuries, means that a batsman must simply love batting. And I mean love. There are a lot of batsmen who like batting, but that is a very different thing.

They are usually the type who score a lot of pretty thirties and forties, unfurling some handsome strokes before chipping a simple catch to cover and then walking off. They are not the match-winners, the centurions usually are. When the going gets tough, the pretty boys get going. To the pavilion.

And that is not the place to score runs, as thousands of sages over the years have always advised. As Andrew Sandham, once Jack Hobbs' opening partner and a Test batsman before becoming Surrey's coach and then scorer, advised a young John Edrich: 'You can't get hundreds sitting in the pavilions,' he said. And Edrich did go on to make 103 first-class centuries.

So too Geoffrey Boycott's famous Uncle Algy, who said to Boycott as a youngster: 'Stay in, because you can't score runs in the pavilion. It's better your team-mates are watching you bat than you are in the pavilion watching them bat.'

It is obvious counsel, but it is always worth reiterating to a batsman because there will for ever be times at the crease when things become very hard. Say the fast bowler just will not tire. You have done everything you think you can in fending him off, but he keeps coming. The easy option then is to give in.

The truth is that very good players do not regularly get out in the thirties and forties. If you keep doing that, your average will just not be high enough because low scores are inevitable, of course.

As Graham Gooch says: 'Every player gets low scores between nought and 20. You make mistakes, you get a good piece of bowling or a bad decision or whatever. The trick is that when you get in and have worked out the conditions and you are into your method, your way of playing, then the trick is to stay in that method, stay in that rhythm, don't step outside of it and just go on and on, and not change much. You see so many people get more expansive when they get to 30 or 40, and they nick off.'

Of course, there might be periods in a player's career when it is temporarily a problem. For instance, even Viv Richards once had trouble in that regard. It was in the 1975/76 season and because he kept getting out in the thirties and forties, he consulted team psychologist Rudi Webster. 'We did a whole lot of sessions and went through my thoughts during an innings to try and identify the problem,' Richards said. 'We were looking for the reasons for my success in the past which could be of use now. We discovered through discussion that I wasn't concentrating in the way that I should have been when I reached a certain stage of my innings.'

It cannot have been that much of a problem. Of those players who have 100 Test innings or more, Richards is only 76th on the list of those dismissed most between the scores of 30 and 49. He was dismissed in that bracket in 15.88 per cent of his innings.

Top of that list is South Africa's Shaun Pollock, with 24.78 per cent, which is not that surprising given that he was a very able No. 8 in Test cricket, who averaged 32.31 but with only two centuries.

Next in the list is Australia's former opener Matthew Hayden, with 22.94 per cent. If you think back to the 2005 Ashes series in England, then that is not too surprising either.

Hayden was out five times between 26 and 36 in that series. But if you remember, that was a series in which reverse swing played a huge part. Andrew Flintoff and Simon Jones befuddled the Australians with it, especially with their ability to reverse-swing the ball both ways, as opposed to the more usual method of just reverse-swinging the ball back into the right-hander.

Often in that series Hayden found that he was at the crease when the ball began to reverse-swing. 'Once you knew it was reversing you could develop a strategy for it. But the changeover period was a devilishly tough time,' he said.

However, Hayden made 30 Test centuries, with an average of over 50. He sorted it.

The thing is, though: if the very best batsmen love batting, then they must also hate getting out. And again I mean hate. A strong word and all that.

Take Ken Barrington. 'It's stupid to deny that I like being at the crease and hate getting out,' he once said. 'All successful batsmen must be like that at heart and I suppose I've always had this hunger for runs.'

Once during a Surrey Club and Ground game when he was 51 not out at lunch, Barrington was asked to get out soon afterwards to give the other batsmen some time in the middle. Barrington did get out. For 150!

We cannot all be like the New Zealander Glenn Turner, who altered his game during his career to a freer manner of playing. Turner scored one of the more famous centuries when carrying his bat for Worcestershire against Glamorgan at Swansea in

1977, scoring 141 out of the team total of 169. The next-highest score was seven, and the percentage of the innings total – 83.43 – remains the first-class record.

'I used to hate getting out,' says Turner. 'I'd mope and sulk for hours. Suddenly I realized it was time to change the way I played, to cram more enjoyment into a shorter stay at the crease. I was cheesed off with my style of batting, so heaven knows about the poor spectators. It dawned on me that there were other things to do; write some letters, read a book, broaden my mind.'

I have always hated getting out, even in the most low-key of matches. In 2013 I played in a Glamorgan Past versus Present match at Abergavenny, opening with Hugh Morris again for the first time since he had played his last first-class match, our county championship-winning victory at Taunton in 1997.

Given that Morris had not played for over 10 years and that I had probably not played 10 matches since my retirement nine years previously, it was something of a surprise to see Will Owen, one of Glamorgan's fast bowlers, coming in off his full run. It was even more of a surprise when he bowled me a bouncer in the first over, at which I flapped without making any contact. So much for it being a benefit match!

Anyway, we had managed to put on a few for the first wicket when Ben Wright, a batsman and very much part-time bowler was called upon to bowl. Wright bowls some innocuous right-arm seamers with a particularly round-armed action. For some reason he decided to bowl around the wicket. As he ran up to bowl I suddenly thought to myself: 'Well, there is no way he can get an lbw from there.' As we have already discussed, such a thought is wholly counter-productive for any batsman. I should have just been watching the ball and nothing else. So it was little wonder that I missed that first ball from him, done for lack of pace if anything, as my head toppled towards the off side.

But I was right about the lbw matter, because it is almost

impossible for a bowler like that to get an lbw from that sort of angle. The laws of geometry dictate that it is highly unlikely that the ball will be pitching in line with the stumps if it is then to go on and hit them. The only situation in which it can happen is if the ball is very full and has swung into the right-handed batsman sharply. That was not the case here, but still the umpire, with a smile that made my hackles rise further, gave me out.

I was furious. The umpire was a chap who had kindly paid Mark Wallace, whose benefit match it was, a donation so that he could umpire. He is a life-long Glamorgan supporter who, prior to that, was following me on Twitter and conversing with me there. He had brought a copy of my book *The Plan* with him for me to sign.

I was still fuming when he asked me to sign it afterwards. In fact I was still fuming for some time afterwards. Pathetic? Yes, probably, but I simply could not help it. That sort of reaction was programmed into my head.

It did not matter what the situation, what the match: I hated getting out. Take a match for Glamorgan against Oxford University in 1992. There had been some rain on the first day, but I ended it 111 not out. It was my ninth first-class century.

With the match taking place in June, it was not a full-strength Glamorgan side on show. Indeed in that game we were captained by Chris Cowdrey, son of Colin and formerly of Kent and England. It is easily forgotten that Cowdrey had one season at Glamorgan at the end of his career, mainly on a one-day contract.

On the second morning at Oxford I was expecting that I would be allowed to retire, in order to allow others a bat. Cowdrey had other ideas.

He immediately told the team that he felt obliged to invoke the long-forgotten '15-ball' law of the ground. In other words, if I hit 15 balls for six I would have a double century. I probably didn't hit 15 balls for six in my whole career!

I walked out to bat, slogged at the first ball from Jason Gallian, who went on to play for England, of course (as a batsman, I might add!), and skied it to slip, where Richard Montgomerie (yes, the same one who dropped me early in my triple century) this time took the easy catch.

It was shambolic, and, though it was apparently hilarious for all my colleagues, I was seething. For one I was embarrassed. Secondly I despised the fact that I had just thrown my wicket away in a first-class match.

If I had just completed my century, I do not think that it would have mattered quite as much. County players should not be greedy against the students, in my opinion. The games should never be first class anyway, so to make a double hundred, say, against them is just rude. That might sound strange, given that it goes against the grain of much of the central point of this book, but these are just practice matches. They are not matches in which you should be grinding your way to big scores.

I made five centuries against the students, three against Oxford and two against Cambridge. My maiden first-class hundred was against Oxford in only my third match, in 1987 (I had made my debut in 1985 against Sussex in a match in which I did not get onto the field because of rain), but it says everything about university cricket that it is not an innings that I look back upon with any affection.

I am much prouder of my 43 not out against Sussex in my second match – or first in which I got onto the field – a few days before, when I faced the giant South African fast bowler Garth Le Roux, who introduced me to first-class cricket with three bouncers for my first three balls.

If a decision was taken to strip the first-class status from those five university centuries, I would not be upset. They are simply not worthy of the status. The matter of the six centuries I scored while at Cambridge is different. To me they were genuine first-class innings. The last of them, 131 not out to win the match for the Combined Cambridge and Oxford Universities side against New Zealand at Fenner's, was one of my finest innings, on a turning pitch with the off-spinner John Bracewell snarling and chirping throughout.

The first of them, 151 not out against Warwickshire, was against an attack that included the West Indian Tony Merrick, two England bowlers (even if they were hardly fixtures on the international scene) in Tim Munton and Joey Benjamin, the talented all-rounder Paul Smith and a steady off-spinner in Adrian Pierson.

And only one of them was against a totally second-string attack, against Sussex at Hove, where the members of the opposing attack were Rodney Bunting, John North, Carlos Remy and Brad Donelan – hardly household names – but that innings did come in a run chase that brought a victory for us, so there was some pressure.

Because I went to Cambridge University and thoroughly enjoyed my time there, as well as advancing both my rugby and cricket careers with the standard of fixtures available, you might think that I would stick up for the universities, but sadly I won't. Their games should simply not be first class.

Things have changed. Universities do not possess the quality of sportsperson they once did. I'm not sure the Cambridge team in which I played, even though it included Mike Atherton, wicketkeeper Rob Turner and batsman Jonathan Atkinson, both of Somerset, should really have had first-class status.

But we now have a situation where all six University Centres of Cricketing Excellence – or, because of MCC sponsorship, MCCUs as they are now called – at Oxford, Cambridge, Durham, Loughborough, Cardiff and Leeds/Bradford have first-class status, even if it is only for their first two matches of the season against the counties. And the players involved are generally of nowhere near the standard of years ago.

But don't blame the players. They happily take the status, but only the most foolish don't realize that it is not deserved.

Durham UCCE's excellent coach, Graeme Fowler, has admitted that at the time they started in 2001, 'I never thought we should have been given first-class status.'

Once, Oxford and Cambridge did deserve the status. This was brought home to me while reading the excellent autobiography of Alastair Hignell, a moving and inspirational tale of his hugely courageous battle with multiple sclerosis as well as a remarkable sporting life that saw him play rugby for England and county cricket for Gloucestershire, and then become a hugely respected broadcaster and journalist.

'Cambridge University was a power in the land at both my chosen sports,' he wrote of his time at Cambridge. In his 1974 rugby side, both half-backs, Alan Wordsworth and Richard Harding, would play for England. Centre Peter Warfield had already done so. One wing was an All Black, Mike O'Callaghan, and the other centre, Jim Moyes, played for Canada. At full-back was Hignell himself, who went on to win 14 caps for England before injury cut short his career.

In Hignell's 1975 University cricket match almost half of the 22 players had county experience. There was a current international in the Oxford side, the Pakistani Imran Khan, who was joined by two future England internationals, Chris Tavaré and Vic Marks. In Hignell's Cambridge team was Peter Roebuck.

That is a dreamland now. But that is not to say that there shouldn't be any university cricket against the counties, especially during pre-season. Of course there should. The six MCCUs are superb nurseries. Apparently one-fifth of all current England-qualified cricketers have played for one of them.

It is the MCC, who began their sponsorship in 2004, generously providing each UCCE with £75,000 per annum, that insists on the first-class status. That must stop.

Goodness, Nick Compton made 236 against Cardiff MCCU in 2012. That is gluttonous boot-filling. And on the very day I was writing this chapter in 2013, Gloucestershire's Chris Dent made 203 not out against the same hapless opponents. One cricketer still playing texted me with a word to describe it: 'disgrace'.

I often mock my good friend Mike Powell about this. He made a double century against Oxford University in 1997, but it was his debut and he had no idea of the done thing. At least he went on to surpass the score on two occasions in the county championship.

It is interesting to note now that my next first-class match after Cowdrey's command at Oxford was that dreaded debacle at Luton where I recorded my pair in the same day. They do say that you should not mess with the game.

I do not think I am alone in this attitude about getting out. Once in the middle and going nicely, it is so hard to drag yourself away, even if it is in a university match that does not really matter.

There is a good story about the great Pakistani batsman Zaheer Abbas playing for Gloucestershire against the Oxford students in 1982. Captain David Graveney had made it clear that if anyone scored a century, they were to depart soon afterwards. Zaheer was having none of it, and after passing the milestone continued on his merry way.

Attempts to alert him to the requirements of the situation were to no avail. So in the end Graveney had to stand beside the sightscreen at the bowler's end to attract Zaheer's attention. He was eventually out, very reluctantly, for 144.

Take Geoffrey Boycott too. On the 1970/71 Ashes tour he was 173 not out overnight in the opening state match of the tour against South Australia in Adelaide. Keith Fletcher was 67 not out. Captain Ray Illingworth announced to them five minutes before they went out the next day that Boycott was to get 200 and Fletcher 100, and then they were to get out to give others a chance. Boycott was so angry about it that he was out to the third ball of the day.

Now Boycott could easily have been accused of being selfish there. And it has to be said that it was not an uncommon accusation in his career. Indeed when I googled the words Geoffrey Boycott and selfish, I was immediately given over two million responses. Ian Chappell, when considering Boycott's merits as a truly great batsman, went as far as to say that he could not be considered great because he was a 'selfish bastard'.

Run-outs are often a good indicator of a batsman's attitude to self-preservation, and Boycott was involved in a fair number where it seemed that he cared for no one but himself, most notably when running out local hero Derek Randall at Trent Bridge in 1977.

But then another piece of advice from his Uncle Algy had been: 'When two people get involved in a run-out, one of them is going to be very disappointed. Make sure it's not you.'

They reckon that Hampshire's Philip Mead, he of the previously mentioned 'Mead shuffle' and scorer of over 55,000 first-class runs with 153 centuries between 1905 and 1936, was particularly selfish. Hampshire had a bonus system for fifties and hundreds. And Mead often ran players out when he was on 49 or 99. He was rarely run out himself in such circumstances!

Mind you, Boycott could not follow Algy's advice to the letter in Christchurch in 1978, when Ian Botham ran him out deliberately so that England could push on for quick runs in search of a declaration.

And Boycott was, of course, dropped from the England side in 1967 for slow scoring, as Ken Barrington had been two years earlier after making 137 against New Zealand. Boycott's omission came after he had made 246 not out against India in a Test at Headingley that England actually won.

It might have been his highest Test score, his only Test double century indeed, although he made two higher scores of 260 not out and 261 not out in his first-class career, with 10 double centuries in total, but he was still dropped for it, because it had been made too slowly. 'The decision stunned me,' he said. 'I was morti-fied with embarrassment and filled with an angry, burning sense of injustice.'

Boycott had recorded his only pair in first-class cricket earlier that season – against Kent at Bradford – and was in poor form (sorry, luck!) generally, with his previous nine innings having produced only 124 runs.

So in front of a small crowd of around 5,000 on his home ground at Headingley, he ground it out. 'It was more of an occu-pation than an innings,' John Woodcock wrote in *The Times*. 'A defenceless army was hunted down.'

It sounds a bit like most hundreds against the universities, a view given strength by the fact that India's attack was so weak, having lost two bowlers – Rusi Surti (knee) and Bishan Bedi (thigh) – to injury well before the close on the first day, which Boycott ended on 106 not out, and they did not bowl again in the match.

Was Boycott selfish? Of course he was. Most cricketers are, in my opinion. It is not your usual team sport. It is an individ-ual sport played in a team environment. As I have always said to people, nobody can help you as a batsman once that nasty fast bowler begins his run-up. You're on your own. It is how we channel and sometimes hide that selfishness that counts.

Richard Dawkins knew what he was on about when he wrote his book *The Selfish Gene*. The drive required to succeed in sport has to be self-centred.

That is even though Tony Lewis, the former Glamorgan and England captain who became such a fine broadcaster and jour-nalist, wrote these thought-provoking words in the foreword to *Hooked on Opening*, the autobiography of Alan Jones.

'It was a blessing for Glamorgan that Alan liked run-getting so much,' wrote Lewis. 'In all professional players there has to be an instinct of self-interest, which is not the same as selfishness. Alan had the perfect balance. He was prepared to anchor an innings and it usually meant that he scored more runs than anyone else, but he was always wrapped up in his partner's performance too. "Get on the front foot, AR," he would say as I began an innings. "It's seaming."'

I can believe that of Jones. When I was a young professional and still at Swansea University, he was a huge help to me as a young batsman, spending long and cold hours in the Neath indoor school feeding a bowling machine and offering sage advice at every opportunity. I learnt so much about being a county player in those sessions.

But I never really cared for my partner when I was batting. I was too wrapped up in my own struggles. And anyway, mostly I did not feel that it was my place to offer advice. A lot of batsmen do not like receiving it. And the tales of erroneous counsel are legion. Many an incoming batsman has been advised to beware the ball swinging sharply away from him only to be bowled first ball by one swinging into him.

I was selfish. If I scored a century and the team lost, did I return home that evening desperately disappointed? Of course I didn't.

It happened on six occasions in my first-class career. All but the first, a century for Cambridge University against Gloucestershire, had some significance that meant I was pretty happy with my personal contribution. There was that aforementioned century against Surrey at Neath that came after my pair in a day at Luton. Happy? Yep.

There was 230 not out against Leicestershire in 1995, my first double century even though we lost in a run chase. Happy? Yep.

There was 148 against Warwickshire at Edgbaston after following on and scoring 90 in the first innings (ninth out) against an attack including Shaun Pollock. Happy? Yep.

There was 130 against Worcestershire at New Road in 1997 in a vain run chase. It was my Uncle Gwyn's funeral that day. I obviously wanted to attend, but when I realized I could not, my father said simply: 'Well, you'll just have to get a hundred for me and for him, then.' So I did.

The wake took place in the Cross Inn in Aylburton near my uncle's home, and I'm told that when my father heard that I had scored a century that day, he burst into tears. He was both happy and sad. So was I.

And lastly there was 118 against Middlesex at Cardiff in 2002. It was my only first-class century against Middlesex (I once made 94 in a run chase at Lord's, where I never made three figures, before being brilliantly caught in the deep off John Emburey by Neil Williams), meaning that I only required Derbyshire to make it a full set of centuries against every county. That was something I never achieved, of course, but happy? Yep.

There was an occasion when I carried my bat for the only time in my career when making 61 not out against Leicestershire at Grace Road. We followed on and I was out relatively cheaply in the second innings, but that evening as a team we attended a testimonial dinner for the umpire Ray Julian. I was sitting next to Adrian Dale and mentioned to him that it had been the first time I had carried my bat. I was hardly expressing disappointment that we were just about to suffer a heavy defeat (we eventually lost by 10 wickets). 'Stop that,' he said sternly in rebuking my selfishness.

As captain of Glamorgan I once bowled a bowler I suspected less capable than others of taking a wicket at the end of the day so that I might not have to bat that evening. On another occasion I just refused to bat in the second innings of a match against Surrey.

I was tired from a long season and a benefit function that had gone on late the night before, and so I sent the tyros like Ian Thomas and Jonathan Hughes out to bat when the opposition captain, Adam Hollioake, had already let the game peter out to a draw (although the Australian Jimmy Maher did say: 'If you're not batting, then neither am I!'). The current Glamorgan captain, Mark Wallace, still ribs me out about that today. Waiting to go in at No. 4, he was on a pair. That was seriously selfish from me.

I am not proud of my actions. But I was obsessed about batting and my own performance. You can get yourself into a real mess with selfishness sometimes. Take Sunil Gavaskar and his 36 not out in the first match of the inaugural 1975 World Cup against England at Lord's. That was 36 not out off 60 overs as India crawled to 132-3 in response to England's 334. That has to be the most selfish innings of all time.

But cricket is a game of statistics. Yours matter most, and then, if you are a decent player, the team will benefit accordingly. In the longer game, that is. In batsmen, four-day and Test cricket often foster selfishness. It is mostly harmless. As my father always told me: 'If you score a hundred, then it is more likely that the team will have a decent score.'

So of Sir Don Bradman's 117 first-class hundreds, only eight were in a losing cause. Forty-two were drawn. That is some influence and some indication of the importance of centuries.

Even of Boycott's 151 centuries, only 12 were in a losing cause. Fifty-three were in a winning cause. Boycott made 22 Test centuries and England lost none of the games in which he made those runs.

Wally Hammond made the same number of Test centuries, and England lost none of those games either. In fact only South Africa's Graeme Smith has made more Test centuries that have not been in matches that his side lost. Indeed none of his 27 Test centuries came in a losing cause.

As I write, the next on the list below Boycott and Hammond is Ian Bell, who has currently made 21 Test centuries without England losing in any of those matches. Next below Bell is the West Indian Gordon Greenidge, with all of his 19 Test centuries coming in wins or draws for his team.

My dad was right. Make a hundred and it is likely that the

team will benefit. The best example of that is probably the famous case of Charles Bannerman, who holds the record for the highest percentage of a completed team innings by one batsman scoring a century. His 165 not out for Australia against England in the first-ever Test match in 1877 was 67.35 per cent of the team's total of 245. Since then 10 batsmen have managed over 60 per cent of their team's totals, but no one has surpassed Bannerman's percentage. And his team won by 45 runs.

Of course, centuries do not always mean victories. For instance, of Brian Lara's 34 Test centuries, 14 were made in Tests lost by West Indies. Of Sachin Tendulkar's 51, 11 were made in Indian defeats. Of his 49 one-day international hundreds, 14 were scored in losses, including his final one – the one that made it 100 centuries in all international cricket – against Bangladesh in Dhaka.

Tendulkar is always a contentious case when it comes to selfishness. He had to wait 33 innings without a century before he finally reached those 100 hundreds.

The milestone had been a distraction, and then an impediment. In its wake, he was asked about retirement. 'It's a very selfish thought that, when you're at the top, you should retire,' he said. It was an interesting choice of word at that time.

Nobody likes being called selfish. But as the American preacher Henry Ward Beecher once said: 'Selfishness is that detestable vice which no one will forgive in others, and no one is without in himself.'

Michael Vaughan is interesting on this subject. 'One of my big theories about cricket, if I am being totally honest, is that your first 75 runs are for you, and that after that it is all for your team,' he says. 'By that stage you have already bought yourself two or three games, so from then on it is wholly about the team as you have already made your personal mark. You need to have a selfish streak in you as a batsman – all the best ones have it – but there has to be a balance.'

That goes back to the England team Vaughan became part of in the late 1990s, which were pre-central-contract days when players were mostly concerned with making the team for the next Test.

Sometimes the weakness of your colleagues just cannot be papered over. Of Lara's 34 centuries, 25 were made when no other West Indies batsman made a century in the same innings. He was playing in a poor side.

Boycott played in a pretty poor England team too. That is reflected in the fact that, of his 22 Test centuries, 18 were made in innings where no other England player made a century.

Indeed, according to Cricinfo, of those who have scored at least 10 Test centuries, only Pakistan's Hanif Mohammad has a higher percentage (83.33) of lone centuries in an innings than Boycott's 81.82.

Hanif made 12 centuries in 55 Tests and 10 of those were in innings in which no other batsman made a hundred. Only one of those resulted in a Pakistan victory but none of them was in defeat.

Curiously, though, for all this lauding of centuries, it can be quite fashionable to nominate scores below 100 when looking for a batsman's greatest innings. For example, for all of Sir Jack Hobbs' centuries, there are those who say that his 47 not out against Kent in 1919 was one of his best innings.

Surrey required 95 to win in just 45 minutes and rain began to fall as Hobbs and Jack Crawford walked out to bat. But Hobbs, having begun cautiously, opened his shoulders towards the end, especially against the leg spin of 'Tich' Freeman, and was eventually carried from the field by jubilant Surrey supporters. It was his benefit match too.

It is also said that Hobbs' Ashes 49 in Melbourne in 1928 on an uncovered pitch after an overnight thunderstorm was pretty special.

Sunil Gavaskar always says that the greatest innings he saw

was Gundappa Viswanath's 97 not out against West Indies at Chennai in 1975. Many observers reserve the same hushed tones for Ted Dexter's 70 for England against West Indies at Lord's in 1963 in the famous match in which Colin Cowdrey appeared with his arm in plaster, having broken it the previous day when hit by Wes Hall.

Due to Cowdrey's bravery in appearing as England's last man (he did not face, though), the match was drawn and some have said it might be the greatest Test ever played at Lord's. But certainly Dexter's strokeplay in making his 70 off just 75 balls against the might of Hall and Charlie Griffith has entered folklore.

In his foreword to Steve Waugh's autobiography, India's Rahul Dravid mentions, above Waugh's 32 Test centuries, his 67 not out against India in Delhi in 1996. 'It was an innings that was masterful both in its technique and its complete concentration,' wrote Dravid, who knew a little about both those disciplines as probably the most classical batting technician of his generation, known as 'The Wall' for a magnificent defence that helped yield 36 Test centuries at an average of just over 52.

Over the years I have not been averse to nominating a 'non-century' as one of my colleagues' finest innings. It concerns my Glamorgan opening partner Hugh Morris, and the 54 he made against Warwickshire at Cardiff in 1993. We were pursuing 138 to win in that match, but the pitch was horribly green and Gladstone Small bowled wickedly fast.

Morris was captain that year and we were chasing the county championship; later in the season we memorably won the Sunday League at Canterbury against Kent, Glamorgan's first trophy since 1969. But it is easily forgotten that we finished third in the championship that year.

For that match at Cardiff, Morris had ordered two pitches to be prepared by the groundsman, Len Smith: one the 'green mamba' on which we eventually played, the other a dry, spinning surface that was there in case Allan Donald appeared with the Warwickshire team.

Thankfully Donald was injured. If he had played on that green surface, I'm sure someone would have suffered serious injury. We were rather fortunate to escape some sort of censure because the live grass at the start of the match was longer than any I have ever seen on a county pitch.

I do not think that my friend Adrian Dale will mind my mentioning this but he took a career-best 6-18 in the Warwickshire first innings. Dale was a very good county cricketer, a fine batsman who could bowl useful medium pacers that were especially effective on home Welsh pitches with little bounce, where he could bowl accurately from wicket to wicket and prove very difficult to score off.

But a bowler likely to produce such devastating figures (he bowled 13.3 overs) in a county championship match? No. It was a terror pitch on which Morris batted with remarkable skill and courage in that second innings.

I too could nominate a personal 'non-century'. It was during our championship-winning season in 1997. The match was against Sussex at Swansea on a pitch that began slightly wet. We were duly inserted and bowled out for 172. I thought I played pretty well for my 48, the top score in the innings. That Sussex then only made 54 in total, with Waqar Younis taking a career-best 8-17, confirmed my impression that the pitch was a bit of a shocker.

When we batted again, we made 183-9 before skipper Matthew Maynard decided we had enough. I was 82 not out when he called us in.

Now, Steve Watkin, our opening bowler, was never one for lavish praise. In fact I can rarely remember him getting particularly excited about any of our batsmen's innings, but when I returned to the St Helen's dressing room that day he was lavish in his appreciation. 'Jeez. I must have played well,' I thought. Sussex were then bowled out for just 67, so that my 130 runs in the match had actually been more than the whole Sussex team's 121.

Alan Jones always said that his best innings was not a century but the 95 not out he made at Sophia Gardens, Cardiff, in 1967 against Lancashire.

In a rain-affected match Lancashire's captain, Jackie Bond, set Glamorgan 178 to win in 111 minutes. Before he went out to bat, team-mate Ossie Wheatley said to Jones: 'Come on, Alan, you can play the game of your life out there today.'

With the light poor and the pitch doing plenty, and Ken Higgs bowling with his usual parsimony, it was a tricky chase. But Glamorgan managed it with six wickets down, with Jones still there.

'I had played the knock of my career,' he said afterwards. 'Ossie Wheatley's "prediction" had been fulfilled.'

Sadly for Jones the England selector Alec Bedser had been there on the game's first day, when only five minutes' play was possible, and not on the final day. 'This incident was fundamental in my failure to gain an England place,' said Jones. 'I am convinced that in the course of your career three or four chances will arise that allow you to achieve something special, or make a lasting impression on a game. The importance of taking your chance when it arises must be stressed.'

That may be a comment touching on the luck we were discussing in a previous chapter. But Jones certainly was unlucky. He played once for England, against a very strong Rest of the World team in 1970 in a series that was arranged to replace the scheduled tour by South Africa that was cancelled after public protests.

Jones made just 5 and 0 in the match at Lord's against a side including the likes of Garfield Sobers, Mike Procter, Graeme Pollock and Barry Richards. At the time it was considered an official Test match and had been marketed as such, but later that status was removed, and so Jones remains without a recognized

England Test cap, even though he still has his cap, blazer and sweaters at home.

It was reported that he had been asked to return them. But he never had, and never did. For a player who made over 36,000 first-class runs with 56 centuries in total not to win a Test cap, that is unlucky. Indeed no one has more first-class runs without being capped, just as no one has taken more than Don Shepherd's 2,218 first-class wickets without being capped.

Glamorgan fans have often considered there to be some sort of conspiracy against the county when it comes to England selection. Personally I have never believed that, but you can easily see why when considering the cases of Jones and Shepherd, two Glamorgan greats.

As a batsman Jones had every right to be angry about that treatment, but of all the cricketers I have seen and worked with, Jones is the least likely to lose his temper. You could not wish to meet a more mild-mannered, affable and even-tempered man.

But the truth is that most batsmen are not like Jones, especially when they are out. Hell hath no fury like a woman scorned? Well, hell hasn't seen Nasser Hussain after being dismissed, or Michael Bevan, or Justin Langer, or Mark Ramprakash. The list goes on.

The problem is that the player has to control himself – relatively so anyway – while on the pitch. There will be the odd utterance and expletive, the odd kick of the ground, but these days the batsmen know that they cannot express their annoyance publicly. Not like, say, Chris Broad did when he smashed the stumps down after being bowled by Steve Waugh in Sydney in 1988. He was fined £500 for that.

It would be a lot more today. And it might be administered by Broad himself, who in a delicious piece of irony is a Test match referee. Mind you, in rugby union Wade Dooley is a citing officer. The words 'poachers', 'gamekeepers' and 'turned' spring to mind.

There is usually one bat thrower in every team, with a couple of others capable of acting like a rabid animal if matters turn particularly frustrating. At Glamorgan when I played, it was David Hemp. 'Mad Dog' we called him, and mad he could be, even though I am told that he mellowed in his later years of playing.

I'll admit here and now that I was one that fitted into the occasional bat-throwing category. I could have my moments. I screamed at the groundsman once at Cardiff after a ball had suddenly reared off a length to dismiss me. That was nothing compared to Bevan, who once threw his bat at a supporter when dismissed in a one-day international in Auckland, New Zealand.

Bevan often took dismissal particularly badly. He would take showers fully clothed and, even though he was a left-arm china-man spin bowler, he would also go to the nets to bowl bouncers with no batsman at the other end. Mind you, fellow Australian Michael Slater once tried to flush all his kit down the toilet.

I even waited at the top of the steps at Swansea once to speak to Ryan Sidebottom after I had been dismissed just before lunch against Yorkshire and been given an almighty send-off. Quite what I was going to do I have no idea. As anyone who played rugby with or against me will testify, I was hardly a tough nut. And just behind Sidebottom was his captain, David Byas. Now he was a tough nut.

But in the time after you have been dismissed, you become a different person. It is best not to approach a batsman just out for some considerable time afterwards. The pain and infuriation linger.

Everyone has different ways of dealing with it. Matthew Maynard, for instance, would simply change straight into his running gear, walk down the steps of the Sophia Gardens changing room and jog out to the bank of the River Taff alongside the ground, where he would run until the pain of dismissal had eased.

I was a confirmed fitness fanatic but I could never do that. I always needed my mind to be right to train, and at those moments after being dismissed it was never right. I will freely admit that as a youngster I would cry when dismissed. I just could not help it. That is how much it meant.

Later I would often just sit in the dressing room with a towel over my head, stewing over the consequences. That is what Geoffrey Boycott did apparently after that run-out by Ian Botham in New Zealand.

Mark Ramprakash would rush to the gym and pump weights to rid himself of his frustration. Once at the Oval a young fitness trainer in the gym, who clearly did not know who Ramprakash was or that he had just got out, advised the batsman that he was doing his exercises incorrectly. Unsurprisingly the poor trainer received a response that was not entirely complimentary, or without its expletives!

Ramprakash's temper as a player was legendary. One of his nicknames when playing was 'Bloodaxe', after all. It was during my Test debut at Lord's in 1998 that Ramprakash famously told umpire Darrell Hair: 'You're messing with my career' after he had been erroneously given out caught behind. The ferocity and duration of his fury afterwards was quite remarkable.

Ramprakash was once run out playing for his second county, Surrey, at the Oval. He returned to the dressing room and took out his anger on a helmet. Except that it wasn't his own. It happened to belong to skipper Adam Hollioake.

And when another wicket fell quickly, Hollioake did not know what had been happening to his helmet. He got to the middle before he did realize. Trying to put his helmet on, he suddenly became aware that the grille had been damaged badly. He called for another helmet, and later called in Ramprakash for a chat about his behaviour.

But I did not damage any equipment or myself. Plenty of others have done that. In 2014 England's Ben Stokes returned early from a tour of the Caribbean after breaking a bone in his wrist when hitting a dressing-room locker. He had just been out first ball.

Anger does not ignore greatness either. Steve Waugh once needed four stitches in a hand after getting out against South Africa in 2001/02. He slapped his open hand against a locker, without realizing that there was a protruding hinge. He had to call the team physio with blood gushing out of his hand.

Worse still, Mike Gatting once put his hand through the main dressing-room door at Lord's after being run out and the gash required more than 20 stitches.

When England played Australia in Adelaide in 1998/99 Ricky Ponting was fighting for his place. The ball was reverse-swinging, and as Darren Gough ran into bowl, Ponting got confused as to which way Gough was holding the ball. He thought the ball was going to be an outswinger. It ended up being an inswinger that bowled him.

He returned to the dressing room, placed his Australian helmet on the floor in front of him and chopped it in half with his bat. That's some pretty good helmet chopping. Better than Ian Healy's attack on a poor defenceless bag of apples once given to the Australian team in Auckland. The wicketkeeper pulped the huge bag of them after getting out.

Out of the stroppiness can come some humour, though. One of my favourite stories regarding this involves Robert Croft, my former Glamorgan team-mate, when he was playing for England under Duncan Fletcher, who coached the pair of us at Glamorgan.

England were playing Sri Lanka in Galle and some of the umpiring had been debatable to say the least. Croft was the latest to suffer in this regard and he returned up the stairs to the dressing rooms. He decided to take out his frustrations on the glass door in front of him, crashing his bat into it. Unfortunately for him, the glass smashed and went everywhere.

'Is that bloody necessary, Croft?' said an unhappy Fletcher, who was sitting nearby and whose leg had been cut by the flying glass. Off Croft went, but a few moments later he reappeared, with his batting pads still on, looking very sheepish and pushing a sweeping brush. Fletcher is not as grumpy as many assume, but I do not think he will mind my saying that even he raised a huge smile at the sight of that.

And so did the Australian dressing room in Sydney, more like uproarious laughter actually, when Matthew Hayden once kicked a chair after getting out. His foot became wedged in it and in his anger he began hopping around the room trying to get rid of the chair from his foot. The harder he tried, though, the more embedded it seemed to become. Eventually he had to succumb to the comedy of the moment, lying on the ground and bursting out laughing. Steve Waugh came to his rescue and removed the chair. 'You nuffy,' he muttered.

Hayden also broke his toe once when kicking his cricket 'coffin', an injury that also befell Mike Atherton in Port Elizabeth during the 1995/96 tour of South Africa. Atherton was usually pretty calm after getting out, but in this instance he lost his cool and kicked a set of weighing scales that were placed by the dressing-room door. A little embarrassed, he did not say anything immediately but he was soon shouting to physiotherapist Wayne Morton for assistance.

Inside the changing rooms at Lord's there used to be a comfy chair situated either side of the balcony door (there may well still be so), and on one occasion Mike Roseberry, the former Middlesex and Durham opener, hit one of these chairs with his bat after getting out cheaply. He continued his mood by walking around the room swearing before deciding to sit in the chair. As he sat down, though, the chair collapsed. He had hit the rivets out. Cue the room collapsing as well. In laughter.

It was at Lord's in 2011 that in a Test against Sri Lanka the England wicketkeeper, Matt Prior, smashed a window after being run out in a mix-up with Ian Bell. I ghosted a book for

Prior called *The Gloves Are Off*, so I got to hear in detail about the incident.

Prior's position in the Lord's changing room was seated in one of those comfy chairs, with a window looking out onto the pitch above it. There on the ledge Prior had his four bats. Having been run out, first Prior threw his gloves into his bag and then slammed his bat onto the seat. Then he picked up his bat and went to put it on the ledge with the others, but he did it rather too forcibly. 'I'll admit that I probably didn't put it down as gently as I might have done on another day,' he said. 'But it was only because I couldn't quite reach that I threw it a very short distance rather than placing it down more carefully.'

The bat bounced off the wall and then into the window. 'It must have hit dead centre,' said Prior. 'The next thing I knew, the window had exploded and glass had gone everywhere.'

The noise was incredibly loud, leaving no one in the crowd in any doubt as to what had happened. Suddenly television viewers were treated to the sight of England captain Andrew Strauss, sitting outside on the balcony, shaking his head – 'like a disappointed headmaster,' said Prior – and going to inspect the damage.

There was an almighty fuss, not least because the flying glass had cut the leg of a female MCC member, and some confusion. There was a botched press release saying it had been caused by a glove bouncing up. But the truth was that Prior was a little miffed at being out. There is nothing wrong with that. He didn't mean to break the window. It just happened. These things do.

Just as during an England Test in Trinidad against West Indies. Nasser Hussain, as happened quite regularly to him, got a bad decision and returned to the dressing room to put his fist through a locker in disgust and anger. He could be as enraged as Ramprakash at times, but here his rage got him in a pickle, or rather in a wooden-slatted trap.

According to team-mate Angus Fraser, Hussain muttered,

'Can someone come over here and fuckin' help me?' Fraser did, while nearly crying with laughter, and retrieved Hussain from his predicament.

Back in 2000, only a week after promising not to complain about bad umpiring decisions, Hussain suffered a diabolical lbw decision against Wasim Akram in a one-day international in Rawalpindi, and smashed a dressing-room fridge. 'We have had to take the refrigerator away,' the stadium manager, Farooq Aziz, said. 'I think it was because of that bad decision.'

I am not saying that youngsters should throw bats. It certainly will not help them score any centuries. Most of those who continually indulge in such behaviour are either too highly strung or simply seeking attention. But I would much rather see a batsman deep in disappointment after getting out than whistling merrily as if nothing has happened. It has to matter. You have to care. To the best batsmen, losing one's wicket seems like a form of death.

It is why some simply cannot drag themselves away from the crease when that moment occurs. The late Peter Roebuck was something of an inspiration to me, both as an obdurate opening batsman and as a far more fluent writer. And his wonderful description of Justin Langer regarding this sums it up perfectly for me.

'When Justin Langer finds his off stump akimbo,' Roebuck wrote, 'he leaves the crease only after asking the Met Office whether any earthquakes have been recorded in the region. In any case, he never edges the ball. It's just that his bat handle keeps breaking.'

There are many batsmen in the game who are never out. Not in their minds anyway. We can trace that sort of attitude right back to W. G. Grace and his famous comment: 'Play on. They came to see me bat, not you umpire,' when given out once. But that was in an exhibition match, and he was probably right. The crowd had come to see him bat.

They reckon that Frank Woolley, the great Kent and England

left-handed batsman who made 145 first-class centuries, would, when dismissed, keep looking over his shoulder in the hope that the umpire had changed his mind.

Some were just so sure of their ability that they could never believe that they had made a mistake. I remember thinking that about Ian Botham. He was at the end of his career and playing for Durham against us at Colwyn Bay. The pitch was slow and Botham never came to terms with it, eventually chipping a catch to cover.

He did not depart immediately, though. First he walked down the pitch to tap down the divot that had obviously caused his dismissal. The ball had disturbed the surface and stopped, therefore causing Botham to hit the ball in the air.

After Botham had done this, I thought I would take a look at the pitch. There was nothing there where Botham had tapped his bat. There had been no divot. But a spectator came up to me afterwards and said: 'That Botham was so unlucky, getting a ball that stopped.' He had conned the crowd, and he had conned himself. He was still infallible in his own mind.

Mike Selvey tells a magnificent tale about this. Botham was playing golf in Australia and had an approach shot to an elevated green, which he could not see. His playing partners were watching from above.

Botham hit the shot. It just about cleared a bunker and trickled onto the green a long way from the hole. Botham strode up onto the green, saw where his ball was and immediately walked towards the hole, where, just as he did at Colwyn Bay, he repaired an indentation that simply did not exist. 'Spun back,' he said. 'Too much action on it.'

His partners laughed. Again there was no possibility in Botham's mind that he had played a poor shot. There had to be another explanation, and this was it.

6

Technique

The small portable television at the far end of the Fenner's pavilion was on. It was in that corner where the players would watch the game. I was already out and had done my grieving, and so was ready to speak to some of my colleagues again now.

As I got closer to the television, I could see that it was not showing any usual programme. Instead it was showing footage of a batsman in action in the nets.

You must remember that these were the days long before rigorous video analysis in cricket was applied. I took a closer look at the batsman. 'Doesn't look a bad player,' I thought. 'He's seriously ugly, though. There's an awful lot of movement before the ball is bowled.'

Graham Saville, the former Essex batsman, was the Cambridge University coach. 'You're looking OK,' he said to me. I very nearly keeled over. I took a double take. 'What, that is me?' I thought to myself.

I did not let on, though. I quickly composed myself, mumbling something like, 'Yeah, but my head's still falling over a bit.' And then I took myself away to mull it over.

That was how I looked at the crease. My God! All those years of batting, and I had never realized. You conjure visions in your mind of classical elegance and textbook technique, driving like Viv Richards with a flourish and defending like Geoffrey Boycott with a high front elbow. But instead I looked like some tall, fretting, ever-moving batsman who knew that he probably should be getting forward, but was never sure whether he could.

These days young batsmen probably discover how they look at the crease by the time they are 10, but here I was past my 20th birthday and only then discovering that I was probably going to be one of the ugliest batsmen ever to play county cricket.

I instantly thought that I would never make it. Surely I needed to look better than that?

That is not so, of course. Even the great Viv Richards says so. 'I am a simple individual about what I needed to do on a cricket field,' he says. 'Too many people put undue pressures on themselves. Sometimes I would hear them worrying out loud about the elbow not coming up and other technicalities. You cannot be textbook correct every ball you face from an express bowler or a top spinner. There is not time to be pretty. It is an instinct thing. If you are able to prepare yourself quickly and make quick decisions, these are the solutions for reacting to a quick delivery.'

Looking back, this is a sharp glimpse at how the game has changed, though. It has become so much more scientific and analytical now. Counties video every ball of every game, and analysts log every ball too. I was just watching some grainy footage gathered from a simple camcorder.

For instance, Graham Gooch adopted his famous stance with bat held high off the ground after viewing some video tapes of an Ashes series recorded from the television by his wife's Auntie Grace.

'I watched the tapes again and again,' he said. 'And each time I was staggered. They showed how crouched my style was and how my head kept falling over towards the slips.'

Nowadays the system used by the counties is called CricStat, and you see dismissed batsmen rushing to view it. The problem is that you can pick holes in every dismissal. Anyway, you will see only the consequences of a poor technique, not the causes.

Former England and Glamorgan coach Duncan Fletcher would always use a dominoes analogy. With a batsman's dismissal it is like a line of dominoes having been pushed over but the last one has not fallen. Somewhere along the line one of the dominoes is out of place. Working out which one is the key, and it is not a simple process. An angry batsman viewing a video screen immediately after being dismissed is not going to be able to work that out.

One of my favourite retorts to commentators who describe a departing batsman as having played a poor shot is to ask: 'Have you ever seen anyone out to a good shot?' As it happens, I reckon my pull for four off Steve Watkin at Cambridge, when I clipped my leg stump with my boot, was a good shot, but you get my drift.

And often shots look a lot worse than they actually are. Panic and overcompensation can often ruin the final milliseconds of a shot.

Say, for example, that you are advancing down the pitch to look to hit an off-spinner back over his head. Despite what a lot of observers reckon, that will usually be a predetermined move (as are 99 per cent of sweep shots, in my opinion) and you will be looking to get close but not too close (you can only hit the ball along the ground then) to the pitch of the ball.

For whatever reason, though, suddenly you find that you are too far away from the pitch of the ball, and then, horror of horrors, the ball turns a little. Now you are in serious trouble.

You are already committed to the big shot, and the chances of it coming off now are slim. You panic and look to hit with the spin in the vain hope you might make decent contact in doing so. The result is a horrible heave across the line and probably a 'That is an awful shot there from James, bowled heaving across the line at the spinner' from the commentator.

One of my biggest frustrations is trying to watch one-day cricket on television and not knowing where the fielders in the deep are placed, especially against spinners. So you often do not know why a particular shot has been played, simply because you don't know where the field is.

And often when a batsman is caught in the deep he is not looking to clear the fielder. Yes, in this Twenty20 age, there are some ferociously strong hitters who can do that, but generally batsmen in one-day cricket will look to hit boundaries to untenanted areas.

So, the next time you see a batsman caught at long-off from an off-spinner, please reflect on the fact that he was probably trying to hit the ball over extra cover and maybe it held on him a little. Or if he is caught at long-on, he was probably trying to hit it between deep mid-wicket and long-on, and got too close to the ball.

And you would hope a batsman does not have to watch CricStat to see that. In that regard I'm glad that I did not play in this era. The only reason I would have wanted to view CricStat is to prove that I was not out, but that is a different story.

I certainly could not have viewed it to make myself feel good. It took me an awfully long time to realize that I would never look like, say, Mark Ramprakash at the crease, and that in fact that did not matter. It goes back to the old cliché: 'It's not how, it's how many.' The record books do not record how the centuries have been made, just whether they have been made.

The South African Graeme Smith has probably been the greatest example of that. The hulking left-hander – with his wide-of-feet crouched stance, a grip that lent new meaning to the term 'bottom-handed' and a pick-up that meant the bat face was so closed that it might have been shut for ever – was so ugly at the crease that even Hieronymus Bosch might have baulked at painting him.

Looking good can have its disadvantages anyway. For instance, Ramprakash was probably the most elegant batsman of my generation, and so that meant he was often labelled the 'most talented'. That in turn meant that he carried the most expectation.

Observers like watching such players – David Gower was another – so it is almost as if different standards are set for them. Ramprakash became a truly great county player, but did not cut it at international level. For such a fine player he became the source of a great deal of frustration.

Was he more talented than his contemporaries? Or was it just that he looked more graceful? It was the same with Matthew Maynard at Glamorgan. I have often fallen into the trap of describing him as 'the most talented player I have played with'. Was he? He certainly looked better at the crease than myself and Hugh Morris, but there were shots Morris and I could play that Maynard couldn't, and vice versa.

We all had one thing in common: we had all worked exceptionally hard to develop a technique that worked in the first-class game, that could produce centuries consistently. Maynard had a reputation as something of a dilettante, but, believe me, he worked harder than most. His pre-season net sessions with his trusted coach, Bill Clutterbuck, were ferociously hard and long. He would basically spend two days batting in the nets.

A lot has been written in recent times about talent, for instance by the Swedish psychologist K. Anders Ericsson, who has studied the structure of expert performance in various domains such as medicine, music and chess, as well as sports, and concluded that elite performance is reached through long, deliberate practice where the participant is extended beyond his or her comfort zone. In other words, talent is not inherited, it is acquired by putting in the hours of work.

I agree with that. My father was a decent cricketer, but I did not inherit any cricketing skills from him. He was a bowler who could not bat. I became a batsman who could not bowl. I became a cricketer because I was always in an environment where I could practise the skills required. Others had the same opportunity but simply did not wish to put in the hours required.

Matthew Syed in his book *Bounce* also reiterates that it is relentless hard work – as expressed in Malcolm Gladwell's 10,000 hours of practice in his book *Outliers* – as well as the circumstances in which you can practise which eventually bring about exceptional sporting performance.

Syed, of course, was a British table tennis champion, and he tells the story of how the street in which he lived in Reading (Silverdale Road) produced a remarkable number of Britain's top table tennis players. It was all down to the fact that one of the nation's best coaches, a man by the name of Peter Charters, taught at the local primary school and that nearby was a table tennis club which was open 24 hours a day for those who wanted to use it.

Syed was lucky (that word again!), not least because his parents, who were not table tennis players themselves, had randomly bought a table for him and his brother to play on in their garage.

I was lucky that I was born into a cricket-mad family and was at a cricket ground from the day I was born, but even luckier again that I went to Monmouth School, a public school, where Graham Burgess became coach in my second year.

The production line of cricketers in England and Wales is always an awkward subject concerning privilege and fairness, and, with cricket in state schools having declined so rapidly, I know that I was lucky.

Much has been done of late to encourage cricket in state

schools. There has been the Chance to Shine programme run by the Cricket Foundation, and latterly, to complement that work, the MCC Foundation's creation of 'hubs' around the country to provide coaching to children in state schools. But any benefits from that have not really been seen at the top level. Indeed it is not certain that it is even being seen at club level, with still a very low percentage of players in these schemes progressing to club cricket.

In his book *Luck*, Ed Smith, who went to Tonbridge School in Kent, tells us that when England toured Pakistan in 1987/88, 12 of the 13 players selected were state-educated. He compares that with the England Test team which beat India at Lord's in 2011. It included eight privately educated players and three state-educated ones.

In rugby union, at the 1987 World Cup, 62 per cent of the England team were state-educated. By 2007 that had dropped to 36 per cent.

'Being state-educated makes it about 13 times less likely that you will play for England,' Smith concludes of cricket. 'That really is a waste of talent.'

In 2013 a poll of county cricketers revealed that 119 out of 431 of them were privately educated, which is almost 30 per cent and a large percentage above the 7 per cent of the population that benefits from such education.

When England played Australia in the final Test of their calamitous 2013/14 Ashes tour, there were five state-educated players in the side, but four of them were bowlers (if we include the all-rounder Ben Stokes). Only Michael Carberry as a specialist batsman stood out, and, along with Ravi Bopara, he has been a rarity in recent times as a state-educated batsman playing for England.

As Scyld Berry, my colleague at the *Sunday Telegraph*, wrote in 2012: 'A decade ago 80.5 per cent of England's Test runs were scored by batsmen who had come from state schools, like

Marcus Trescothick, Michael Vaughan, Graham Thorpe and Andrew Flintoff.

'This year the percentage has tumbled to 10.2 per cent. Almost all the batting is done by players who have come from private schools, or South Africa, or both.

'The odds now seem stacked against any English batsman who does not grow up with privileged access to true grass pitches, qualified coaching and the network of first-class counties.'

Yes, to repeat again, I was lucky, not least because of the length of matches played in public schools. I could never have scored a century when aged 12 in a 20-overs match. I simply did not have the range of strokes or the physical strength required. I needed longer, and, fortunately, at Monmouth I got that.

But that is not to belittle the contribution made by my club, Lydney, and it is at clubs such as that where the void must be filled, through their links with local schools.

And I also think that the fundamentals of your batting technique will be established long before you go to public school anyway.

The story of Sir Donald Bradman is famous. As a young boy he would practise by using a stump to hit a golf ball rebounding off a water tank that was mounted on a curved brick stand. It was on a paved area behind the family home, and the golf ball would rebound at speed and at many different angles off the curved brick facing of the stand.

Bradman would hold the stump in his left hand while throwing the ball with his right hand, then quickly put his right hand onto the stump before hitting the ball. To me, then, it is unsurprising that Bradman ended up playing cricket with a rather unconventional grip, with his left wrist further behind the handle than usual – as he himself wrote in his book *The Art of Cricket*: 'I unhesitatingly admit that the left wrist could be more towards the front than mine and be perfectly correct. W. G. Grace and Sir Jack Hobbs both favoured this latter method.'

When grasping a stump one-handed it is almost natural to do so with that sort of grip, especially when you are young and relatively weak in the arms. The more conventional cricket grip does not feel strong enough with one hand. It is something I did as a young kid with a tennis racquet, holding it in my left hand with that sort of grip while throwing the tennis ball against a wall with my right hand and then putting my right hand onto the racquet quickly.

Bradman also had a slightly unorthodox pick-up that was probably derived from that practice too. 'My back lift was usually in the direction of second slip,' he said. 'This is what might be termed in golfing parlance, a slightly shut face. I think it helps to keep the ball on the ground, especially when playing on-side strokes.'

My grip changed a lot over my career, but we will come to those tinkerings shortly. Most batsmen's methods, especially the very basics of grip, stance and pick-up, are ingrained young.

Their technique is honed early and it never becomes any less important throughout their career. As Duncan Fletcher says: 'A batsman must make sure that his technique looks after him when he has made an error. That is what happens with the great batsmen. Their excellence is manifested in their technique getting them out of trouble when they make an error of judgement, rather than them playing shots more perfectly than others.'

If you are going to score a lot of centuries, you are probably going to make a lot of mistakes along the way. You need a good basic technique to see you through those tricky periods.

For the early development of a technique, take the great Sachin Tendulkar. He always gripped the bat low on the handle and adopted a short back lift. That is because when he was five, he was already using the bat of his brother Ajit, who was much older. The bat was too big and too heavy for him, so this was the only way Tendulkar could grip it and pick it up.

This is always discouraged in young batsmen – I can still hear the voice of my father in his sports shop advising parents that they must never let their son 'grow' into a cricket bat, as they might an item of clothing – but here it worked rather well.

Thereafter Tendulkar always used a heavy bat, and that suited the low Indian pitches. His coach Ramakant Achrekar tried to get him to change his grip, but eventually relented. The best coaches do not force a player to change against their will, after all. And while such a grip does suggest bottom-hand dominance, his top (left) hand was always very strong. He writes with that left hand.

At least Tendulkar had some formal coaching. Bradman did not. He mainly taught himself in a rather solitary upbringing in the rural town of Bowral in the Southern Highlands of New South Wales.

Bradman also thought Tendulkar to be the player in the modern era most similar to himself. 'I saw him playing on television and was struck by his technique,' he once said of Tendulkar. 'So I asked my wife to come look at him. Now I never saw myself play, but I felt that this player is playing with a style similar to mine, and she looked at him on television and said yes, there is a similarity between the two . . . his compactness, technique, stroke production . . . it all seemed to gel!'

Bradman and Tendulkar met eventually, on the occasion of Bradman's 90th birthday, when Tendulkar went along with Shane Warne to meet him. Bradman told Tendulkar that he was surprised that he had been coached.

'Anybody who has been through coaches is told to play with the left elbow pointed towards mid-off,' he said. 'You don't do that. I didn't do that. That gives you flexibility to play in any direction anywhere.'

Brian Lara was largely self-taught, too. At his family bungalow in Santa Cruz in Trinidad, there was a large porch with a low wall. Lara used to bounce a marble against it and hit it with his bat or a ruler.

And, yes, I know that the left-handed Lara had a grip that was very much around the front of the bat, unlike Bradman's, but maybe that was because there was not the uncertainty about the direction of the ball like there was for Bradman. And anyway it was a grip that did cause Lara a few problems in his career. Indeed Sir Garfield Sobers at one stage specifically advised him to alter it because he did not feel he was strong enough to keep control of the bat with it.

Just like Bradman, at an early age Lara was sharpening some remarkable reflexes and acquiring some excellent hand–eye co-ordination. But he was also doing something else here.

'There were a lot of pot plants dotted around and I put them in fielding places,' he says. 'When I hit the marble, the idea was to miss them.'

Lara was also learning to place the ball. You don't just hit cricket balls to score a century, you have to miss the fielders, find the gaps.

In my time as a player and a journalist, I have never seen a batsman place the ball as cleverly and with such pinpoint accuracy as Lara. The title of his autobiography, *Beating the Field*, was most apt.

I will tell you a little story to illustrate. When Lara made the previously mentioned 147 against Glamorgan in 1994 at Edgbaston, myself and Adrian Dale were fielding in the covers for much of it. Lara's placement was ridiculously good. Time and time again he would thread the ball between us and we would not so much as get a fingertip on it.

So we decided to do something rather different. Instead of walking in as the bowler bowled, we decided to walk sideways so that we could close the gap between us, and maybe actually stop one of Lara's drives.

So we did just that. And you know what happened? Lara just hit the ball into the space I had vacated. He looked and laughed as if to say 'Good try, boys, but you can't fool me!' Remarkable.

I'll give you an example from my generation in David Hemp, whom I've mentioned before. He did not have any bread-and-butter shots. He hit the ball better than anyone of my era, yet so many of his shots would either find fielders or shoot through the covers in the air. He was always hitting balls, not placing them. He could have done with practising as a kid like Lara did.

Lydney has always been a ground with low and slow pitches, and even when my friends and I created makeshift pitches on the outfield (there were no nets in those days at the club), there was little bounce then either.

No surprise then that I was a front-foot batsman, even if I probably never went as far forward as I should have done. Wilf Wooller, that legend of Glamorgan cricket as well as of plain speaking, who passed away before we won the county championship in 1997, spoke to me only once about my batting. 'You're a tall lad, for God's sake get further forward,' he said.

I was also renowned for guiding the ball down to third man. The title of my autobiography was *Third Man to Fatty's Leg*. The second part of that was a rather obscure reference to a gammy knee that finished my career via a quote from the Welsh cult film *Twin Town*, but the first part was undoubtedly confirmation of where opponents considered that I scored the majority of my runs.

I had quite a reputation. In 1996 when I scored 235 against Nottinghamshire at Worksop (which I later discovered, thanks to Chris Arnot's excellent book, *Britain's Lost Cricket Festivals*, beat Geoffrey Boycott's ground record of 214 not out), I was being watched by England coach David Lloyd. Mike Atherton was England captain at the time. At a break in play Lloyd spoke to me. 'Athers has been on the phone,' he said. 'He wants to know why they haven't got a third man!'

I always thought that scoring runs to third man was the poor man's method of scoring. It made me feel inferior. In fact I would go as far as to say that I possessed a serious complex about it. It goes back to the start of this chapter and the issue of aestheticism. I thought that the best players drove elegantly down the ground, when the truth is that, because they usually play with such 'soft' hands, most opening batsmen at the higher level score a lot of runs down to third man, even if that fact is still only recognized mostly in jest.

Andrew Strauss and Alastair Cook used to say to the rest of the England team that they should get paid more for the jobs they did at the top of the order, facing the new ball and laying the platform for the stroke-makers later. To which the frequent response apparently was: 'You can't get paid much for edging the ball down to third man!'

Likewise, when John Edrich passed 30,000 first-class runs, his Surrey team-mate Robin Jackman joked: 'Yes, 28,000 have gone through third man!'

It is mostly assumed that to play the ball down to third man requires an opening of the face of the bat, which is always a risky manner in which to play. But I did not always do that. What I did was play the ball so late that it would run off a straight face of the bat that was not quite yet vertical to the ground.

It was only when Duncan Fletcher arrived as coach at Glamorgan in 1997 that someone really praised me for being able to play that shot so skilfully, especially as regards its benefits in rotating the strike in one-day cricket. 'It's a real skill to be able to do that,' he told me. No one had ever told me that before.

It is also assumed that quicker pitches produce more runs to third man, but it is actually just as easy to score in that area on slow and low pitches, and you can actually open the face a little more if you want because the chances of an edge to slip are much reduced.

We develop techniques to suit our surroundings. Sometimes that can be good, sometimes that can be bad. Justin Langer wrote an interesting article on this matter in 2001. Langer was brought up in Western Australia, of course, and in particular the WACA ground in Perth, where the pitches mostly bounce like a trampoline. You cannot survive on that without a back-foot game.

Anyway, Australia had just played a tour match at Hove against Sussex in 2001 in which Richard Montgomerie had scored a century. And Langer was musing whether the prolific Montgomerie might one day be given a chance at international level. He mentioned me in the piece, actually calling me a 'run machine', which was nice, but he was clearly comparing my technique to Montgomerie's when he wrote: 'Day in day out, a player like Montgomerie plays county cricket on pitches like we are playing on at Hove this week. The surface is very, very slow, with very low bounce and a lightning fast outfield.

'The chance for someone like Montgomerie to develop a technique and temperament ready for Test cricket is limited. After all, he will rarely be placed under the same pressure that he could expect when he enters the Test arena.

'Although Brett Lee, Damien Fleming and Ashley Noffke were bowling their hearts out, the ball rarely lifted above bail height. And the pace of the ball gave scant encouragement for the bowlers trying to build pressure on the batsmen.

'The reality of Test cricket is that the pitches usually give some assistance to the fast bowler and, as a batsman at that level, you can expect to play a large majority of balls faced off the back foot.

'If a county batsman is rarely tested on the back foot, then it is unreasonable to expect them to be able to do it at the highest level.'

It is a very fair point, and it is an issue I tried to address halfway through my county career. My response to the short ball had always been to duck or sway. I was never a hooker or puller, although I would cut if the ball was well outside off stump.

And I remember talking to Steve Watkin about it. 'If a batsman doesn't hook or pull, I always know that I have got somewhere to go,' he said. In other words, if he found himself under pressure, which, I have to say, did not happen that often because he was one of the most accurate seamers of my generation, he could always resort to a short ball to relieve that pressure.

As it happened, Watkin was a tail-end batsman who had particular problems with the short ball. He would often turn his head away from the ball and thrust the bat, held in only his top (left) hand, hopefully at it. He once hit Wasim Akram for four doing that – he said he had 'hooked' him! – but it was not a method that was ever going to be sustainable.

So together we decided to do something about this. One winter we spent session after session at the Neath indoor school working on the short ball using the bowling machine there.

I had been playing professional cricket for a number of seasons by then. Matthew Maynard had played only a handful of games when Glamorgan's overseas professional, Javed Miandad, advised him that he had to work on an attacking method to play the short ball.

One of the reasons why I had never hooked or pulled was because I never felt that I had the reaction time to do so. But apparently there is little difference between the reaction times of the general population and top-level athletes.

As Peter McLeod, mentioned earlier as a member of Oxford University's Department of Experimental Psychology, says: 'There is surprisingly little difference between top-class athletes and good, fit ordinary people. In laboratory tests of reactions using unskilled tasks, most people show much the same reaction time of about a fifth of a second.'

But still in my opinion the hook and pull shots are two of the most difficult shots to play. The truth, though, was that I had never really tried to play them.

So Watkin set the bowling machine at quite a high speed, say about 85 mph, and angled it so that it was pointing halfway down the pitch. We used the slighter, softer type of machine balls so that if I got hit, which I did frequently, especially at the start of the process, it would not hurt too much. And I decided that I was going to hook or pull every single ball.

At first I could barely hit a ball. It was just too quick. I could not extend my arms fully out in front of me, which is the key to both shots. But gradually I started to hit one or two. And then more and more.

Somehow I developed my own technique of jumping in the air to ensure that I could hit the ball down. It was hardly textbook stuff but it actually became reasonably effective. Bowlers were surprised. They no longer had their get-out clause.

It was no coincidence that the next season was my most fruitful in first-class cricket. I scored 1,766 runs and followed it with 1,775 the following season, 1997, when Glamorgan won the county championship. And I did not get hit either. When looking to duck or just avoid the bouncer, you can easily take your eye off the ball. When looking to attack it, you simply have to watch it. 'Always look to play the ball first,' says Graham Gooch. 'You watch it for longer then.'

But a confession. I became a 'happy hooker'. I was not like, say, Herbert Sutcliffe, the great England opener and celebrated partner of Jack Hobbs, who used to hook in the air, but could be selective enough not to hook until he had made 40 in an innings.

Or Gooch, who says: 'Before, say, Malcolm Marshall has bowled to me, I have decided whether I am hooking or not. I have assessed the conditions, I have assessed how quickly he is bowling, how old the ball is. If it is up front in an innings, I may have to duck or get out of the way.'

In other words, by the end of my career, I could not help myself. Anything short I went after. It occasionally got me into trouble, even though I got away with a lot because I always looked to hit the ball down. That was what the jump was for.

There was one match against Gloucestershire at Cardiff when we had just a couple of overs to bat before the close of play. Mike

Smith, the left-arm swing bowler, who was given just one cap by England, was bowling.

Now, throughout my career, I had a problem with left-armers, especially when they could swing the ball back into me. It was because my natural set-up was to position my body towards extra-cover. That was where my front foot and shoulders were aiming when the ball was delivered. I would press with my front foot but would not reciprocate that with a complementary back-foot movement, as you should do to align yourself pointing back down the pitch.

So with the angle of a left-armer from over the wicket, if the ball swung into me late, I was always going to struggle because I would end up playing across the line. 'Play it back to where it comes from,' Graham Burgess would always urge me, and he is right.

And it is why the common advice for right-handed batsmen when facing left-arm over-the-wicket bowlers is to open up your stance. But with my set-up it was not always that easy. You still have to worry about the ball slanting across you, therefore you often end up still getting into the same position as you normally would.

It was quite heartening for me to hear Mark Ramprakash talking about this. I had just made my Test debut against South Africa at Lord's and Ramprakash was discussing his next county championship match for Middlesex. It was against Essex, who had a left-armer, Mark Ilott, in their ranks. 'He gets me out all the time,' lamented Ramprakash. 'Just watch now.'

As it was, Ilott did not get Ramprakash out in that game at Southgate in 1998. It probably helped that Mike Gatting (241) and Justin Langer (166) put on 372 for Middlesex's first wicket before Ramprakash got to the crease, mind.

But the left-armer problem was one that never fully went away for him. In his autobiography he tells a good story of the championship match, against Somerset at Taunton, after he had scored his 100th first-class hundred, in 2008, and of a battle against the left-armer Charl Willoughby.

He had been having throw-downs with team-mate Scott Newman, a left-handed batsman, and he found himself considering why Newman did not fall over when he threw his right-armed throw-downs at him. He imagined himself being the mirror image of Newman and indeed, that evening in his hotel room, practised in front of the mirror, opening up his stance and ensuring that his front foot was pointing at the bowler, not down the pitch. Ramprakash scored 200 not out in that game!

Anyway, back to Cardiff and Smith. I was certain that he would be looking to swing the ball into me late and trap me lbw, as he had done on a few occasions before. That was all I was thinking about. I was thinking: 'Don't move too early. Try to play the ball back to him.'

And then from nowhere he bowled a bouncer. The pitch was typical of Cardiff at that time: horribly, horribly slow. Smith almost had to pitch the ball on his toes to ensure that it bounced high enough.

I saw it pitch and immediately thought: 'That is going to bounce about hip-high – chest-high at most – and I am going to pull it in front of square for four. What a great way to finish the day.'

So the ball bounced and began rising. I got into position for the stroke. This was a freebie. A short ball on such a slow pitch. 'Oh hang on, this is getting a little high,' I suddenly thought. It was at that moment that I should just have pulled out of the shot. It would have been so easy to do. The ball was, with all due respect to Smith, slow and looping.

But for some reason I carried on regardless. The ball was well above my head and I thought I could still play a tennis smash and hit it down through mid-wicket. In truth I had no chance. The top edge was as inevitable as the humiliation that followed. The ball was caught at fine leg by Jon Lewis.

This was now the last over. So, as everyone knows, if you lose a wicket in the last over, that is it for the day. I could not even endure my shame alone. I trudged off with Gloucestershire fielders yelping around me, disbelieving that such an experienced player could make such a schoolboy mistake. Behind me was my young partner, Dan Cherry. I was supposed to be setting an example to him. I was ashamed. It was undoubtedly one of the worst moments of my career.

I know how Alastair Cook felt when he fell hooking Mitchell Johnson from only the seventh ball he faced as England attempted to save the Test against Australia in Adelaide in 2013. And that was nowhere near as high a bouncer either.

On a tour that was already showing signs of a shambles Cook was lambasted. 'That's totally out of character,' said the BBC's Jonathan Agnew on *Test Match Special*. 'Alastair Cook? Caught hooking in the second over of an innings, when England are trying to survive? That's not Alastair Cook. That's not how he plays.'

Well, actually it is. Cook is a very fine puller and hooker. Those shots are very much part of his game. Statistical probability tells us that he will fall to those shots at various stages in his career because every shot, even a defensive shot, carries some sort of risk.

Yes, you could say that it was early in his innings to be attempting the stroke and especially when England had to attempt to survive for a draw, but that would be a hugely simplistic argument. Just because you need to play for a draw does not mean that you cannot play any attacking strokes whatsoever. You still have to try to score runs.

There is a saying that the best players are positive in defence as well as in attack. What that means is that it is easier to defend when a batsman is in a positive frame of mind and looking to score runs. That is because he will then get himself into better positions at the crease.

Passive defence usually only ends in one place: a horrible, deep hole from which there is simply no escape. Hardly any centuries emerge from there.

Few are the batsmen who can go out with just defence on their mind. Geoffrey Boycott, maybe, or Sunil Gavaskar or Chris Tavaré, but even Mike Atherton has confessed to playing better when thinking positively.

In my career I managed to play one innings with only defence on my mind. It was actually my first second-team century for Glamorgan, and it was at my home ground of Lydney against Gloucestershire.

In a three-day match we had been bowled out cheaply on the first day on a pitch with some dampness in it. Gloucestershire had then made a big score so that, with four sessions remaining, our only hope was to survive that time. I did so. I batted 135 overs for 125 not out. In cricketing vernacular I 'blocked the shit out of it'.

That I could do so was down to that previously mentioned low and slow pitch, as well as some naivety on my part. I was still learning the professional game then and my own game was horribly limited. I could be so defensively minded because in truth all I was doing was playing my game. I did not have a range of shots beyond that.

It was an important innings for me, however. First of all it taught me that I could score a century at that level, and that I could concentrate for that length of time, but it also taught me that I had to expand my range of strokes if I was to be successful. I never played an innings like that again.

But that is not to say that defence is unimportant. On the contrary it is absolutely crucial, even for the most flamboyant and attacking of batsmen. For instance, when Kevin Pietersen made his Test debut, against Australia at Lord's in 2005, it was his defence that immediately struck me.

Glenn McGrath was wreaking havoc from the Pavilion End with his off-cutters darting down the slope and most of the

England batsmen could scarcely lay a bat on him. But as soon as Pietersen entered the fray it almost appeared as if an altogether different game was taking place.

Taking a huge stride forward with an impeccably straight blade, Pietersen smothered all of McGrath's projected perils. If a man cannot defend, he cannot play. And that is what happened to Pietersen when he had that awful trouble with left-arm spinners later in his career.

Because of the arrival of the Decision Review System and a greater number of lbws for left-arm spinners as right-handed batsmen pushed forward, Pietersen suddenly found that he could not trust his defensive stroke. And it led to a horrible case of sinistrophobia.

The great Viv Richards had an immaculate defence when he wanted. He will always be remembered as the master persuader of balls from outside off stump towards the leg-side, but we should not forget his solid, technically perfect defence.

Bowlers talk of his sometimes unexpectedly blocking a whole over, as if just to take a break from his coruscating strokeplay. Ah, to be that good.

But I can also talk about being asked to throw him balls one day after play at Chesterfield and his blocking every single ball. Yes, he did not play one single attacking stroke. It must have been an awful disappointment to the large crowd that had gathered to watch, but Richards had something in mind. He wanted to tighten up.

I have also seen Sachin Tendulkar perform a practice session where he has placed a semi-circle of cones around him in his stance and tried to ensure that the balls thrown to him did not advance outside those cones.

He was practising 'soft hands', something that does not come readily to today's players. 'Batters go hard at the ball because of the way they are brought up now,' Worcestershire's director of cricket and former England wicketkeeper, Steve Rhodes, says.

'When the ball's moving around, the seamers are going to get the batters nicking off.'

You simply have to be able to defend. If you think about scoring a century in say 180 balls (which was quick for me, I might add), you will probably defend or leave 130 of those balls. That is over 70 per cent of your innings spent on defensive measures, playing either a forward defensive stroke, a back-foot defensive shot or simply disregarding the ball as it passes through to the wicketkeeper.

Leaving the ball is such an important part of playing any long innings. Nothing frustrates a bowler more than seeing a batsman blithely disregard all the effort he has just put into that delivery. It makes the bowler reassess, and often alter, his line. It is a game of patience. The batsman is saying: 'I'm not coming to you, you will have to come to me.'

As Graham Gooch says: 'It was always part of my plan. One of my little sayings was: "If it's wide, leave it." But I was always looking to play first. Leaving was the second option. It should not be seen as a negative option.'

Gooch's 'little sayings' have become imbedded in current batting terminology. We will come to his 'daddy hundreds' later, but for now just let him recount the story of one of his first meetings upon becoming England's batting coach in 2009 (he was a consultant until 2012, when he took up a permanent position, before departing in 2014).

It was on a tour to South Africa and he gathered the players around in East London. The then team director, Andy Flower, had articulated to Gooch that he liked short, sharp messages being given to the players. So Gooch just said: 'Play late, play straight, be great.'

It became a catchphrase for the team. 'They always took the mick out of me about it,' admits Gooch. 'But the point is that the players have to work it out for themselves, what is best for them. It has to be a short, sharp message.'

Although not necessarily one of Gooch's sayings, 'Knowing where one's off stump is' has also become a fashionable phrase, but it is vital if a batsman is to play a long and successful innings. After all, the bowlers are generally urged to hit the top of the batsman's off stump, so it is rather a good idea that the batsman himself knows where the bowler is aiming!

The best way for a right-handed batsman to do this is to ensure that, once his pre-ball movements (his 'triggers' as they are called) have been completed, his right eye is over his off stump.

As Gooch says: 'I took a leg stump guard, with my toes on leg stump. Where your bat is is irrelevant to me. It can be in the air, outside off stump, it's where your feet are that counts.

'Whatever your trigger movements are, when you get in the "ready" position, your head needs to be on off stump. That's where you pick your line up from. I went back, not so much back and across, but the ball of my foot would be on middle stump and my head on off stump.'

Matthew Maynard ensured that he knew where his feet were by marking a line down the pitch rather than back towards the stumps. 'At the end of my career I would take middle and leg [guard] and then draw a line out from the crease,' he says. 'Most people draw a line back to stumps. I stood with my bat between my legs so it was a little inconsistent – I had left the ball occasionally and it had hit my off stump. It was important that I knew where my feet were, then my trigger back and across to middle and off.'

I too tapped my bat between my legs in the later stages of my career. I found that it helped my balance, and had done it for no other reason than because a friend at Swansea University, Neil Pritchard, who played a few games for Gloucestershire, had suggested it at a time when I was struggling.

When the Australian coach Jeff Hammond arrived at Glamorgan in 2000, he was not impressed with this at all. He called it the 'Glamorgan way' and was unhappy that two such senior players as Maynard and myself were doing it, because it influenced all the young batsmen. He reasoned that it was not conducive to a good pick-up because you have to take your hands away from your body first from that original position in order to begin your backswing.

'Tuck your wings in' was his constant refrain, which basically meant to keep your hands close to your body in your pick-up. It worked for me, though, and if you have ever seen a photograph of Donald Bradman in his stance, you might notice that he too tapped his bat in between his legs.

You must also ensure that your eyes are level and that your head is still at the moment of delivery from the bowler. That stillness is absolutely crucial. A moving camera takes blurry pictures.

As previously mentioned, in the worst periods of my career, when I was standing with my bat upright, I think I was moving my head often as the ball was bowled. I was taking some seriously blurry pictures. If you want to see how the position of the head should be as the bowler delivers a ball, then you need look no further than a picture of Sachin Tendulkar at that very moment.

Mind you, if you wanted to base a batting technique on anyone it would probably be Tendulkar. The grip on the bat might be low, as is the pick-up, but the feet are shoulder-width apart, the knees flexed and the balance perfectly formed on the balls of his feet. And that head is so still, those eyes so level.

Leaving on width is obviously a crucial factor, but doing so on length is just as important in my view. For instance, much of my game was based on looking for width from the bowlers, whether that was to drive off the front foot or cut off the back foot. But I also had to be very careful, especially early in an innings, not to drive at balls that were not quite half-volleys.

But for me the ability to read length is often what distinguishes the very best players from the pack. Timing is what distinguishes the best in terms of aestheticism. Think of Brian Lara, Colin Cowdrey, David Gower, Mark Waugh and Sourav Ganguly.

According to Angus Fraser, we should not think of Mike Atherton, who was, apparently, 'a natural mistimer of the ball'.

That is a little harsh because Atherton could time the ball nicely. He had to really, because he was certainly no power player.

But quite what timing is and how it is achieved is something that is very difficult to explain, and it is certainly even more difficult to coach. We all know when we have timed a cricket ball. The ball hits the middle of the bat and speeds away with the minimum of effort. It is a truly wonderful feeling. But how did we do it?

As with the correct execution of any cricket shot, it is a combination of factors coming together at the precise moment, mostly born of a solid technique: a fluent, well-timed backswing that accelerates through the hitting zone, ensuring the bat is still gripped tightly at the moment of impact and ensuring that one's weight is moving into the ball rather than away from it.

And it will also require the correct reading of length. You will struggle to drive a ball too short for the purpose, and you will also struggle to play any shot of consequence off the back foot if the ball is too full.

We touched on reading length earlier in the book when considering the constant demand of 'Watch the ball' from a batsman to himself. The ball is not usually watched all the way, so instead it is about how and how quickly a batsman uses the visual cues given to him. As Peter McLeod, the Oxford University psychologist, says: 'It lies in how they [batsmen] use visual information to control motor actions once they have picked the ball up.'

You can have the very best technique in the world, but if you cannot then read the length of the ball, it will mean nothing.

And on bouncier pitches, you can leave on length too. That is nowhere better seen than at the WACA ground in Perth where balls pitched in line with the stumps can be left alone with impunity, even if it might require some contortions of the body to avoid being hit.

As Gooch says: 'People who leave the ball well, it looks as if the ball is cutting them in half. Mark Taylor was a great one for that. My first big change was when I was asked to open the batting five years after I started. Suddenly I had to be tighter. I had to think about how I left the ball and had to play straighter. It was a massive part of my evolution as a batsman.'

Of course, openers will naturally look to leave the ball more as they aim to set the tone for the innings. If you were thinking that I might write 'see off the new ball' there, then you were badly mistaken.

That phrase annoys me more than most in cricket. What on earth does it mean? To me it is nebulous nonsense.

At Glamorgan we would sometimes have meetings in which roles were established. Always when it came to the opening batsmen, on the board would appear 'see off the new ball'.

I would love to know the precise moment when a new ball is seen off. Can the opener raise his bat then? Can he just walk off?

I think it is disrespectful to ask an opener merely to see off the new ball. That was never my job. My job was to score runs. I never felt as if I was some blunter sent out before the stroke-makers. I was there to score centuries.

Yes, opening is the toughest job for any batsman. I have certainly always felt that. The 'tough nuts' is how I used to describe us, as opposed to the 'prima donnas' hiding lower down the order.

But 'to see off the new ball'? Does anyone really go out there with that purpose? 'To see off the new ball is a negative tactic,' says Gooch. 'That's survival. If you bat well as an opening batsman you do a number of jobs. You progress the score, you build a platform, you protect the middle order and you set the game up.'

Mike Atherton agrees. 'I don't think it is necessarily the opener's job to get a dour 15 and make way for the pretty boys who can play in the middle order,' he says. 'If you are going through levels of technical competence then openers are supposed to be technically sound and competent. So if there is more movement off the seam, you are more likely to survive than perhaps some other players. But obviously when you get in, there is the same expectation to go on and get a big score.

'Fundamentally your job is to go out and score runs. How you do it is down to you. Maybe you expect the No. 5 to get runs quicker than the No. 1, but it is the same job at the end of the day.' Too right it is.

In a way I was fortunate to have to expand my game rather than constrict it. Over time, and it certainly does take time, a batsman has to work out his game. Alastair Cook has continued hooking since that Adelaide mistake because he knows that it is a shot that will bring him more reward than failure.

Others in history have ditched that shot, mind. Geoffrey Boycott did so, as did Steve Waugh. They considered it too risky, even though both could actually play it very well.

Andrew Hilditch wanted to ditch it, if you will excuse the pun, but never could. The Australian famously could not help himself hooking, especially in the 1985 Ashes when Ian Botham served up bouncer after bouncer.

Hilditch is an intelligent man, even if he copped huge flak in an unsuccessful stint as Australia's chairman of selectors. He is a solicitor, no less. But his intended cure for an addiction to hooking was not particularly intelligent. Apparently he listened to audio tapes with the repeated command of 'Don't hook'.

Shame that no one told him the mind's subconscious always ignores the negative part of such a dictum. All he was doing was urging himself to commit more sins of self-destruction. As Graham Gooch says: 'He should have been telling himself: "Leave the ball" not "Don't hook."'

Gooch also mentions Tendulkar's famous 241 against Australia in Sydney in 2004, when he eschewed the cover drive for so much of the innings. 'I watched part of it and he didn't play a shot on the off side,' says Gooch. 'I asked him about it and he said he hadn't been playing that well, so he decided to say to himself: "Leave well." He didn't say: "Don't play any cover drives." The point is never tell yourself not to do something.'

In truth, what Hilditch was doing was playing outside of his limits. He was not a good hooker. It was not a shot that should have been part of his game plan. He should have worked that out much earlier than he did. Working out one's game is a long and, at times, painful process, but it is absolutely vital if you are to become a consistently successful batsman and score the centuries we all crave.

You must know how you are going to score your runs, and also which shots you are going to eschew in order to avoid dismissal.

It is what Ricky Ponting brilliantly calls learning to 'swim between the flags'. At the end of his career he said: 'I'd worked out that to be a successful batsman I had to "swim between the flags". At the beach the lifesavers decide where it is safe to swim and they put the flags in the sand to mark those boundaries. Drift outside those flags and even the strongest swimmers can get into trouble. I had to work out what shots I could play, when I needed to defend, when it was prudent to be bold. If I stayed within my limits, I was very hard to dismiss and I had the skill to score runs at a reasonable rate. However, if I ventured outside my flags, I might be OK for a while, might even play a big innings or two, but sooner or later I'd get into trouble. Eventually, I'd drown.'

It is a wonderful summation of the art of batting, indeed the art of centuries. As Jack Birkenshaw, the former Yorkshire, Leicestershire and Worcestershire off-spinner, said when talking about the art of batting when manager of Leicestershire in 1994: 'Look at Allan Border. He's scored 10,000 runs and he's only got three shots: the cut, the cover drive and the pull.'

The left-handed Border actually scored 11,174 Test runs, crouched in his baseballer's stance, with his bat raised ready to hop back and pull and cut. But the point was that he did not care how he looked or how he scored those runs.

As John Edrich also once said: 'Far too many cricketers try to do things they can't manage; they go out of their depth. I reckoned I could get away with about three main shots, plus the knack of being able to pick up ones and twos here and there.'

The last part of that quote is crucial. Picking up ones and twos is so important for any batsman. Those are his bread-and-butter shots, his release valves when the going gets tough.

How much to tinker with your technique, though? It is the hardest question for any batsman to answer throughout his career. As you move up through the levels, new and much stiffer challenges always present themselves and it is a question of how you adapt to them.

But the fundamentals remain. As Graham Gooch says: 'There are different styles but there are a lot of basics for every player – you have got to move your feet, keep your head still, get your bat delivery pretty much coming straight – those basic principles, you have to keep them going.'

I'm not sure about the moving of the feet, because there have been some fine players who have not moved their feet a great deal – for example, Marcus Trescothick. The key in such an instance is the distribution of weight and the position of the head. Trescothick can drive beautifully when his weight is going forward and his head going into the ball.

My problem was that I always felt that the grass was greener on the other side. It is all too easy to think that a small technical change will bring huge rewards. I learnt the hard way that this is not the case.

My natural grip on the bat was very much like Donald Bradman's in that my left wrist was behind the handle. It is a grip that is good for leg-side play but not so good for off-side strokes. So at school I was known as a good leg-side player but one who was not so strong through the off side.

But in my early days as a professional I decided to alter that. In fact it was between my first and second years at Cambridge

University. I decided that I wanted to become a better off-side player and reasoned that the best route to achieving that was by changing my grip. So I brought my wrist round to the front of the handle. I consulted no one on this. I just did it myself.

It was to prove calamitous, very nearly costing me my professional career.

The problem was that my wrists and arms were not strong enough to facilitate such a change. What transpired was horrible. When the hand is too far round the front of the bat, it is very difficult to keep the front elbow up without opening the face of the bat. So the blade of the bat became very open in my pick-up and then started to waver out towards the slip cordon, resulting in a dreadful 'inside-out' movement.

As I was also persisting with a raised-bat method at the time, as previously mentioned, with my head moving around, this just got uglier and uglier. Even more so when, after finishing at Cambridge, I returned to Cardiff's low pitches to dream up another variation, which was to stand with my front foot pointing down the pitch, opening up my shoulders in the vain hope of avoiding lbws.

If I thought I looked ugly on that television screen at Fenner's this was something else altogether. In 1993 Glamorgan famously won the Axa Equity and Law Sunday League title at Canterbury, beating Kent in a glorious finale to Viv Richards' career.

There is an excellent video tape of that day, but I have watched it once and will never do so again. I cannot bear the sight of my batting, however brief my role in that day was – I scored three and was dropped once in the process of making that many.

Somehow I managed to score some runs with this method, but how different it was from my original method is probably best summed up by the response of Graham Burgess when I went to see him at Monmouth School one day to work on my game. 'What have they done to you?' he said in exasperation.

He thought the various coaches working with me had

changed my technique. They hadn't. It had been all of my own making.

Eventually, after a lot of hard work, I got my method back to a state in which I could operate consistently. I did that by simply going back to basics; by tapping my bat on the ground and somehow achieving a straighter pathway for it after my pick-up.

It was a harsh lesson about the possible effects of trying to make radical changes to a technique. But I know now that I was hardly alone in my faulty thinking.

Far, far better players than me have fallen into the same trap. Take Andrew Strauss. In 2007 he worked a lot with the then England coaches Peter Moores and Andy Flower on driving the ball. Strauss had never been a particularly strong driver and opposition bowlers were no longer bowling short balls so that he could pull or cut, just as he had done when announcing himself so wonderfully on the Test stage in 2004.

The result? Strauss kept getting out driving and hardly scored any runs off the back foot. 'I ended up going after balls that were far more dangerous to play,' he wrote in his autobiography. 'My far more productive back-foot game had been neglected and so my bread-and-butter shots were not coming off as often. No wonder I didn't score many runs that season.'

And then the killer advice that I wish I had been offered before I began my uneasy journey through technical hell.

'If a player came to me for advice about altering their game, I would always counsel against rushing into making wholesale changes to their technique,' said Strauss. 'Certainly, if you have reached international level, your technique, which has evolved over a long number of years, has got you to where you are. Your problem would have to be very serious indeed to throw away all that evolved knowledge. More often than not, your issues will lie with shot-selection, despite what the commentators might say. That is something that is controlled by your head, not your technique.

'Looking back on my career it still frustrates me that I tinkered with my technique as much as I did. Perhaps that is inevitable if you are practising for thousands of hours every year, that you will try different things in practice in the constant search to become a better player. I think I would probably have scored more runs if I'd constantly honed my own technique rather than searching for a magical cure.'

I could not agree more. But that does not mean that little technical adjustments do not catch on.

Graham Gooch's upright stance was copied by many, myself included. Justin Langer once got into the habit of twisting his head at the very last second to face the bowler. In Perth this soon became all the rage and before long the likes of Mike Hussey and Ryan Campbell were doing it.

There have been some more bizarre technical adjustments. John Wright, the former New Zealand opener who coached India, and was an endless fidgeter, for ever stopping the bowler because something or someone tiny had moved behind the arm, used to glue his top glove to the handle, in order to hold his grip in that position. And I'll admit that I toyed with that idea when I was struggling with my grip. Thankfully I resisted.

Clive Rice, the South Africa and Nottinghamshire all-rounder, apparently wrapped strips of lead around the top of his handle to balance his very heavy bat.

Then there was Adam Gilchrist's famous use of a squash ball in his glove when making 149 from just 104 balls in the World Cup final of 2007 in Barbados against Sri Lanka. Gilchrist put the ball in his bottom, left-hand glove to stop his hand turning on the handle.

Gilchrist had a very high grip on the bat, which can lead to a slightly whippy effect and a loss of control, especially if you are trying to defend against spinners. England's Alastair Cook had a high grip like this (as did my opening partner at Glamorgan, Hugh Morris, and also the New Zealander Glenn Turner), and changed it when advised to do so by the then England coach, Duncan Fletcher.

But Gilchrist's bottom-hand grip was unusual in that the hand was prone to going too far behind the handle. The squash ball was used to prevent this.

It was only the second time Gilchrist had done this, having previously made a domestic one-day hundred for Western Australia against Queensland using it.

The idea was the brainchild of Bob Meuleman, the former West Australian cricketer and selector, who coached Gilchrist.

'I went to a squash centre before he went off [to the World Cup] and got him six squash balls that were a bit broken and were not as hard as a new ball,' said Meuleman. 'You don't want it to crush right down but be a bit flexible. He had a few hits before he went off for the World Cup. He didn't have the squash ball in and he hit them like he couldn't even play fourth grade. He put it in and he then hit the ball so well.'

Upon reaching his century Gilchrist pointed to his bottom glove, but not many people realized the significance of that gesture until afterwards.

As Gilchrist said: 'Bob's last words to me before I left the indoor training centre in Perth were, "Well, if you are going to use it, make sure when you score a hundred in the World Cup final, you show me and prove to me that you have got it in there". So I had to stay true to that.'

If only all centuries came on demand like that.

7

For Openers

It was always the same at the old Sophia Gardens ground in Cardiff. I would be inside the dressing room, preparing myself, fidgeting and jumping around. My opening partner, Hugh Morris, would be outside on the balcony, sitting calmly and adjusting his eyes to the light.

My rituals had been done, my equipment put on. My batting shoes (half spiked, half rubber) had been tied with the laces pulled so tightly that the blood was barely able to reach my toes. Then my box, thigh pad and inner thigh pad had been put on.

That last piece of protective equipment was important. If I can offer any young opening batsman one piece of advice it would be to wear an inner thigh pad. I took so many fearfully painful blows on my right thigh before beginning to wear one well into my professional career, and they all could so easily have been avoided. The new ball moves around. It does not have to nip back too much to avoid the bat, or catch its inside edge, and thud into that fleshy region at the top of your back leg.

One must not be wary of wearing protective equipment. As

long as you feel comfortable with it, wear it. It is with a shake of the head that I recall that I did not wear a helmet regularly until I played county second-eleven cricket. Today's Health and Safety would certainly not have approved.

I did not wear a forearm guard until Yorkshire's Darren Gough nearly broke my arm at Cardiff. I always wore one after that. It seems to be out of fashion these days, though. Maybe that is evidence of the lack of fast bowlers, but that is another argument.

The one thing I did not wear was a chest guard, although I did borrow one in the second innings of my Test debut against South Africa in 1998. Having been caught down the leg side in the first innings off Allan Donald, captain Alec Stewart urged me to wear one in the second innings. I took his advice, but wished I hadn't. I was out for a duck and felt uncomfortable. You need to become accustomed to such things in practice, not try them out in a Test match!

It is remarkable how the use of equipment has evolved, and how much better protected the modern batsman is. There were obviously no helmets until relatively recently, and even the gloves used offered little protection, with either some sausage padding or rubber spikes stitched onto the fingers.

Donald Bradman did not even wear a thigh pad. 'It is not essential,' he said. 'And, in fact, I only wore one when facing certain types of bowlers such as the left-handed Bill Voce, whose pacey in-dippers could give you a nasty rap on the thigh.'

The West Indian Carl Hooper never wore one either, just a handkerchief in his pocket. It helped that he has thighs like tree trunks, mind. Often batsmen would just fold a towel and use that as a thigh pad.

My left pad had been put on before the right. Next was the helmet, then lastly the batting gloves, with the Velcro on the left done up (I would never do the Velcro on the right until just before facing my first ball), and I picked up my bat.

The bell would go. Morris and I would make our way to the door. I was always first, tapping the sign above our heads. It wasn't quite the 'This is Anfield' sign at Liverpool Football Club, but it bore the names of the 15 Glamorgan players, including myself, to have played Test cricket for England (Simon Jones became the 16th in 2002), and so it had sufficient resonance.

We began to descend the stairs. Out onto the field we went, exchanging a brief 'good luck' with each other before I played a couple of shadow drives as I walked. I have no idea what Morris was doing at this stage. I was in my own world as I walked to the striker's end to receive first ball and he went to the non-striker's end.

We did this 180 times in first-class cricket apparently, amassing 7,606 runs as an opening partnership with an average of 43.96. Without wishing to brag – even though I'm pretty proud of it! – at the time of writing that is 34th in the all-time list of partnership averages, just behind the Michael Slater/Mark Taylor alliance. Only 95 pairings have made more than 5,000 runs together.

I have always said that Morris and Alan Butcher were a much better pairing for Glamorgan, and so it is proved by their presence on the list at fourth, with an average of 59.38, behind only the partnerships of Jack Hobbs and Herbert Sutcliffe, Jack Fingleton and Bill Brown, and Bill Lawry and Bobby Simpson. That is some effort.

Morris and I, though, were like an old married couple, able to predict each other's every movement and always knowing what to say at the right time.

I would always take first ball because that was what I wanted, and being No. 2 was what Morris wanted. That was OK for me until the Australian Matthew Elliott arrived at Glamorgan after Morris' retirement, and he too wanted first go. An uncomfortable compromise had to be reached: take it in turns. I didn't like that.

As already mentioned, on my Test debut Mike Atherton let me face the first ball. He made a duck. But he took first ball in the second innings and I made a duck. It was probably not coincidence. Familiarity breeds comfort.

I genuinely cannot see why anyone would want to be No. 2 when they could be No. 1. As Graham Gooch says: 'One of the great things I enjoyed about opening above all else was that you are given the opportunity to set the tone, to dictate the game. The game is not set for you, you are doing the setting. I liked that. So when I was batting with Boycs [Geoffrey Boycott] he said: "You go one." I wanted to be No. 1 – it's a mental approach.'

Every opening partnership has its quirks. Morris and Butcher hardly spoke. In those days they never got on that well, although I'm told that has thankfully been rectified in recent years. Chris Broad and Tim Robinson at Nottinghamshire were another superb opening partnership (15th on that list) that barely said a word to each other.

Matthew Hayden and Trevor 'Tank' Barsby opened together at Queensland, and they averaged 55.40 as a pairing, putting them ninth in the list. Barsby would walk out first and he would always smoke a cigarette before doing so.

'Even though I wasn't a smoker – my lungs couldn't handle it – I loved smelling the final deep drag of his cigarette as he walked on,' says Hayden. 'It took me back to my country cricket days, when I was a boy playing against men, and just as I was about to face up for the first ball the umpire would call play and the old crinkle-faced wicketkeeper would have one last puff and throw away his durry.'

Hayden's famous and successful opening alliance with Justin Langer for Australia was slightly different. For certain you cannot imagine the fitness fanatic Langer smoking before batting!

Instead religion played its part. Langer would make a mark on middle stump before he faced the first ball. Then Hayden would cross it when he took strike.

At the bowler's end Hayden would mark centre, and Langer would then cross it. 'It was an anchor in our relationship,' said

Hayden. 'When we marked the sign of the cross at the crease I would always say a silent prayer: "*Whatever happens today is in your hands.*"'

And that last part is actually the bit that matters. Australians in general often peddle an over-effusive line of two players joining spiritually, emotionally and physically to do battle against 11 bloodthirsty fielders. But it is blithely forgetting that once the bowler begins his run, you are on your own. Only then can you score your runs. A century is made by you, and you alone.

I loved opening the batting with Hugh Morris, but I'm pretty sure that he never helped me score any runs. Yes, we were a right-hand/left-hand partnership and supposedly that sort of alliance is king. But haven't some of the greatest opening partnerships been of the same bent, whether dextral or sinistral?

Jack Hobbs and Herbert Sutcliffe (who stand top of the partnership averages with 87.81 together in Test matches), and Gordon Greenidge and Desmond Haynes (who scored the most Test runs – 6,482 – as an opening partnership in Tests) represent the former, and Matthew Hayden and Justin Langer the latter. Bowlers at the top level simply should not be overly inconvenienced by rapid transitions in line, the common reason given why right-hand/left-hand partnerships should prosper more.

Batsmen are more likely to have a negative effect on a partner than positive. For instance, if one just simply is not scoring, it will put pressure on the other. It happened for England in 2013 when both Nick Compton and Joe Root were rendered strokeless at times by New Zealand and then Australia, and so Alastair Cook felt that pressure at the other end. It made him feel as if he should play outside of his natural game, which is never a good thing.

The best partnerships arise because they are made up of the best batsmen. It really is that simple. I always remember Duncan Fletcher making an interesting comment at the end of the 1997 season, in which Glamorgan had won the county championship.

Much had been made of the starts given to the team by myself and Morris, and indeed we averaged 57.92 as a pairing that season with five alliances of over 100, but Fletcher said that it was the fact that we had dovetailed with our individual centuries that was most important. I made seven centuries that season and Morris four, but only once, against Durham at Cardiff, did we score hundreds in the same innings.

Mike Atherton agrees that batting is a personal battle. 'Batting is an individual thing,' he says. 'Yes, partnerships are important if you put together a big partnership and the other team is not getting wickets and a lot of good partnerships do go a long way to winning the game, but your mate can't help you. A bit of chat maybe, and you probably feel more comfortable with some partners than others. Some you might run with better than others – I remember running well with Goochie at the start of my career, but he couldn't help me keep the ball out. It's like when people talk about a batting unit, I never quite understand it. Maybe a left-hand/right-hand or an aggressor/accumulator combination can be effective, but it comes back to the point that batting is an individual exercise.'

Kevin Pietersen may not be the greatest example for obvious reasons, but his reply on debut in the 2005 Ashes to Geraint Jones, who wanted a middle-of-the-pitch chat, has always made me laugh. 'Sorry, china. Can't talk now. Too pumped,' he said.

There is a lot of mystery behind those mid-wicket conversations between batsmen, and they are deemed in many quarters to be vital to a partnership's function. Well, sorry to be a spoilsport, but they are generally made up of only nonsense chatter.

'Well played', 'Keep going', 'It's swinging away a little', 'Don't worry, I didn't think you hit it' after the most blatant edge. You get the drift. It is hardly cerebral stuff.

A player once told me that batting with Mike Hussey at Northamptonshire was not a pleasurable experience. 'Too intense' was the complaint. That probably says more about that cricketer's mindset than any failing on Hussey's part, but there is an important point to be made in that you must know and understand your partner. Some like to be cajoled constantly, others prefer just to be left to themselves.

Murray Goodwin liked batting with Hussey at Western Australia. 'We are very similar characters with our cricket,' Goodwin says. 'Off the field we are probably not, but the thing I liked about him was that he was a left-hander and they had to adjust to him, he was so good at getting off strike.'

As I've said, I think that is a little simplistic, but Goodwin is certainly a player who feeds off the other player in a partnership. 'Partnerships help in my focus to keep the other guy going,' he says. 'Also when you've got a partnership going you can see the fielders and the bowler, they start losing that little bit of energy and bite. Especially if you are batting with someone who is not quite the same player as you, so he might be a better front player than me [Goodwin is a renowned cutter and puller], so I am a foil. As well as batting a lot with "Huss", I remember batting with Andy Flower [for Zimbabwe], especially in a huge partnership in Sabina Park – he was so good at rotating strike too.' They put on 176 against West Indies in that match, with Goodwin making 113 and Flower 66, and they also once put on 277 against Pakistan at Bulawayo, with Goodwin 166 not out and Flower 100 not out.

Matthew Maynard is another who extols the virtues of partnerships. 'They are a big thing for me,' he says. 'Any partnership of 150 can put you right in the game. The easiest period I had in my career was when I was batting with Viv [Richards]. He had this fear factor.'

I do not doubt that partnerships have huge numerical benefits. Of course they do. But I always felt that the bowlers saw each batsman as a new battle rather than a dual dispute. I did bat very occasionally with Richards and the reaction when he walked out to bat was quite something. You could hear the chatter among the opposition, and they would always turn to watch Richards' entrance. It did create a warm feeling inside knowing he was on your side.

But I'm not sure I would have liked to have opened the batting with Leonard Hutton. The story goes that he was once walking out to open with a young partner. Hutton asked his partner what he was thinking about. 'Nothing,' was the reply. 'Well, let me tell you what I am thinking. I'm thinking about how the wicket's going to play, which bowler will have the breeze, what shots I will not try in the first hour, which fielders aren't too quick on their feet and I'm wondering about those sightscreens. You've got to think it through, you know.'

Or you've to keep it a little more simple than that. Yes, those are all things that you need to consider as an opening batsman, but all in one go and just as you are walking out to bat? It is surely too much information.

One player I did like batting with was Glamorgan colleague Adrian Dale. And that was because we ran so well between the wickets. Despite my reservations about the value of right-hand/left-hand alliances, it probably also helped that we were very different players. Dale was very good off his legs, and my game eventually became based on using width outside off stump.

When my game was at its worst technically, I used running between the wickets as my way of saving my game, scoring runs in one-day cricket simply by being prepared to take singles and twos that few others were willing to risk.

Dale and I had played so much cricket together, from Glamorgan Colts upwards, that we did not need to call. There was just a look and off we would go. It helped that there were some other excellent runners in the Glamorgan side at that time – like David Hemp, Tony Cottey and Matthew Maynard.

Hugh Morris was a little reluctant at first but even he bought into it eventually, so that when I made my Test debut against South Africa in 1998 he sent me a message saying: 'Many congratulations – thoroughly deserved. I'll be running every one with you! I only hope Athers can run as fast as your old opening partner!'

As for Atherton, he had other ideas. He said to me, partly in jest it does have to be said, the night before the match: 'Remember this is not county cricket; don't try any quick singles to [Jonty] Rhodes.'

We had run together decently at Cambridge, I think, but there had been one incident when I had nearly run him out and he had become unusually flustered. We made up, of course, and are still good friends today as journalistic colleagues.

But running between the wickets can cause jitters for a batsman. It is easy to lose one's nerve. Even Dale and myself had our wobbly moments. You have to take risks and sometimes you misjudge and a run-out ensues. If it is your fault, then the guilt can weigh heavy (although we have already seen that some of the more selfish players have appeared to deal with that rather more easily than others), and one's nerve can be tested in the next few innings.

And in today's power-obsessed game, running between the wickets can often be neglected. I thought the Test match partnership of 124 between the two young Yorkshiremen Joe Root and Jonny Bairstow, against New Zealand at Headingley in 2013, was quite magnificent for its running. It renewed my faith that the modern game is not all about that muscle and power.

What I have never fully understood is when people talk of deliberately rotating the strike, either in one-day or longer-form cricket. It is evinced in Bobby Simpson's views on his partnership with Bill Lawry. 'As a definite plan and policy we would rotate the singles,' he said. 'We would share the strike as near to 50-50 as we could; to keep giving the bowler a different target, give him as few chances as possible even to bowl a full over at you so he could never work out his game plan with any consistency, never get a prolonged shot at you. The singles and threes are the vital scoring shots in cricket, not the twos and fours.'

That was never something I considered, although there was one instance when I took up my partner's offer of a quick single to change ends. It was in a second-team match for Glamorgan against Leicestershire at Grace Road in 1987. I was young and still coming through in the game, while my partner, John Hopkins, was at the other end of his career.

Hopkins was a solid opening batsman, whose figures at the end of his career were not necessarily that flattering, but one thing one could never doubt about his batting was its courage. I had first seen this when watching him face Greg Thomas in the indoor nets at Neath, where the surface was always lively.

Thomas, who went on to play for England, was seriously quick, if also erratic, and Hopkins would goad him to bowl faster and faster at him, with Thomas pulling the net at the back of the hall away so that he could run in further from the changing rooms behind. Hopkins never flinched.

Anyway, playing against us in the game at Leicester was the West Indian fast bowler Winston Benjamin. Those were the days when counties employed two overseas professionals and one would play in the second team. I also faced the likes of Allan Donald and Tony Merrick at Warwickshire, and it was invaluable learning for me on my route to first-team cricket. It was scary, but such wonderful experience.

Consider also that Les Taylor, the former England seamer, was opening the bowling with Benjamin that day and you can see the world of difference from today's county second-team cricket, which, from what I gather, is full of schoolboys and triallists.

The only problem with the second-team matches was the standard of umpiring sometimes. And so here at Leicester, Benjamin got mightily miffed because the umpires would not change a ball that he considered had gone out of shape. His response? To bowl bouncer after bouncer. And I mean bouncer after bouncer. I happened to be at his end for two overs, and faced 12 bouncers, with the umpire doing absolutely nothing about it.

It was then that Hopkins came to me and said: 'Try to get something on one, and I'll run through for the single.' It was not an offer I was going to refuse. So I got as far back on my stumps as I could, and got as high as I could to the next ball, gloving it down on the leg side as Hopkins came rushing through for a single.

Benjamin went rushing down with him, picked up the ball and hurled it at the stumps at the non-striker's end to which I was running. Unfortunately for him, nobody was backing up and the ball went for four overthrows as well! I'd got five runs and I was off strike. What a result. I have never seen a fast bowler more angry, though. Poor old 'Ponty', as he was known, really copped it in the next few balls.

Surely batting is never about rotation. You just take the runs that are available. For instance, take the example of a quick bowler bowling and the wicketkeeper standing a fair distance back, with no short leg in place.

If the batsman defends a ball with soft hands and it drops down beside him, that is a single. For me that was always a no-brainer, in whatever form of cricket. But it is the non-striker's single. He is the one who will call that run, and can only make it if he is backing up and alert to the opportunity.

I still find myself watching a game these days and I will shout: 'Run!' when I see such a chance wasted. Batsmen who do not back up cannot consider themselves batsmen in my view, and I see so many top players not doing so.

It is simple. If the bowler is right-armed and bowling over the wicket, you stand with the bat in your left hand. You begin inside the crease, obviously, but as the bowler approaches you move forwards so that by the time he releases the ball your feet are outside the crease but the bat is still touching inside the crease line.

Once the ball is delivered, you set off a couple of paces down the pitch in anticipation of a run. If the ball is drilled back towards the bowler, you simply move back, stretching your left arm, complete with bat, towards the crease. Those complaining that they will be run out if they back up too enthusiastically are talking nonsense. It never happened to me once in a professional match.

It is no disgrace to run your way to a century. Indeed Graham Thorpe did just that for England against Pakistan at Lahore in 2000. He hit just one boundary in his century (though he hit one more before being dismissed on 118), the fewest ever in a Test century, and ran 51 singles, as well as seven threes and 12 twos.

Three batsmen have got to a first-class century without hitting a four. Alan Hill, mostly of Derbyshire and a renowned blocker, did so for Orange Free State against Griqualand West in 1976/77, as did Paul Hibbert for Victoria against the touring Indians in 1977/78. And on Australia's tour of England in 1926 Bill Woodfull scored a century against Surrey without hitting a boundary. He did hit one afterwards before being out for 118.

Centuries come in many different ways.

8

Conversion

My first-class batting average was 40.63. Without wishing to drown in any more braggadocio, and I will admit that maybe I have been getting a little wet in it for purposes of illustration in this tome, I'm pretty happy with that. It's better than W. G. Grace's 39.45 anyway. Yes, yes, I know you cannot compare, but that does not mean I cannot mention it.

But it could have been so much better. My average should really have been 45.96. That is not to say that there has been some horrible miscalculations over the years – and Dr Andrew Hignell, Glamorgan's esteemed statistician and scorer, might be fretting a little at the moment – but rather that some detailed analysis of my statistics has proved that.

Who has come to that conclusion? 'Numbers', that's who. That is Nathan Leamon, England's team analyst. Leamon is the former Cambridge University mathematics graduate, Eton school master and qualified cricket coach, whom the then England team director Andy Flower appointed to his backroom team.

Flower himself had been appointed assistant coach by Peter

Moores in 2007, and had been heavily influenced by the *Moneyball* book – Michael Lewis' compelling account of how the Oakland A's baseball team achieved remarkable statistics-driven success under manager Billy Beane – that Moores had once given him to read.

When Moores was sacked in 2009, after a nasty episode in which captain Kevin Pietersen was relieved of his position too, Flower took over, and Leamon became an integral part of England's successes, as they won three Ashes series and rose to No. 1 in the Test rankings.

Central to Leamon's involvement was the use of the Monte Carlo simulation, a computer program invented by Stanislaw Ulam, a mathematician who was part of the Manhattan Project at Los Alamos during the Second World War.

It forecasts the probability of various outcomes. So, for example, when England played Australia at Melbourne in the 2010/11 Ashes series, Leamon played that game many times in advance using the simulator, concluding that England were 15–20 per cent more likely to win if they bowled first.

It is always a big decision to insert the opposition in a Test match, especially one so important as this one, with the series score standing at 1-1 after England had lost the previous Test in Perth. But England took Leamon and 'Monte's' advice, inserted Australia, and the home side were rolled out for just 98. With England finishing the first day on 157-0, the game was as good as over. England had retained the Ashes.

But, of course, on their next trip Down Under in 2013/14, England did not fare quite as well. Indeed they were hammered 5-0. Flower departed as team director, to be replaced, in a strange piece of irony, by Moores. Perhaps not surprisingly, the take on Leamon's statistics was suddenly rather different. Now it was partly to blame for England's demise.

It was nonsense. Yes, earlier I criticized the use of too much video analysis, but that is not to say that it should not be used.

And this is not to say that statistics should not be used. Of course they should. Why would you not want the sort of knowledge England possessed before that Test in Melbourne?

Cricket is a statistical game, and its use of statistics has always been pretty archaic. The arrival of Leamon and his like should be greeted warmly, not treated with scorn.

So I had no compunction in seeking Leamon's advice on centuries for this book. Of course, he was not going to give away a slew of trade secrets, but he was good enough to give me the mathematical formula he uses to determine the probability of a batsman scoring a century, even if he was a little reluctant at first, saying it might be a bit 'too geeky'.

It is not too geeky. It is fascinating. 'Individual scores are approximately geometrically distributed,' he says. 'So the probability of a batsman scoring a hundred is $(1-1/a)^{100}$, where a is his career batting average.'

So, take the greatest of all, Donald Bradman. His Test batting average, as we all know, was 99.94. So, using Leamon's formula, his predicted percentage of centuries in terms of innings played is 36.6 per cent. And in fact he scored 29 centuries in 80 Test innings, which is a percentage of 36.3. That is pretty good work by Leamon, I reckon.

Just to make sure, let us look at some other examples. Graham Gooch had a Test batting average of 42.58, with a predicted percentage of hundreds of 9.3. He actually made 20 Test centuries in 215 innings, and so his percentage was, you guessed it, spot on with 9.3!

In first-class cricket I am an exception, apparently. I averaged 40.63 as previously mentioned, so my predicted percentage is 8.3. But I made 47 centuries in 424 innings, so scoring centuries in 11.1 per cent of my innings. Thus my average should have been 45.96.

The reason for this? I was a decent converter. Spending long hours as a youngster place-kicking at the posts at Lydney

Rugby Club, I had dreamed of being a converter of a very different kind.

But, once past 50, I was pretty good at going on to make a century. I made 58 first-class fifties and 47 centuries. That is a conversion rate of 44.76 per cent.

Subconsciously I was following my father's advice about making centuries to get noticed. Consciously I did not realize that I was quite as good at doing it until Matthew Maynard mentioned it one day.

I really must stop bragging but I cannot help but state that that figure of 44.76 is actually the 25th-highest figure of all time. That is in first-class cricket and for batsmen who have made more than 50 fifties. Bloody hell. 25th! The hairy, skinny-forearmed, third-man expert from Lydney!

I can't believe that, if I'm honest. I'm nestled just below Steve Waugh, and above such greats as Jack Hobbs, Leonard Hutton, Brian Lara and Sunil Gavaskar. I could go on. I am even above Mark Ramprakash, who may have made 114 centuries but his conversion rate was 'only' 43.67 per cent. In Test cricket it was a miserable 14.28 per cent, of course, as he only made two centuries and 12 fifties.

Donald Bradman is top, of course, at 62.90 per cent, with his 117 centuries and 69 fifties. Wally Hammond is the first Englishman on the list at 12th with 47.44. Graeme Hick is at 18th with 46.25 (and he is a Zimbabwean really, of course), and the next Englishman? Well, I did have to justify myself in writing a book about centuries.

By the way, the worst of those ever to have scored 50 fifties? Step forward Geoff Miller, the former England all-rounder and national selector until the winter of 2013/14. He made a whopping 72 first-class fifties, yet scored only two centuries. That is a conversion rate of just 2.70 per cent.

In Test cricket Bradman again naturally rules with the top percentage of 69.04, and the highest Englishman is Peter Parfitt, the Middlesex left-hander who made seven centuries and six fifties in his 37 Tests to give him 53.84 per cent, but four of his centuries were against a weak Pakistan side in 1962. Dennis Amiss, Chris Broad and Michael Vaughan all have an impressive 50 per cent record.

But it is in Test cricket that we probably remember the worst converters. First to spring to my mind is Stephen Fleming, the tall, dark-haired, handsome New Zealander, a shrewd captain and elegant left-handed batsman. They called him Mr Tickle during his stint in county cricket at Nottinghamshire, on account of his extraordinarily long arms, just like the character from the Mr Men series. But he could not extend them around too many Test centuries, making just nine and 45 fifties. That is a conversion rate of 16.36 per cent.

At one stage of his career it stood at two centuries and 31 fifties, and was the worst in world cricket. It was a reputation he never shed, even though three of those centuries were double centuries (plus a score of 192), including a remarkable 274 not out against Sri Lanka in Colombo. He was always the great non-converter.

It is a bit like England's Ian Bell and his reputation for 'soft' centuries. It was an oft-repeated statistic that Bell's first eight Test centuries had all come after a colleague in the side had already scored a century in that innings. In other words he was seen as the great 'piggy-backer' of the time, a player who preferred the back seat to the front. At the time of writing, he has scored 21 Test centuries at an average of over 45. Soft players do not possess that sort of record. Bell is beautiful to watch, and therefore can be frustrating if he does not produce. That, rather than softness, surely explains much.

So Fleming was certainly not as bad as Ramprakash, or indeed Chris Tavaré, who stands alongside with the same percentage of 14.28. Or indeed, as I write, Australia's Shane Watson, whose percentage is 14.29. Look further down the list and you find Sri

Lanka's Arjuna Ranatunga at 9.52 per cent and Pakistan's Ramiz Raja at 8.33 per cent.

What is the secret then? How do you become such a good converter? The answer, sadly, is that there is no secret.

One day in 2005, the year after I had retired from first-class cricket, I was covering a county championship match between Gloucestershire and Surrey at Bristol for the *Guardian*. It was a gloriously sunny day so I decided to leave the press box for a while and sit in one of the chairs just outside the pavilion.

I was in that awkward period where a player is just becoming a journalist, and sometimes it was difficult to know how to approach a player, and, presumably, vice-versa. Anyway, Surrey were fielding and Alistair Brown had just wandered down to third man in front of me, and said hello before quipping: 'I'm in your favourite position here', when I received a tap on the shoulder.

It was Alex Gidman, the young Gloucestershire batsman. I did not know him well, but had played against him at the end of my career, giving him his maiden first-class wicket at Cheltenham in 2002 when pulling his medium pace to mid-on.

Gidman had just been out for 93. And the previous season he had made nine fifties without converting one to a century. He clearly had a bit of a problem. 'How do I score hundreds?' he asked.

I was taken aback, firstly because Gidman was even seeking my advice. And secondly because I had no ready-made answer.

So we talked. One thing I did mention was that I often applied reverse psychology to my batting. For instance, the common wisdom is that the placing of fielders in certain positions usually dictates that a batsman should desist from playing a particular stroke.

Therefore, say I was facing a left-arm spinner, and the opposing captain placed two men on 'the drive' on the off side, that would not stop me driving through the off side. My mindset would be:

'Let's hit it between them. I am not letting them prevent me from using one of my strengths.'

So too with the scoring of centuries. The common wisdom is that, having passed 50, you should knuckle down and work harder, maybe even tighten up. I would do the opposite. I would actually relax a little and try to play down the importance of making a century. I knew in the back of my mind that it was important, but I always felt that there was little point in putting undue pressure on myself.

I suppose it was like the start of an innings. There you are supposed to be cautious and watchful. But, amid my nervousness, I would often begin with a flurry of boundaries, and then settle down a little.

As Steve Waugh says: 'Often you'll see a batsman start recklessly, but once his safety barometer has been reached, normally somewhere between 10 and 20, he will settle down and consolidate for the long task at hand. My "trigger" was always 15, because by that point I'd usually faced at least 30 balls and felt very settled at the crease. I would have adjusted my shot selection according to the pace and bounce of the pitch, probably faced most of the opposition's attack, and been familiar with what they were trying to achieve. At the end of my career I saw a statistic that where I got to 20 I averaged around 90.'

Twenty was a key figure for me too. If I got to 20, I knew that I had not had a horrendous day. That might sound terribly unambitious, but it probably demonstrates how difficult the mental travails are at the start of an innings.

The same figure resonates with Graham Gooch. 'Twenty was the first target for me,' he says. 'I always kept an eye on the scoreboard, only inasmuch as, if my runs did not go up on the scoreboard, I would know that because I knew what my score was.'

For Brian Lara there was a different target. 'All I ever try to do at the start of an innings is play 60 balls,' he once said. 'If

I get through those 60 balls, doesn't matter how, I feel like I'm okay.'

Patience is often seen as a key word in batting, and especially in batting for long periods. It was a word often associated with my batting. But it used to make me laugh, if I'm honest. You only have to ask my family about my patience. I am one of the most impatient people on this earth. Traffic jams? Oh my word.

It is instructive here to recall a conversation between two top Australian batsmen. It was before the third Ashes Test in 2006/07, when Michael Clarke said to Justin Langer: 'I've finally got it. My problem is that I can't conquer haste. I want everything to happen right now and in the process I forget what is important today and the steps I have to take before I get where I want to be. JL, it's like when I go out to bat I want to be a hundred before I even get off the mark. I am not patient enough when I know I should be.'

That was before play on the first day. Clarke scored his fourth Test century that day. He went back to the changing rooms, winked at Langer and said: 'It's amazing what happens when you conquer haste isn't it, old fella?'

Langer entitled a chapter in his motivational book, *Seeing the Sunrise*, after that 'Conquering Haste'. Mind you, Clarke has a range of shots that means he has to conquer haste. I did not have that problem.

I suppose it boils down to what Mark Ramprakash says: 'I don't want to play the shot of the day, I want to play the innings of the day.'

Anyway, back to Gidman. Away he went after our chat, and soon Gloucestershire were following on. He made 142 in the second innings, only his second first-class hundred, after making his first three years previously. I have no idea if I had had any effect, but he went on to score two more centuries that season. As I was putting the finishing touches to this book in September

2014, he made his 23rd and highest first-class century, with 264 against Leicestershire.

OK, so now we have done the chest-puffing bit about conversion rates. But what about the counter-argument? I was actually a horribly inconsistent batsman, with long periods of low scoring, interspersed with exceptionally high scores. Might it not have been better for me to have scored more fifties and fewer hundreds?

I remember during my last full season as a professional receiving a letter from an irate Glamorgan supporter stating that I should be dropped from the side. We had just been hammered by Northamptonshire at Northampton in a game in which I had scored just 20 and 12. My correspondent's gripe was that I never scored runs when the team needed them most.

At the time I had over 1,000 runs in the season and was averaging over 50. I replied saying as much, and did so with some venom too.

But deep down I was thinking: 'Maybe he is right.' That season I made four centuries (including 249 and 184) and just three fifties. I made 1,111 runs at 52.90. On the surface it looks like a good season, but might it have been more useful to the team if I had made, say, nine fifties and just one century? I might have been labelled a poor converter, but I might actually have been aiding my team a little more.

I have a very relevant comparison. Two years later, in my first season as a full-time journalist, Warwickshire won the county championship. I watched them quite often.

It was something of a strangely unpopular victory, as they only achieved five wins. But they were unbeaten and their success was forged upon racking up huge first-innings totals.

Jonathan Trott was then an emerging batsman with the county. That season he made 1,120 runs at an average of 53.61. But he made 10 fifties and just one century. I remember writing at the time that he was a poor converter.

One day, off the record, a member of the Warwickshire management questioned that statement. The suggestion seemed to be that they were pretty happy with Trott's contribution. Trott had been consistent. They knew what they were getting.

I was not consistent. For instance, backing up a century with another: I could not do that. I only achieved twin centuries in a match once in my first-class career. That was in 1997, during Glamorgan's county championship-winning year, when I made two centuries in the match at that wonderfully picturesque (and nice and small for a batsman!) ground at Abergavenny. It concluded a spell where I had scored four centuries in five first-class innings (with the 'failure' being 69). That was the most golden and, as previously mentioned, probably lucky spell of my career.

Six centuries in consecutive first-class innings is the record held jointly by, unsurprisingly, Donald Bradman, C. B. Fry and Mike Procter. Everton Weekes holds the record in Test matches for his five successive centuries in 1948.

Mostly I could not keep churning out the big scores. The mental effort was often too much. Thus I have great admiration for the likes of Mark Ramprakash, who achieved twin centuries on seven occasions, the same figure as Wally Hammond. Only Ricky Ponting and Zaheer Abbas, with eight each, have done it on more occasions.

Ramprakash's Surrey coach, the Australian Steve Rixon, once said that Ramprakash's greatest strength was that he was 'suspicious' – of bowlers, of pitches, of what might get him out. 'Even if I have scored a hundred the day before, I will never just go out there and try to hit the ball on the up from the off,' says Ramprakash. 'I need to go through the process.'

It was not that I went out trying to smash bowlers everywhere. I rarely did that anyway. It was just the mental upheaval required again.

So, often I would follow glorious success with ignominious

failure. Take my 235 at Worksop against Nottinghamshire in 1996, followed by 0 in the second innings.

What about a match against Warwickshire at Edgbaston in 2000? At the end of the third day I was 165 not out. The following morning I added just one more run, and we had to follow on. I immediately got a duck. A friend of mine had travelled up for the day's play. 'To me you have only got one and nought in this match,' he joked.

Usually when beginning a day's play with a century to my name, I was good at going on – we will come to that later – but this was a different scenario in that there was that possibility of having to bat again, to start all over again with nought to my name. That definitely affected my thinking.

So I did something in the changing rooms that day of which I am not proud. Having been dismissed in the first innings I threw my bat, helmet and gloves down into my cricket case and stomped out to the shower area at the back of the old Edgbaston changing rooms and screamed at the top of my voice: 'F****** c***!!'

Yes, it is disgraceful language to be using, and for that I apologize, but the thing was that the second word was used in the singular, which gave the impression that I was berating myself, when in fact I was angry with my team-mates for not helping me avoid the follow-on, and so I really wanted that word to be in the plural.

As I say, it is not a moment of which I am proud. But I just knew that my sometimes strange psychological make-up would find it mightily difficult to go again. I was destined for failure in that second innings. It was little surprise that I made a duck.

I suppose David Gower sums this up neatly. 'For me, one of the hardest things was getting into the right frame of mind to perform well day in, day out,' he says. 'Playing one good innings was both very difficult and very satisfying. But to repeat it was another challenge altogether, especially because if any little self-doubt surfaced it was not difficult to use it as some sort of excuse for saying: "Er, well, I got a hundred yesterday. Do I really have to do it again?"'

Unsurprisingly, Graham Gooch has a rather different take. 'If you are playing well, the one thing you want to do is keep playing well, so you keep the wheels oiled, keep the engine ticking over,' he says. 'I don't think going in again is a problem after a big score. I looked forward to it. It's important to get into that frame of mind.'

Gooch then raises an interesting point. Sometimes in order to reach that frame of mind that he mentions there, he had to rouse himself, even if that meant involving himself in a war of words with a member of the opposition. Yes, we are talking 'sledging' here.

'I was always a better player if I had a contest going on,' he says. 'A little bit of niggle, I quite liked that. I liked someone "sledging" me. "Sledging" is about them [the opposition] trying to get you to play the man not the ball. I would take it as a compliment. They are worried. That would sharpen my senses.

'Some days you are not right. To get me into that a bit of needle with the bowler would be spot on. I didn't get a lot of "sledging" from the Australians at the end. It was like: "Good morning, Mr Gooch."

'I once initiated some "sledging" with Kevin Shine in a match [for Essex against Middlesex in 1994]. I wasn't feeling great, but it was nothing to do with him. I got 100 [140 actually] at Uxbridge. I tried to sledge him. It's a risky strategy.'

It was one also employed by Mike Atherton against Pakistan at Lord's in 1996 when he did something similar to substitute Moin Khan in order to rouse himself.

It was not something I could ever have done. I will freely admit that I did not like 'sledging'. I don't think anybody does, if they are being totally truthful. Being abused is no fun.

Did it distract me? For that is its primary intention. Occasionally it might have done. Often it roused me too. Sometimes I might chirp back at a bowler. The problem with that is that more often than not the bowler will have the last word. At some point you will have to depart the scene, and, as you do so, it is so easy for the bowler to send you on your way.

There is nothing more irritating than that happening, actually. It is not particularly brave, in my view. It happened to me once, as I have already said, at Swansea against Yorkshire when the bowler Ryan Sidebottom did just that.

I actually think that 'sledging' is a hugely overrated concept in the game. For one it is often associated with toughness, but most of the 'sledgers' I encountered were among the most cowardly players on the field. There seems to be a perception that the professional game is laden with stand-up comedians who spout side-splitting gags out in the middle at every opportunity. Nothing could be further from the truth.

Often at question-and-answer sessions I am asked about the best 'sledges' I have heard or received in the game. And it is a tricky one to answer, because most 'sledging' is just abuse, and the better stories are often apocryphal.

'Sledging' is just an extension of the background noise that accompanies every cricket match these days. I do not really get that either. Noise equals energy apparently. But that is forgetting that some people operate better in silence. I was always being encouraged to be noisier in the field, but I never understood how constantly shouting such inanities as 'Come on, boys, let's get number five!' was going to help anyone.

But, sadly, that is the way now. And the saddest part of all this is that club cricketers probably 'sledge' more than any others. They think it is the way to play cricket. It is not. But with poor officiating, it can easily get out of control.

Aggressive cricket does not have to be noisy cricket. The late, great Malcolm Marshall barely used to say a word to the batsman, but, having faced him on many occasions, it did not take anything from the battle or indeed his ferocity. You knew that you were in a battle, all right.

After retirement I toyed with the idea of playing a little club cricket. Lisvane Cricket Club is near my home so I turned out for them occasionally on Wednesday evenings in a 20-over midweek league. It was going fine – I batted low down and did not try to be a big influence on matches – until we played against Cardiff one evening. They had some young lads with a bit of attitude. They fancied knocking the old pro off his perch.

As soon as I arrived at the crease one of them, whose name I know but will not repeat here because he does not deserve any recognition, shouted out loud that I had never been a particularly good starter of an innings.

It was nothing, really. It was not abusive, but this was coming from some third-team-standard club cricketer in a piffling nondescript match. I was angry, and got angrier when he aimed a throw at my end, glaring at me as I took a single. I got even angrier still when I was out soon afterwards. To a pretty decent yorker, as it happened.

I aimed a few well-chosen words at the chirper, and his father, later, and only played a couple more matches. Was I wanting too much in expecting a little respect? Probably. But it is a sad indictment of where the game has gone.

My advice for an aspiring young batsman on how to deal with sledging? Try to ignore it. The bowler and fielders want a reaction. Do not even make eye contact with them. That annoys them even more when they feel their efforts are being totally disregarded.

And my advice to the fielders and bowlers? Don't do it. Don't 'sledge'. It is not big and it is not clever.

9

The Less Important Centuries

Quite often at the end of one-day matches for Glamorgan I would get out deliberately. Yes, I would get out deliberately. There, I've said it. And I had never even heard of spot-fixing, and I had certainly not made the acquaintance of any Indian bookmakers.

The reason? I wasn't very good at one-day cricket in general. I was even less good at slogging at the end of a one-day game.

I would hoick hopefully across the line. It was even uglier than my usual array of strokes. 'That's not what they taught you at Cambridge,' exclaimed one exasperated bowler as the ball once farted its way towards mid-wicket.

So I would often feel that it was better that I was not around at the end of an innings; set the platform and then leave.

Centuries did not matter. They really did not, despite everything I have said so far. I only made seven List A (remember that means all limited-overs cricket bar Twenty20) centuries in my career, and in 1995 I actually set a Glamorgan record of 1,263 one-day runs in a season without scoring a century.

Fourteen fifties, but not one hundred. It is in stark contrast to my first-class conversion rate.

One-day centuries are nowhere near as important as first-class centuries. That is fact. Obviously for club players there is no choice. Their centuries have to be one-day efforts, but for the professional there are different grades, heightened further by the advent of Twenty20 cricket.

'Four-day hundreds are what you are measured on,' says Matthew Maynard. And to illustrate the point I give you the story of a friend of mine. His name is Ian Thomas. He was a powerful left-hander who played 32 first-class matches for Glamorgan between 1998 and 2005. He made his county championship debut in 2000 and scored 82 that day. He never made a higher first-class score.

But what he did do was score a Twenty20 century against Somerset at Taunton in 2004. It was only the fourth Twenty20 century scored, and was Glamorgan's first. Indeed, as I began writing this book it was Glamorgan's only Twenty20 hundred. In 2014, however, Jim Allenby scored 105 against Middlesex at Richmond to become the club's second Twenty20 centurion.

That Thomas feels a strange mixture of pride and embarrassment about it tells a significant story.

'It's great to have got a Twenty20 hundred but I almost feel guilty about it,' he says. 'I find it embarrassing, purely because of how I view hundreds. I think the first benchmark for any batsman who wants to have a status in the game is a first-class hundred. You haven't arrived until you have got a first-class hundred.

'I'm lucky enough to still work in the game [as a national personal development manager with the Professional Cricketers' Association] and I think players of today have still got a traditional view of hundreds. I know there is an emphasis on strike rates and effectiveness in one-day cricket, but, if they are honest, they will say their first goal is that first-class hundred.'

Being a Twenty20 specialist might have its financial benefits, but in cricketing terms it can still carry a stigma. The Nottinghamshire opener Alex Hales is an example. He became England's first T20 centurion at the ICC World Twenty20 in Bangladesh in 2014 (he had previously made 99 against West Indies in 2012 and 94 against Australia in 2013), but was struggling so much with first-class cricket in early 2014 after a poor 2013 season (averaging just 13.94 in 10 matches) that he was loaned out to Worcestershire by Nottinghamshire.

'I think it is a little bit harsh if people are already pigeon-holing me as a T20 specialist,' he said at the time. 'OK, I had a shocker last year with the red ball but up until then I averaged 40 opening at Trent Bridge which isn't a bad record at all. I'm keen to learn from last year and put it behind me and move on. I feel it's too early to be pigeon-holed and I'm working hard on the other aspects of my game.'

And, in fairness, he did eventually sort out his first-class game in 2014, returning to Nottinghamshire, averaging over 50 and scoring three centuries.

Consider, too, Kieron Pollard, the big-hitting West Indian, who has never played a Test match. 'I'm not a specialist,' he says. 'Everybody says I'm big and strong and suited to Twenty20, but when you look at cricket, the game is changing so much. A few years ago they said David Warner was a T20 specialist but look what he has achieved in Test cricket. Think back to why I was called up in the first place to the West Indies side too. It was because I made centuries in four-day cricket.'

Indeed Warner was the first player to be selected for Australia before he had played a first-class match, when he made a stunning debut at the Melbourne Cricket Ground in 2009, hitting 89 off 43 balls against South Africa in a T20 international. At one stage he had played more T20 matches than Sheffield Shield games.

But he knew what he wanted, and at the time of writing he has got it, having played 36 Tests and made 12 centuries. 'I want to play Test cricket,' he said. 'That's always been my dream as a kid and that's what I want to do. I can't be one of those who's just going to play Twenty20 cricket.'

No one wants that tag. But you need to score first-class centuries to get rid of it. Thomas could not, and his desire to do so became almost overwhelming. In the second team he rattled up centuries for fun, even making 267 against Somerset second eleven (he also once made 255 not out in a club match), but the milestone at the higher level in the longer form of the game would never come. It became a millstone.

How much time did he spend thinking about scoring a first-class hundred? 'I was thinking about it all the time, obsessively,' he admits. 'I had something stuck in my head from second-team cricket. Graham Reynolds [a coach at Newport CC and Glamorgan scout who is sadly no longer with us] said to me: "Once you get your first hundred, the rest will come." It took me a while to get one in the second team. I got 96 on debut against Essex but then it took me three years to get a hundred, but then they came. So I always thought that if I could get a first-class hundred then the rest would come.

'It was a big problem. I had a mindset that built nerves and anxiety. I used to try all sorts. "Don't think about it" – that was stupid because what are you thinking about?

'I could never take the relaxed mindset of the second team into the first team. It was 80 per cent mental, even though I admit that my technique could be loose. I got told so many things. I look back and realize that I listened to too many people.'

Thomas tells the story perfectly of how difficult it is to score a first-class century. Just one. In one-day cricket he was given a role at the top of the order to make use of the power-play overs.

'I felt no pressure compared to first-class cricket,' he says. 'I was given freedom to play the game that suited me.'

Twenty20 centuries are still rare. Remember that that form of the game was only introduced at professional level in 2003, when

English county cricket took a leap into the unknown. That year there was only one century, from Gloucestershire's Ian Harvey, made off just 50 balls and an even more remarkable effort considering that his side were chasing only 135 to win against Warwickshire.

Indeed only eight players have scored more than two Twenty20 centuries. Unsurprisingly, Chris Gayle stands top of that list by some distance with, as I write, 13 to his name. Next are David Warner and Brendon McCullum with five. Luke Wright has four, and then there are eight players – Harvey, Adam Gilchrist, Richard Levi, Hamilton Masakadza, Ahmed Shehzad, Dwayne Smith, Suresh Raina and Rassie van der Dussen – with three each.

Not that there is any lack of opportunity these days. You have only got to look at the teams listed in brackets next to Gayle's name on that Twenty20 centurions list – Bangalore T20, Barisal Burners, Dhaka Gladiators, Jamaica, Jamaica Tallawahs, Kolkata Knight Riders, Matabeleland Tuskers, PCA Masters XI, Royal Challengers Bangalore, Stanford Superstars, Sydney Thunder, West Indians, West Indies, Western Australia – to realize that there are rather a lot of Twenty20 tournaments being staged these days, and many players, like Gayle, are willing to freelance around the world.

I never played Twenty20, not professionally anyway. For it was easily forgotten that when it was introduced it was not some new form of the game. Players have been playing 20-over evening cricket for years.

I did have my county Twenty20 kit in 2003, but, having played one first-class match that season, I never played again because of my dodgy knee.

I was captain of Glamorgan that season and we had no specific plans at the start of that season for Twenty20. I am not sure anyone had. At least one county suggested that it might play an under-strength side in the competition, such was the initial ambivalence towards the concept.

Would I have been any good at it? It is a question often asked of those who never played it. The answer is probably not. A Twenty20 century would have been way beyond my capabilities, I think.

I would not have minded batting with today's bats, though. They are huge. They are so big in size and yet do not weigh any more than those used by my generation and those before, and they pick up just as lightly.

They make my old bats look like toothpicks. Those players who were once colleagues but are still playing today, like the Glamorgan wicketkeeper and captain Mark Wallace, mock me incessantly whenever they see one of my old bats.

Long after I had retired from playing I gave one of them to Peter Mitchell, my former sports editor at the *Sunday Telegraph*, and a man to whom I owe so much for my journalistic career. He passed it on to his son, Alex, who arrived at the wicket in one school match to be greeted by the 'sledge': 'Is that your grandfather's bat?' Ouch.

But many much better players than me have struggled to come to terms with the Twenty20 game. Ricky Ponting played 48 Twenty20 matches and did not score a century. At the time of writing Kevin Pietersen has played over 100 matches with only one hundred.

Murray Goodwin, though, scored two Twenty20 centuries. 'I found them the hardest for me,' he admits. 'I only got them because I batted up the order [both for Sussex; one against Essex in 2007 opening, and one against Surrey in 2011 batting at No. 4, but he was at the crease in the second over]. That is the best place to bat in T20. I had a huge responsibility. I'm not a big hitter of the ball and I find it a huge challenge. I've had to use my belief in T20 in a very different way from the modern cricketer. Guys like [Kieron] Pollard just tee it up and hit it anywhere. I can't do that. I've tried and I get caught.'

By the end of my one-day career I was batting in the middle

order anyway, a move begun by Duncan Fletcher when he came to Glamorgan.

One-day cricket was already beginning to change significantly by then, when he first arrived in 1997. The Sri Lankans, who won the 1996 World Cup, had ensured that, with their pinch-hitting tactics at the top of the order and with Sanath Jayasuriya and Romesh Kaluwitharana promoted from the middle order to take advantage of the fielding restrictions in the first 15 overs. It had actually been tried during the 1992 World Cup, with Ian Botham performing the role for England, as well as Mark Greatbatch for New Zealand.

Indeed it is easy to forget how much one-day cricket has changed over the years. It was played in white clothing once, you know, with red balls. There were even breaks in innings for lunch and tea. Today's generation, reared on coloured clothing and white balls, might not even know that!

The first Gillette Cup match was played on 1 May 1963, at Old Trafford, when Lancashire faced Leicestershire in a play-off match to trim the then 17 counties to 16 so that it could continue in knockout fashion, and in some quarters that is touted as the birth of one-day cricket.

There was, though, a competition the year before: in 1962, when a Midlands knockout tournament was played between Leicestershire, Nottinghamshire, Derbyshire and Northamptonshire.

The game was 65 overs per side. Sixty-five! That was one heck of a long day for everyone involved. I never played a one-day match over 65 overs, but I did play in the days when the premier one-day competition lasted 60 overs per team, and that was long enough – especially when you had batted first against a minor county and watched them block aimlessly in pursuit of some unattainable target.

I must admit that I did not play much 60-overs cricket, though. Otherwise my statement about centuries not mattering in one-day cricket would look rather silly. There is ample time in 60 overs to score a century and much, much more.

You could never have matches lasting 60 overs per innings, let alone 65, these days. Were sides compelled to bowl that many overs in a day they would need to begin at dawn to finish before dusk.

I looked up the scorecard from that first match in 1963 – won by Lancashire by 101 runs – and expected to find some embarrassingly low scores considering the number of overs bowled, but was pleasantly surprised to find that the home side made 304 for nine, with the late Peter Marner contributing 121.

But that sort of score was not the norm then. One-day cricket was very different. In fact it was played just like a first-class match, with slips, gullies and men saving ones. Boundary fielders? They only came later apparently, in numbers anyway, with M. J. K. Smith of Warwickshire being one of the first captains to use them.

We have had one-day innings lasting every multiple of five from 65 overs down to 40 since then, without including Twenty20, of course.

And we have had all sorts of one-day experiments, mostly begun in the international game, which started with the first officially recognized one-day international, between England and Australia in Melbourne in 1971. Among others, there have been different fielding restrictions (at one time six fielders were permitted on the leg side, which was most desirable for the off-spinners, especially before the reverse sweep became fashionable), differing numbers of bouncers permitted, restricted run-ups, power plays, one ball at each end, and the great calamity – supersubs. They were introduced in 2005, whereby a batsman or bowler could take over a colleague's batting or bowling duties during a match. It was not trialled properly, though, and it became obvious very quickly that the side that won the toss also had an advantage when it came to the supersubs.

One of the biggest changes has been the reduction by one of the number of fielders permitted outside the fielding circle in non-powerplay overs. It is down to four from five but that one fielder missing from the boundary has made a huge difference. Captains are finding it almost impossible to defend in the closing overs. Batsmen with that one extra boundary option are very hard to stop.

Anyway, the point is that by 1997 the one-day game had already changed dramatically. It was very different from when Mike Gatting wrote a book on the limited-overs game in 1986 and declared: 'It is not the biggest hitters who make the most effective batsmen in one-day cricket. Brain is more important than brawn in what often resembles a chess match.'

He was especially praising his Middlesex colleague Clive Radley, and even today there is still much cat-and-mouse work in one-day cricket, with the shifting of fields and the corresponding ball – yorker, slower ball, etc. – to be bowled accordingly. But power is now very much the most important element when it comes to the shorter forms of the game.

Players do more weight training than ever before. I did a lot of that sort of training in my career; it had a hugely positive influence on me, but it came late, as initially I had been reluctant to use it because someone – it might well have been Mike Atherton – told me that weight training might affect my timing! And sadly my most significant advances in strength came in my legs and chest, and not the forearms.

Of course, you can still hit a cricket ball a long way without having huge forearms. The Indians as a race show that. They are usually small men but they have incredibly fast hands and supple wrists. The Somerset wicketkeeper Craig Kieswetter (who hopefully will return to the game after taking time out in 2014/15 with an eye injury) hits the ball as high and as far as anyone in the game at present, but I am reliably informed that he is no powerhouse in the gym. His hand speed is, though, quite remarkable.

These days sides practise 'range-hitting', which is something that first came to public attention in the Indian Premier League but had been used previously by individuals such as Australia's Andrew Symonds.

'We get the guys to work just like golfers on a range,' said captain Paul Collingwood before England's triumph at the ICC World Twenty20 in the Caribbean in 2010. 'They go out to the middle of the stadium and get someone to give throw-downs so they can hit the ball into the stands. The confidence you can get from knowing you can clear the ropes is huge. If a guy can hit a ball 80 metres that is a six on any ground now.'

Kieswetter was in that squad and hit the ball further than anyone else.

Power was required at the top of the order, and I was never going to provide that. As I have mentioned, Fletcher liked my running of the ball down to third man and thought I could run the ball around in the middle overs after the harder hitters had done their business at the top.

So I batted at No. 5 or No. 6. I could orchestrate run chases with relative calm, as long as the run rate did not get too high – in other words, too far above six runs an over.

That was always the tipping point in the old days, as even Graham Gooch attests: 'In one of my very first one-day games – I was still an amateur coming in at No. 8 – we needed 48 off eight overs and I thought: "How're we going to get that?"'

But this was a tactic that worked well for Glamorgan, with the likes of Robert Croft, the aforementioned Thomas and Keith Newell going hard at the top of the order, and then Matthew Maynard, Adrian Dale and myself coming in later.

Glamorgan won some one-day titles around that time – the National League second division in 2001 and its first division in 2002 and then again in 2004 after I had retired, as well as reaching the Benson & Hedges Cup final in 2000.

But often in early season, especially in the Benson & Hedges

Cup, the formula fell down, with a clatter of early wickets on seaming pitches leading to low scores. It summed up the problems of playing one-day cricket in England. In early season it really has to be played to a different set of rules (and I mean rules, because I know that cricket has Laws not rules). It is one reason why England have been so poor at international one-day cricket, and have never won a global one-day trophy.

There have been many other reasons too, such as the domestic game not mirroring the international, although that was at last altered in 2014, when the county one-day competition became 50 overs again. It was not before time. The main argument against it seemed to be that some counties liked the 40-over format because they could serve Sunday lunches to their members beforehand. I kid you not!

But the overriding reason is that one-day cricket has always been regarded as a second-class citizen in this country. I am proof of that with my attitude towards it, and I was, and still am, hardly alone in that sentiment. It even extends to groundsmen, who have often produced sub-standard pitches that have not been given the required attention.

And my attitude reveals another important factor: we are just not very good at making centuries in one-day cricket, whether internationally or domestically.

A look at the list of those to have made most centuries in international one-day cricket is rather depressing. Sachin Tendulkar is unsurprisingly top with 49, but he did play 463 one-day internationals. That is more appearances than any other player, with Sri Lanka's Sanath Jayasuriya next on 445 (Paul Collingwood has made most for England with 197).

You have to scroll down to 25th on the centuries list to find the first Englishman, Marcus Trescothick, with 12. No other England player is in double figures, with Kevin Pietersen next on nine, then Graham Gooch with eight. David Gower made seven and Andrew Strauss six.

Look at the list for all List A cricket around the world and there is some cheer, in that Gooch is second behind Tendulkar's figure of 60 with 44. And in eighth place is Nick Knight, who made a very impressive 30 List A centuries. Close behind are Trescothick with 28, Robin Smith with 27, Wayne Larkins with 26, Chris Adams with 21 and Alistair Brown with 19.

But, as my colleague at the *Sunday Telegraph*, Scyld Berry, said in 2008, when Kevin Pietersen took over as England captain: 'What Pietersen has yet to beat is the system: the system of English domestic one-day cricket which has failed to supply him with three top-order batsmen who can take advantage of the 20 overs of power-play, instead of turning them into push-plays and prod-plays, then go on to three figures. Robert Key has played 170 innings in limited-overs games of more than 20 overs and scored four hundreds; Matt Prior in 160-odd such innings has made four hundreds; Ian Bell, in the same number of innings, three hundreds; and Alastair Cook, in 50-odd innings, two hundreds.'

And sadly Berry was having to bang the same drum in 2014, when England were looking for new inspiration in their one-day batting. 'So who are the young English century-makers?' he asked. 'Just as the Walrus found after eating all the oysters, "answer came there none". The only England-qualified batsmen to have hit 12 or more hundreds in List A cricket (i.e. 40- and 50-over matches) have come, been and gone internationally: Kevin Pietersen, Owais Shah, Vikram Solanki, Jonathan Trott and – far and away the biggest century-maker of them all with 28 to his credit – Marcus Trescothick.'

How important are one-day centuries then? Best to ask Nathan Leamon. 'In terms of one-day cricket, centuries are pretty influential,' he says. 'If one of your top four scores a 100 you have a 75–80 per cent chance of winning the match, depending on where you are playing, and assuming a fairly even contest to begin with.'

But when Andy Flower was in charge of England it was not apparently a stated objective of his one-day team for one of the top three or four batsmen to score a century, as was often assumed. 'To be honest it is not one of our goals,' he said. 'We set slightly different goals, but I can't say what.'

He told me that in 2013. A year earlier, during England's tour of Sri Lanka, I had dinner in Colombo with him, Leamon and Mike Atherton.

We got on to the subject of one-day cricket and Leamon might just have been about to explain England's unique method of analysing players' worth in one-day internationals when Flower piped up with 'Don't tell them that!'

I did, though, ask Leamon where Jonathan Trott scored in that reckoning. 'At the top,' came the instant reply from Leamon.

Trott, batting at No. 3 and given the anchor role, has been a constant source of debate during his one-day international career. Prior to his selection for the England Lions tour in the winter of 2014 he played 68 matches and made 2,819 runs at an average of 51.25, with a strike rate of 77.06 and four centuries.

That average of 51.25 is one of the highest in the history of the one-day international game. Indeed as I write only four players have achieved a higher figure. And, with all due respect, Ryan ten Doeschate is top of the list with 67.00, but that was achieved playing for the Netherlands in mainly Associates cricket. The others are Michael Bevan, Hashim Amla and M. S. Dhoni.

Reading through some clippings of things I have written about Trott I came across this line about one-day cricket: 'When Trott scores runs, England usually win. Enough said.'

Well, that wasn't particularly well researched, to be honest. Of Trott's four centuries, two were in a losing cause. He also made three nineties and they all resulted in losses, and of his four scores in the eighties, two brought defeat. Oops!

It should also be noted that his last T20 international was against Pakistan in Dubai in 2010. Opening the batting, he made 39 from 51 balls, so that England only made 138 and were beaten by four wickets.

He was summarily dropped. As Flower told me in an interview not long afterwards, and just before the ICC World Twenty20 in the Caribbean that England won, with Craig Kieswetter and Michael Lumb opening the batting instead of Trott and Joe Denly: 'We've had some honest discussion about that, one-on-one and in front of the team. He [Trott] got that innings wrong – no doubt about it – and that was a contributing factor to him not being in the side right now.'

Trott was often blamed for England's one-day batting ills, earning himself his own hashtag on Twitter, which always insisted that it was #trottsfault.

In 2013 the New Zealand bowler Mitchell McClenaghan almost served the ultimate insult by suggesting his side might prefer Trott at the crease rather than in the pavilion. 'In terms of control we're quite able to contain Trotty,' he said. 'He's not one of the easiest batsmen to get out – you need to get him early. But he's not overly a threat when he's out there. It's more about really attacking the guy at the other end and putting the pressure on him.'

But as Leamon said, Trott's value to the side was mostly misunderstood. The 2013 Champions Trophy, held in England, was a classic case in point. Trott was lambasted for his slow scoring in that tournament, yet only three players scored over 200 runs overall. India's Shikhar Dhawan was one, and he was named man of the tournament for his 363 runs at an average of 90.75 at a strike rate of 101.39, helping his side become champions.

The other two? Sri Lanka's Kumar Sangakkara, with 222 runs at an average of 74 and a strike rate of 80.14, and Trott, who made 229 runs at an average of 57.25 with a strike rate of, wait for it, 91.60. I do not remember Sangakkara, who made a magnificent match-winning century against England at the Oval, being criticized for slow scoring.

'People feel better pigeonholing you,' said Trott. 'Fifty

overs is a lot longer than people think. The role that I play has a part in the 50-over game. Obviously you have guys who come in a bit lower down the order who can smash it over the ropes. But the outfields are pretty quick these days! You don't have to hit the ball in the air to score quickly. Two new balls; power plays: I think I'm well suited to playing one-day cricket.'

One-day batting, especially scoring one-day centuries, is not easy. As Graham Gooch says: 'Sometimes one-day batting is more difficult to organize than long-form. In long-form cricket there is a set process – they are trying to get you out and there is no time pressure. In one-day cricket you have got to take calculated risks – and it is a question of when to take the risk. Getting fielders back, when to knock it around – a lot of mental aptitude is required, handling the pressure is big in that.

'It's about the skills but it's about the presence of mind to handle the pressure and organize one's game well. You wouldn't say Dermot Reeve is one of the most talented players to have played the game but would I want him coming in at No. 6 in a tight situation to win a one-day game? Yeah, I think I would. Neil Fairbrother was another one. He could also manage a situation well.'

But the problem arises when a conflict appears between the needs of the individual and the team. We have talked about self-ishness already, but it can be at its most destructive in one-day cricket. And that can often reach another level when a batsman is approaching a milestone, especially a century.

I have seen so many examples of players discarding their team, even if only for a short period, while turning their attentions to achieving a century. It is wrong. It just should not happen.

In my view milestones should be meaningless in one-day cricket. You should not really notice them if you are doing your job, which is ensuring that the team, not you, are scoring at a decent enough rate. Of course, the crowd will probably want to celebrate your milestone with the appropriate applause and you should acknowledge that with a cursory wave of the bat – we will come to celebrations in detail later – but that should be it.

I like the story Murray Goodwin told me of a one-day century he scored for Western Australia in 2001. In fact it was more than just a one-day century. It was 167 in a then record partnership of 257 with Mike Hussey, who made 94 in the match against New South Wales.

'I did not know I had got a hundred,' said Goodwin. '"Huss" congratulated me and I did not know. I have played for a hundred in one-day cricket before, but I was in the moment and in the partnership there. Individually one-day hundreds are nice but it has got to be for the team.'

As Matthew Hayden once said: 'In one-day cricket, if you get to 70 or 80, you can obviously get a hundred by just batting carefully, but we [the Australian team] just don't do that. It affects a batsman's statistics, but we just don't go for those personal marks.

'But countries like India suffer from that. We back ourselves against those countries because they'll get two or three players in the seventies and beyond, and they'll be eyeing off that personal landmark and it'll cost their side 40 or 50 runs as a result. Pretty much all the sub-continental sides are like that. They really can waste a lot of time, and there's no time to waste. Every ball has got to have a priority stamp on it.'

Mike Atherton agrees. 'I think in the sub-continent they have a greater infatuation with statistics. Hundreds are important and should be celebrated in the right context. But even here [in England] in one-day cricket you see a lot of players dawdling to a hundred.'

And as Ian Thomas says of that Twenty20 century of his: 'In the nineties I started to think about a hundred. I did dab a few around, selfish runs, to get to a hundred. I remember dabbing one down to third man and thinking: "I could have whacked that."'

'Milestones in one-day cricket are not as important,' says Andy Flower. 'They are remembered and recorded in the same way.

THE ART OF CENTURIES

Cameos, though, are hugely significant too, but are probably not recognized as such.'

Mike Hussey's batting plan for one-day cricket, as revealed in his book *Mr Cricket*, is also interesting:

'0 to 15 overs: Play straight, be patient, run hard,' he wrote.

'15 to 20 overs: Be busy, work the ball, run hard, keep cool and calm, get to 40 overs.

'40 to 45 overs: Positive risks, use feet, run hard, keep cool and calm.

'45 to 50 overs: Think straight, pick areas and bowlers, watch the ball, keep shapes. If it's not there, get bat on ball and run.'

There is no mention of scoring a century, just as you would expect. Hussey was one of the most unselfish, team-oriented batsmen the game has seen. But check his pre-season goals for first-class cricket earlier in his career. One of them was 'Make 200s (think about it).' Therein lies the difference. And rightly so.

As Matthew Maynard says: 'One-day hundreds don't matter. Maybe in the top three you want someone to anchor the innings. But if you have one person scoring at a strike rate of 75/80 you can't have three doing that, on a decent wicket. Alastair Cook has realized that and has played more aggressively and still got hundreds (before Cook's omission from the England one-day side in late 2014). The secret of one-day cricket is that you don't want two fresh people in.'

It is indeed. That is always the cardinal sin, allowing that to happen, because precious time can be wasted while both players get themselves in. In Twenty20 you barely get that time at any stage. The adage is that 20 overs is a lot longer than you think. Well, it is not really.

It is why the games are often not as close as the marketeers would have us believe. Once you are in trouble in a Twenty20 match, it is difficult to extricate yourself from that mess. The regrouping period often seen in 50-over matches is simply not possible.

It is why I much prefer the 50-over game, despite the constant criticism that it receives. It is 'proper' cricket in my view. Twenty20 is actually quite boring, because it can be horribly formulaic in the sense that the field set reflects the ball likely to be bowled and therefore the batsman's stroke in response.

But what effect is Twenty20 having upon batting, especially longer-form batting and the art of scoring centuries and beyond in that form?

Ricky Ponting was in no doubt of its harm as he observed the young batsmen in the game at the end of his career. 'Most of the batting techniques I was now seeing in Shield cricket were nowhere near precise and consistent enough to guarantee success in Test matches,' he said. 'They were good enough for T20 matches. My guess is that young cricketers aren't learning the right techniques at the right age. This had become a "hobby horse" of mine. Growing up – except at primary school, when they'd made me retire at 30 – when I began an innings I was batting until a bowler got me out. If it took them a week, that's how long it took.

'This happened all the time in family contests at Rocherlea, when my brother, Drew, and I had some serious arguments because he couldn't get me out. Mind you, I reckon he developed into a reasonable junior bowler as a result of having to bowl to me all the time! Everything about my development, on the field, in the nets and in the backyard, was about setting me up so I could bat for ever. It set me up for the days when I had to grind out hundreds in Colombo, Cape Town, Port-of-Spain and Bangalore.'

It is a theme taken up by Graeme Hick, who, as I mentioned earlier, is now High Performance Coach at Cricket Australia's centre of excellence in Brisbane. 'There has to be a desire to spend time at the crease and want to be that person who scores the majority of the runs,' he says. 'Concentrating and adjusting to the three forms of the game are also key. If you're a top player you should be able to do that.

'I think there is a little shift in the mindset more towards Twenty20 and the one-day game and the faster forms of the game,' he says. 'I don't know if they're not willing, but players don't seem to be spending as much time at the crease in the four-day games. We're not seeing as many big scores as we used to. That's something I need to have a look at and hopefully I can make a difference.

'In England I think maybe the younger players come through in the first-class system and play more four-day cricket. They've got more fixtures. Here you get your 10 Shield games and that's it, so that may have a little bit to do with it. I just think, in general, everyone is wanting everything to happen a lot quicker.

'I think it's maybe just educating them on the decisions they're making during their innings. You can certainly play both [short and long formats] quite comfortably, it's just the decisions you choose to make during your innings. When you're approaching thirties and forties it's about making sure you carry on.'

This was Gideon Haigh's take before the 2013/14 Ashes Down Under: 'In the 1993–94 Sheffield Shield, there were 60 centuries scored; last summer, only 31,' he says. 'Century-scoring is a habit we have fallen out of in this country at every level. Batting all day just seems a bit too much like hard work. When Will Bosisto was named Australia's under-19 captain, he had made precisely one hundred in his whole career, in under-15s. A friend of mine, a first-grade coach in Melbourne, recently professed that he was "fed up with coaching talented young cricketers who can play every shot in the book, and a few that aren't, but have never made more than 55 in their entire lives". It's arguable that we used to overestimate the significance of hundreds. Now, I fear, we're apt to do the opposite.'

And here is Graham Gooch on the same subject: 'It's the whole package of not only having the technical skills but having the attitude, the mental toughness, the discipline, the concentration. Anyone can concentrate for 15–20 minutes, but to score Test hundreds you have to concentrate for a long period of time.

'Those skills I think worldwide are being chipped away at the edges by the amount of one-day cricket and T20 cricket.

'If you're a traditionalist and like Test cricket and think that's the pinnacle and the benchmark, you can see with the number of competitions that are popping up and the rewards that are available in terms of finance . . . you can see the possibility of it chipping away at the edges of the traditional game. The players, they want to take those rewards. And that's the same for every country.'

However, the counter-argument comes from Ian Harvey. 'I don't agree that Twenty20 is a threat to Test cricket, quite the opposite,' he says. 'I think the whole standard of Test cricket is being lifted by T20 – you only need to look at the new shots the guys are playing to see the innovations that the game is making. It forces bowlers and batters to think and to improvise and that's really exciting for the spectators. New players are not scared of trying things.'

It may surprise you to learn that I am more on the Harvey side of this argument than the others. For instant evidence I give you the example of New Zealand's Brendon McCullum, who launched the Indian Premier League in 2008 with a blistering 158 not out for Kolkata Knight Riders in the competition's first match and in 2010 scored the second T20I century, against Australia (Chris Gayle had scored the first for West Indies in the ICC World Twenty20 in 2007).

Yet in the space of a couple of weeks in 2014 McCullum recorded Test scores of 224 and 302 against India. His triple century was the eighth-longest innings (775 minutes) of all time.

That hardly suggests a batsman suffering from the excesses of Twenty20. In my opinion the modern-day players are excellent in adjusting. When Twenty20 was first introduced, I felt it sensible that it was played in a block, away from the 'proper' cricket. It could operate in a vacuum, and then everyone could go back to the real stuff.

But in 2014 it was decided that the Twenty20 competition played between the counties should be spread out over most of the season, mainly so that Friday nights could be the prime times used for these fixtures. It makes absolute sense commercially – Twenty20 is the counties' only real way of making money from domestic cricket – because Friday nights are most popular with the spectators. And it is not a nonsense in cricketing terms, simply because the players can now transfer their skills from Twenty20 on a Friday night to the county championship starting on a Sunday.

You would think that concentration spans would have shortened and the long innings of yore would be gradually phased out, but McCullum is a shining light in this regard. And maybe batting standards are rising because of the rise of Twenty20.

Young batsmen growing up can watch a range of different techniques by the same batsman in different formats. I was interested in some comments by Greg Chappell about Sachin Tendulkar recently and how he had been lucky to see only Test-match technique when he was young.

'The big difference I guess from when Sachin was growing up is that back then he would have largely been watching Test cricket, and even one-day cricket as it was played had similarities to Test cricket in a lot of ways,' Chappell said.

'His heroes, and the heroes of the guys he was playing against as a teenager, would have been the players who had established themselves primarily as Test cricketers. But as a young cricket fan today, particularly in India, you would be watching a lot of 20-over cricket. And that in itself promotes the glamour and excitement of batsmen clearing the fence, and playing those sorts of innovative, higher-risk shots.

'I have no doubt Sachin could cope with whatever form of the game he set himself for because of his incredible talent, but

I guess the bigger question would be: "whose game would he choose to model himself on?"'

It is a good question. I always thought of Tendulkar as the batsman to bridge generations while the tempestuous winds of Twenty20 were swirling. In my dear father's later years, when his health was failing, a Tendulkar innings was bound to cheer every time. I would always call him when I spotted Tendulkar batting well on television.

'Are you watching my mate?' he would ask in reference to the 'Little Master'. And off he would go in another paean to Tendulkar, with particular emphasis upon the fact that he batted 'properly'.

And he was right. At a level above McCullum, Tendulkar was proof that, for all the changes Twenty20 purports to bring, the basics of the game have changed very little. Tendulkar was the bridge between generations. A batsman with a robust technique will still enter the battle best prepared. He is more likely to prosper in all forms of the game. And after all, what is technique?

There is technique in big hitting, too. The likes of Chris Gayle and David Warner do not hit balls by fluke. They have a technique to do so. AB de Villiers is another who is adept in all three forms of the game.

It might involve clearing their front leg out of the way (something I could never do – 'protect your stumps' was a mantra too heavily ingrained in my brain), but there will still be a solid base, involving a strong core position (often overlooked in power hitting), a clean swing of the bat with feet, hips and shoulder in sync.

One-day batting is often not as complicated as it is made out to be. It is also not as important. Especially when considering the scoring of centuries in it.

10

No Sweat

It is an astonishing thought. Graham Gooch thinks that, were he playing in today's game, he could have been so much better than he was. That is even though he scored more runs – 44,846 in first-class cricket and 22,211 in List A games – than anyone in the history of the game.

The reason? The help today's players have with their fitness training. 'I would have been a lot better player if I had had the back-up they have today – why wouldn't you be better?' he says. Although I should point out, of course, that the bowlers will say exactly the same, so it may be evened out.

Gooch almost single-handedly changed cricket's approach to fitness. 'I realized I needed to be fitter and stronger, so I started running,' he says. His legendary obsession with running made him the player that he became. 'To be successful as a run-maker I believe that you have got to push yourself,' he says. And, boy, he did push himself.

He also tried to push others when England captain, as already mentioned when famously falling out with David Gower over this.

Cricket was incredibly pompous in its attitude to fitness back then, and to some extent still is, as the old-timers guffaw at the work done by today's players. Their era was the one I walked into when joining Glamorgan in the mid-1980s.

Fitness was a dirty word. There was one fitness test at the beginning of April. It was simply a three-mile run that had to be completed in 21 minutes, which is not very quick at all.

Some players took short cuts. One player used to wear his new batting shoes so that he could wear the spikes in on the concreted part of the run. It was a joke.

Goodness, Ian Botham, when captain of an England tour in the Caribbean, once tried to stop Gooch running in the mornings. 'It's making you tired in the evenings,' said Botham. 'I've noticed a few times that you're nodding off after supper.'

What nonsense. So it was not good that Gooch was unable to indulge in the evening's festivities? Gooch does easily nod off of an evening – I have seen it myself, at the dinner table once in South Africa when he was batting coach with England – but that is only because he will have worked so hard during the day.

But Gooch's problem in those days was that he had no back-up, either in promoting the benefits of fitness training or indeed in the structuring of his own fitness work. It resulted in his doing a lot of unnecessary training.

'I had to work it all out myself. I had no help fitness-wise,' he says. 'I took my own dumbbells to India. I used to run up stairs, then go back down in the lift, and do it again and again. When Essex were playing at Ilford, I lived eight or nine miles away and I used to get someone to pick my bag up and then run to the ground in the morning. It was madness!'

The problem with fitness in cricket is that you can get away with not being particularly fit. You do not have to be fit to score a century. I think it helps, especially when looking to go on to even bigger scores, but it is not essential.

It is also difficult to have a structured training programme.

Most athletes have times in the year when they peak and when they taper. For a batsman, for example, it is very difficult to know when to peak. How can you possibly know when your longest, most energy-sapping innings is going to be? The answer is that you can't.

You simply have to keep topping your fitness up as the season progresses, hoping that it will help when that huge innings comes along. Low scores can mean more training. 'I could do my running then,' says Gooch. 'It was the one opportunity to do it if I got out early as an opener.'

But, as the old-timers always say, there is a difference between gym fitness and cricket fitness. For instance, I'm not sure how fit Sachin Tendulkar was. There was always the hint of some extra baggage around his midriff, but he was 'cricket fit'. He spent hours in the nets and at the crease, and, allied to some top-up work in terms of core stability and flexibility, that was enough.

Mark Ramprakash is another interesting example here. I always heard a lot of talk about his fitness, but when I trained with England he was certainly nowhere near the fittest in the squad.

On a tour to West Indies Ramprakash once fell out spectacularly with the team fitness trainer, Dean Riddle, about extra fitness sessions he was being asked to do because he was not in the side.

But that is not to say that he did not train. 'I have never been above 12½ stone in my whole adult life,' he says. 'I've always looked upon keeping fit as a necessity for batting.'

Even though he never did more than 12.5 on the Bleep test (an endurance test done over 20m shuttles, which become quicker as you have to try to beat the bleeps, until you can keep up no longer), which for a long time was the stated minimum level requirement for an England cricketer, he always thought that to be enough to reach the standards he required in his batting.

I actually agree with that. There was certainly a period during my career when players became obsessed with their scores on the Bleep test. There is much more to fitness than mere endurance, especially as cricket involves interval running rather than continuous work. You work hard – say run a two as a batsman – and then you rest. Then you go again.

That is why most teams do not now do the Bleep test, instead preferring something called the Yo-Yo Intermittent Recovery test, which is very similar in that it is conducted over 20m shuttles, but the difference is that there is a 10-second rest after completing one run of 20m and back. As with the Bleep test, the bleeps come more quickly as the test goes on.

There is also weight training, which has taken considerable time to be taken seriously in cricket, even though it is obviously a game where players' performances can be enhanced by power.

Much of this acceptance has been down to Huw Bevan. He was a rugby union hooker with Bridgend, Cardiff, Swansea and briefly Llanelli who went on to become the England team's strength and conditioning coach, before departing in 2014, even though newly appointed coach Peter Moores wanted him to stay, to return to rugby with Newport Gwent Dragons.

Bevan says: 'I tend to focus on basic lifts, such as squat and deadlift and if they increase muscle that's just a bonus. When I played rugby there was a misconception that weight training was all about bodybuilding. There's probably still that misconception among some rugby coaches. Speed, strength and power are the real purposes.'

Altering perceptions, and especially taking bowlers out of the game and the relentless international schedule in order to build up their strength, has proved a challenging business for all involved. Remember that England's cricketers do not have something called an off-season.

In 2010 both Stuart Broad and Steven Finn were given periods out of the game to work in the gym, and it understandably caused uproar. But as Bevan said at the time: 'I was asked whether it would be of benefit and said yes. Because of all the cricket we play, it is difficult to make any gains in terms of strength, and any gains you make are difficult to maintain.

'Other sports will have an off-season, which we don't necessarily have, so to make real improvements you need a block of time to train. We are trying to build up each of the players' training age. By that I mean if you do weights for 20 years then stop training, you won't lose strength rapidly. But if you only train for a short period of time, you will make gains quickly but also regress quickly.'

Circuit training is now also widely used, especially what are called 'metabolic' circuits, which build strength but also burn fat and improve general conditioning. So you might perform six exercises, working for 30 seconds and then resting for 30 seconds, completing the circuit four times. The six exercises would be combinations, often using dumbbells; for instance, one of the exercises is a step up onto a bench with the dumbbells in your hands and then performing an overhead press once you are standing on the bench.

Even though its technical basics may not have altered too much, there is no doubt that the game has changed in many other respects. The dynamism and athleticism required in the field for a start dictate that high levels of fitness are required.

Those quotes above from Bevan were from an interview I did with him in Australia in 2010/11 on England's victorious Ashes tour. It was obvious on that trip how fit England were compared to their opposite numbers and how much that was helping them. It was also obvious how much the game had moved on in that respect. Bevan was understandably reluctant to say that publicly, so I said it for him.

'A look at the replays of the 1986/87 tour being shown over here says as much,' I wrote. 'Body shapes, athleticism and intensity have all moved on markedly. Cricketers must be athletes;

professionalism demands no less. And no cricketer has ever become less effective by becoming fitter. Plenty might have been a whole lot more effective had they been fitter, though.'

The balance between net practice and fitness work has altered. There was once no balance at all. It was all net practice.

But when the former New Zealand batsman John Wright was coach of Kent during the 1990s he had an interesting conversation with the club president, Colin Cowdrey.

Wright wanted to make the Kent players fitter, and, upon being told this, Cowdrey told a story of once having had lunch with the then Prime Minister, Sir Alec Douglas-Home, who surprised Cowdrey by having a glass of wine with his lunch.

Cowdrey asked him about this and Douglas-Home replied that as long as he had three glasses of water to every glass of wine, he would be fine. So that was Cowdrey's advice to Wright. He told him that the Kent players should spend three hours in the nets for every hour in the gym.

It may even be closer than that these days, or it is often that fitness work can be interwoven into the net practice, especially for batsmen. Players risk not being selected if their fitness is not up to scratch. An obvious example is Samit Patel with England. 'These days fitness is second nature,' says Graham Gooch. 'If you're not fit, you don't get in the team.'

I know that fitness made me the player I was. Weight training made me more confident as a person, and a batsman who could then hit the ball in front of square as well as deflect it behind square. But it was the ability to run shuttle after shuttle that allowed me to play long innings.

After every net session I would run 60 shuttles. That is 60 runs from crease to crease. I would do three blocks of 20, with a walk of two in between. In each block of 20 I could run anything between a one and a five (overloading is no bad thing!), with a walk of one in between. Sometimes I might do that set of 60 twice a day.

When I first began doing it, I would do it without cricket kit on, which was rather silly. I then saw Jack Russell running shuttles in his full batting kit one day at Bristol, and the penny dropped. That was not a bad idea. It was a fully logical idea, in fact.

Mind you, even the realistic nature of shuttles had taken some time to catch on with me. Like everyone else, I had just done long-distance running before then. Of course, that has its benefits for building up an endurance base, and I always remember Alan Jones saying that long-distance running was good for him in building up concentration. And that is true. On any fitness session of lengthy duration, some serious thinking can be done. Most of my articles these days are born on long bike rides.

There were some sprint sessions, especially with my partner-in-crime at Glamorgan, Tony Cottey, who, of course, had been a professional footballer on the books of Swansea City, so he knew a lot more about fitness training than me.

Others joined in so that very soon at Glamorgan we had one of the fittest squads in the country. Wicketkeeper Adrian Shaw had played a lot of top-class rugby for Neath, Matthew Maynard always trained much harder than his carousing reputation implied, Adrian Dale was always keen, Steve Watkin could run like the greyhound his frame suggested and even Robert Croft was a better long-distance runner than most would imagine.

When Duncan Fletcher arrived in 1997, he increased our fitness levels even further, mostly by encouraging games of touch rugby after play, where he carefully selected sides to ensure optimum competitiveness. He also introduced some fielding routines that burnt your lungs like no other cricket-related fitness ever had before. It is amazing how exhausting twisting, turning, bending and sprinting while watching a cricket ball all the time can be.

Fitness incorporated into skills training can often be the most beneficial. Graham Gooch used to do that with the England batsmen. 'I make them run or do press-ups between "overs", do burpees or carry bricks,' he has said. 'All this is about is taking them out of their comfort zone so that they have to step back into their role as a batsman, compose themselves and use their powers of concentration to focus back on the art of scoring runs.'

Sometimes if a batsman was out in the nets, Gooch would make him do 10 burpees. If he was out a second time, it would be 20 burpees. That is seriously tough work. Just try doing a couple of burpees, which for the uninitiated are a body-weight exercise, where you begin in a standing position, then perform a squat thrust before returning to standing. You can even go to the floor as in a press-up too. Whichever variation you use, it is an extremely demanding exercise.

Or as Ian Bell described another session with Gooch: 'The routine consisted of 20 overs of batting with exercises in between each over. Sometimes I'd be wearing ankle weights while batting and there would be different tests at the end of each over.

'So I'd face an over, then complete six runs, and face another over. After that, I might do eight burpees and face a third over. When that's finished, there would be eight press-ups and you'd rotate the whole routine until you'd batted for 20 overs.'

You do have to be careful, however. In February 2014 Rupert Williams wrote a guest blog for Cricinfo about his son's trial at a county. It did make rather worrying reading, particularly these three long paragraphs:

'Recently, he [Williams' son] trialled with a first-class county, and after a single session lasting less than three hours, he was left injured and demoralised for more than a week afterwards,' he wrote. 'The injuries were because the session seemed to be less about cricket and far more about physical punishment. If a bowler failed to hit the cone, hurdle or pole that was acting as a target in the drill in question, he faced punishment. If a batsman failed to hit the bowling machine ball back between the cones provided, he would face punishment. If a fielder failed to complete the drill faultlessly, he would go back to the queue, because for the second half of the session, fielding drills were the punishment.

'Aside from the worrying aspect of fielding being used as a deterrent, it was by far the least damaging of the sentences on offer. In the first half of the session, the weapons of choice for the coaches were heavy medicine balls, which would be added to regular stretches and drills to make them that bit more punishing. Presumably, this was supposed to help to create a pressure situation, as well as to gauge "the non-negotiable fitness levels required". Instead, when added to a half-hour long "light" warm-up, it served to leave my son too tired to perform anywhere near his best and with much of his body in spasm.

'Two players spoke out against the ritual punishment that was going on in the session, both of them regular county players. One of them was given a frankly humiliating dressing down in front of all present, while the other was told that he should "work harder to rise to the challenge" and "turn his anger into positive energy". My son, meanwhile, went through an entire session without bowling at a batsman or batting against a bowler. Quite how this gave the county in question any idea about his abilities, I have no idea. He left a county cricket session, something that should have been a superb experience, both emotionally and physically shattered.'

Hopefully this was just an isolated and exaggerated incident. It sounds like awful coaching, of which there is undoubtedly plenty at all standards. There is a difference between encouraging high fitness levels and running military-like boot-camp activities.

And I should add that at school I was not particularly keen on fitness. I just wanted to play in those days. The need for better conditioning only became apparent later. Realization comes at different times for different people.

Mentally, of course, fitness is hard, but the discipline required to drive oneself to higher levels of conditioning can be hugely beneficial for batting: the idea of a healthy mind in a healthy body – 'mens sana in corpore sano', as Juvenal wrote. Often when I was in the middle of a big innings, I would say to myself: 'This is why you do all that training. You can do this.'

'The hardest thing about training is getting out of the door at 6 a.m.,' says Gooch. 'It is easy to say: "Not today." But the massive spin-off that I didn't realize at the time when I was playing is that it is character-building, it makes you a tougher competitor.'

It was only at the end of my county career that clubs started employing fitness coaches full time, and then most of them only did so because they were given £25,000 per annum by the England and Wales Cricket Board specifically for that purpose.

Otherwise it was part-time employment. At Glamorgan we were lucky that a former rugby league player, Andy Harrison, now British Cycling's programmes director, was working at the Welsh Institute of Sport next door at Sophia Gardens. He helped us out, for the first time doing rigorous testing for all aspects of fitness rather than just the dreaded Bleep test that had become the norm.

And then when I became captain in 2001 I enlisted the services of the aforementioned Huw Bevan, who was then working with the Ospreys rugby team.

Both of them were very good at their jobs, even if they were very different in their approaches, but as good as any fitness coach is, the desire and drive to get fit still has to come from the individual. As Gooch says: 'The back-up is there but you still have to drive it forward yourself. The player is the master. The coaches can only help if the player wants to be helped.'

And there is no better example of this than current England Test captain Alastair Cook. His desire to train and practise was evident even during his time at Bedford School. As his teacher Jeremy Farrell says: 'He always had a burning drive to make the most of his ability. Some of us teachers who were getting a bit older would go down to the pool in the morning for a swim a few mornings a week. Alastair said: "Can I come?" because he knew he wasn't fit enough. He would have been 14 or 15 at the time. At first we were looking over our shoulders nervously to see if he would make it to the other end, but soon he was flying up and down.

'He was the only pupil who came. On the other days he would be dragging Derek Randall (the school coach and former England batsman) out of bed to do 60 minutes on the bowling machine before the boarders had their breakfast at 8 a.m. That was his attitude. In 22 years of teaching I've never seen anything quite like it.'

When talking of fitness and long innings, Cook has become famous for one thing in particular: the fact that he does not sweat.

As he has said: 'I'm quite lucky – I don't really sweat that much. It helps in hot countries, because it means I can retain my body fluids more easily than others. When you're dehydrated or struggling with cramp, it's the concentration that goes first. And as a batter, I need to concentrate. A cool body certainly helps me.'

When Cook made a century in Adelaide in the second Test of his record-breaking Ashes tour in 2010/11 he admitted that he had used only one pair of gloves. Cook made 148, while Kevin Pietersen made 227 as they shared a partnership of 175.

'I only wore one pair of gloves all day, while Kev was changing them every other over,' said Cook. 'I'm built in a way that I don't get too hot, and don't really sweat – so it was all right.

'It was hot, around 38°C, the hottest I can recall playing in, so it was a question of keeping yourself going.'

I am unconscionably jealous of Cook. I went through pairs of batting gloves like Henry VIII did wives. I was the worst-case scenario for a glove manufacturer: a heavy sweater who liked to grip the bat very hard. Most sponsorship deals with bat firms wanted to give me between two and four pairs of batting gloves a season. I needed at least 10, and it was only in my latter years with Slazenger that I got that many.

'Alastair is incredible,' says Kirk Russell, who was the England team physiotherapist from 2002 to 2011. 'I have never seen anyone like him. You worry a bit because sweat is your mechanism to cool you down, but he is a very fit man.'

Wicketkeeper Matt Prior sweats profusely, like other former England colleagues such as Pietersen and Jonathan Trott, and has suffered with severe cramps. 'We have regular sweat tests,' Prior has said. 'Unsurprisingly they show that I sweat a lot. In the Test in Colombo against Sri Lanka in 2012 I lost 3.5kg in weight between the start of play and lunch on one of the days. They also show that Alastair Cook hardly sweats at all. That's just ridiculous. He doesn't know how lucky he is.'

A revelation, though: Cook does get cramp, or at least he once did. Or maybe it was that he did once. Anyway, the evening after his double century for Essex against Australia in 2005 he went to a Paul Grayson benefit function. Unfortunately he got cramp and had to leave his seat during a speech by Geoff Miller. 'I hope he didn't think it was a comment on the quality of his speech!' Cook wrote when Miller was still an England selector.

But you suspect that Cook's attitude towards hydration and nutrition has improved, as it has for most cricketers now. When Andy Harrison first conducted urine tests at Glamorgan, he was shocked by the results. Most cricketers then used to drink copious amounts of alcohol of an evening and then think that a cup of coffee in the morning would fix everything. Harrison reckoned that some players were so dehydrated that, had they been in hospital, they would have been immediately placed on drips.

Of course, that is what happened to Australia's Dean Jones when he was rushed to hospital after losing seven kilograms during his famous 210 in the tied Test against India in 1986 in Madras.

Jones was 56 not out at the end of the first day, with Australia 211-2.

'I didn't drink water overnight,' Jones says. 'One hour into day two I knew I was in trouble. I didn't drink anything apart from a cup of tea or coffee. We didn't know anything about dehydration and rehydration back then. Then I just batted from memory basically. I can't remember much from 120 on. I know nearly every shot in every innings I played. I can't remember a thing after 120 in that innings.'

It was when Jones had made 170 that there came a now well-known comment from captain Allan Border. Jones was in such a state that he was unsure whether he could continue his innings.

Border was adamant that Jones should continue, and he taunted the Victorian with the line 'we'll get a Queenslander out here', meaning the next man in, who was Greg Ritchie.

Jones replied: 'Yeah, right, you've got no chance.' He stayed at the crease. 'That moment forced me on to my 200,' he says. 'Looking back, it's great and I wouldn't change a thing, but back then I was a complete mess.'

Even though he was vomiting regularly and urinating involuntarily, Jones made it to tea on that second day, when he was 202 not out.

'I didn't want to come out after tea,' said Jones. 'I was 202 and I was just gone. They [his team-mates] dragged me into the shower, because I literally couldn't put two steps together. But afterwards they padded me back up and pushed me out the door again – only to discover that they hadn't put my box or thigh-pad back on! All I had was my pads, gloves and a bat, but I was only up against the spinners, so it wouldn't have mattered too much.'

Steve Waugh was sitting next to him in the changing rooms. 'I'll never forget how, after more than eight hours at the crease, his physical appearance had changed,' Waugh wrote afterwards. 'He was gaunt and pale in the face and had a vacant expression that suggested he was in serious trouble, his body bordering on completely shutting down.

'He was like a walking corpse. He had lost control of his

bodily functions, and was slumped in his chair saturated in urine, shaking uncontrollably and virtually incoherent.'

It is a remarkable story. But it was not over. Jones went back out to bat.

'Simmo [coach Bob Simpson] and AB [Allan Border] just pushed me out and said, "You're batting,"' Jones says. 'When you're urinating in your pants and vomiting 15 times, you've got massive problems. It wouldn't happen now because of litigious players and workplace safety. Should we be playing in 42 degrees? We go off for rain but we don't go off when it's 42.

'I was out shortly afterwards, and it was then that I started to cramp up real bad. I went into a ball, as everything started to tighten up – my neck, my hands, my stomach muscles, my toes, my hamstrings, my back, my forearms . . . everything.'

'I could have killed him,' Border said later. 'Instead, I made him a legend.'

Kirk Russell tells a rather humorous tale about Rob Key when the Kent batsman made a double hundred for England against West Indies at Lord's in 2004. Key was 90 not out at tea, but because both teams were meeting the Queen during the interval, Key forgot to take the requisite liquids on board.

'The whole hydration thing wasn't what it is now,' says Russell. 'He went out and suffered a migraine. He was seeing double. And I couldn't get out to the wicket because the Queen was in the Long Room. I had to go round the side. We eventually got some medication out to him, hydrated him and he went on to score a double hundred.'

There was also the case of Owais Shah's Test debut. He was not supposed to be playing in the third Test against India in Mumbai. It had been the series in which Alastair Cook had made his debut, scoring a century in Nagpur, but on the morning of the third Test he fell ill. 'Alastair was sick in the morning so Owais turned up not expecting to play and hadn't done the hydration,' says Russell. 'He got 80-odd [88, to be precise] but I think he might have got a 100 if it hadn't have been for that. He was cramping up badly.' That remained Shah's highest Test score.

When England played a one-day international against India in Jamshedpur in 2006, two players ended up on saline drips in the dressing rooms. One of them was Matt Prior, who was keeping wicket for England for the first time, having previously played just as a batsman, and the other was Andrew Strauss, who set up England's victory with 74 before having to retire hurt because of cramps.

It was horribly hot – the temperature in the nearby city was recorded at 43°C – and, with India batting first, Prior really struggled.

'I was due to open the batting, but I returned to the dressing room in a right state,' Prior wrote later. 'I remember sitting in a chair and my whole body was cramping, and by that I mean every single muscle. It was horrendous. I looked down at one of my thigh muscles and it was horribly deformed. It was bulging out, and I was in complete agony.

'I'd seen Owais Shah in a similar state once on an England Lions tour. Sometimes those watching find people cramping funny, but it is not funny at all, I can tell you. Owais was there in Jamshedpur too, but he was not playing. But I remember him coming out as twelfth man when we were fielding, with a cold towel to put over my head, a drink and a sympathetic tap on the back. He knew what I was going through.'

I used to get cramps in my arms when batting, especially when starting again after an interval, but it was nothing compared to what Prior, Shah and more recently Michael Carberry have been through while playing for England.

In fact Carberry was not selected for some time because of his cramping, which often occurred in conditions when it was not that hot and he was well hydrated. He did, of course, have other serious health issues, being found to have life-threatening blood clots on his lung, meaning he was unable to fly to Australia in

2010/11 as part of the Academy squad which accompanied the senior Ashes squad that winter. He missed much of the following county season.

The problem with cramps is that there is no one definitive reason for them occurring. And often they are viewed, as Prior suggests, with jest, or, worse still, scorn, because they are merely considered a result of poor fitness.

Advice on dealing with cramps has varied over the years. In Jamshedpur Prior was told to jump into an ice bath. 'I knew that was the wrong thing to do because I knew that once I got in there I would just cramp more,' he says. 'But I obeyed my instructions, and guess what happened? I got worse.'

On another occasion, in South Africa, Prior was told to drink the energy drink Gatorade all day to avoid cramps. 'I drank the stuff all day; I got cramps. I knew I would,' he says.

Drips are no longer permitted at grounds. 'They are obviously unhygienic in dressing rooms,' says Kirk Russell. 'But in an emergency you might have to do it.'

And Prior, although not having had cause to use one for some time (although both he and Shah again cramped very badly on the one-day tour of India in 2008), bemoans their banning.

'It's a shame that we are no longer allowed to be put on drips,' he says, 'because they can obviously rehydrate you so much more quickly.'

Thankfully things are very different now, though. 'The education of the players has changed dramatically,' says Kirk Russell. 'Their awareness of hydration levels is far greater. You have to be hydrated at the start of the day so that you are not playing catch-up.'

There is much more testing and monitoring. Players are weighed at the start of the day and at every break, and they have regular sweat tests.

'The thing that has moved forward in cricket is looking at specific hydration protocols for each player,' says Russell. 'The tests give an indication not just how much they sweat but of the salt concentration too. So you give different drinks to each player. It might be a different quantity or a difference in the isotonic concentration.'

So each player has a hydration plan to which he is advised to stick rigidly, especially in hot countries. For instance, Prior: 'Every night before a playing day I mix up two litres of electrolyte drink,' he says. 'I aim to have drunk all that by the time we start practising at the ground the next day. So I will be up early, and I will start sipping from one of my two bottles as soon as I wake up. Hopefully I will have finished one bottle by the end of breakfast, and then I can take the other with me to the ground. If I don't need to go to the toilet by the time we get to the ground, then I know I'm behind the eight ball! I'll also nip off at the end of warm-ups to relieve myself. Again that is a good sign!'

And, unsurprisingly, Cook is no less diligent. 'At breakfast, I force down a litre and a half of sports drink, even though it's not a particularly pleasant thing to do at 7.30 am,' he says. 'But you have to stay on top of hydration, otherwise you have no way of catching up.'

Determining exactly how cramps come about is difficult. 'They still don't know exactly what causes cramps but it is a combination of factors,' says Russell.

Much research has been done, though, and in a recent report the Medicine and Science teams of the England and Wales Cricket Board concluded: 'Cramping is likely to be a consequence of muscle fatigue with a number of contributory risk factors.'

Those risk factors are manifold. Top of the list is lack of endurance, and when you look at three of the England players named so far, you can see that this might have been a problem at various stages.

Though Owais Shah was a very fine hitter of the ball, especially to leg in the one-day game and Twenty20 games, his fitness was always poor, and that was ultimately why he was dropped from the England one-day side in 2009 after the ICC Champions Trophy in South Africa. This was even though he had made 98 against South Africa in that tournament before finishing his ODI career with scores of 3 and 0 against New Zealand and Australia.

Then there is Matt Prior. By his own admission, there was a time when he was probably more concerned with looking good via beach weights than building endurance. 'I did get too caught up in the weights at one stage and got a bit too heavy,' he says.

That has changed in recent times since he has found road biking as a hobby. Indeed that work, combined with using a Wattbike (an indoor bike developed by British Cycling that produces extensive data) at home, meant that before the 2013/14 Ashes in Australia Prior had lost 8kg and produced personal bests on most of the tests done at Loughborough by the England team. He does not get cramps any more either, although an Achilles injury troubled him in 2014 and eventually forced him to take a break from international cricket.

Michael Carberry is another who is very strong in the weights room, probably one of the most explosive players when in the England squad. And he is also quick over the ground, having done some work during his career with Donna Fraser, the Olympic 400m runner, with whom he grew up in Thornton Heath in South London. But his endurance? I am told that it is not outstanding.

Other risk factors are obviously the heat, dehydration, electrolyte depletion and a history of cramping in a player's family, as well as others like late nights, excessive alcohol, jet lag, poor sleeping patterns and poor recovery after prolonged exertions.

Muscle tension is also a risk factor, as being nervous and tense, as well as making you grip the bat hard, is likely to produce local muscle tension and neuromuscular fatigue.

'Nasser Hussain suffered a lot with cramps through this stress element,' says Russell. 'He gripped the bat really hard. He was incredibly intense. But that was what made him too. He used magnesium tablets a lot. He found that helped.'

Training for acclimatization to hot countries can be done much more realistically these days too. As Ian Bell explained before going to Sri Lanka in 2012: 'I did some work in a heat chamber at Birmingham University, which is not too far from where I live,' he said. 'You go in and there is a bike and a treadmill, and when I was there, the temperature was set to 34°C and the humidity was between 70 and 80 per cent. I did five fitness sessions and I found it really beneficial.

'When you bat in places like Sri Lanka, the heat and humidity are a huge factor. You sweat a lot, so your shirt will be wet and heavy and you have to be prepared for that. You also need to know how to cool down during an innings and how to lower your body temperature during a drinks break.

'The Birmingham sessions were arranged for me by Huw Bevan, and it's certainly far better than training in a normal gym during the English winter. It meant I felt ready to go when I landed in Sri Lanka.'

I wish that I could have had that sort of preparation when I went to Sri Lanka with England A in 1998. I trained hard beforehand but I was wholly unprepared for the heat and humidity. In the first match we played there, I made 50 before lunch, but returned to the dressing rooms absolutely shattered.

I was drenched in sweat and I was squelching as I walked, so it was no surprise that I tipped large quantities of sweat out of my boots when I took them off. In my first three first-class innings of that tour I made three fifties without scoring a hundred. So much for my conversion rate. The heat was too much.

Nutrition is also highly important. When I played, advice on that was negligible. We certainly had no idea about the benefits of eating protein. We were told to avoid too much meat if anything. I think I was fairly typical of my generation in that I felt I could out-train my poor diet. In other words it did not matter what I ate or drank, as long as I trained hard enough afterwards it would be fine. It was nonsense, and what happened was that I spent a lot of time training just for weight loss, which was exhausting and time-consuming.

It is a view shared by Matt Prior. 'I've realised the effects of nutrition now,' he says. 'It comes from experience. When you are 21 you can almost eat and drink what you want. And I've always trained hard, so I thought that, if I ever did overindulge, I could then train any excess off. What I've realised now is that if you get your diet 100 per cent spot on, you don't have to train so hard. You just don't have to punish your body as much.'

So the England team are given a sheet containing 10 nutritional and lifestyle basics in order to be in their best possible shape. These days they are fairly obvious and well known, but I am sure that they would have been highly useful, and a little revelatory, to me during my playing career.

We are not talking here about the ridiculous 82-page document of catering demands that was sent to Australia before the 2013/14 Ashes tour. That was quite rightly lambasted, as it contained among its 194 dishes such things as mini mushroom and spinach bhajis, quinoa with roasted butternut squash, apricot and parsley, piri-piri breaded tofu with tomato salsa and mung bean curry with spinach. Goodness me!

No, these are more just common-sense guidelines.

They are:

1. Drink plenty of water.
2. Never miss breakfast.
3. Get enough sleep.
4. Eat more protein (at least 1.5 grams for each kilogram of body weight).
5. Limit refined carbohydrates (like white rice, white bread, white pasta, sweets, biscuits, soft drinks, which should only be eaten within two hours of hard activity).
6. Eat some essential oils (from, say, sardines, salmon or mackerel).

7. Limit junk and processed food (pies, pasties and cakes).
8. Limit alcohol.
9. Don't look for short cuts (in other words, plan your meals, especially when travelling).
10. Apply the 90:10 rule. In other words, you can have treats but make sure that at least 90 per cent of the time you are eating healthily.

I would have liked to have been able to drink the protein shakes that are available these days. Whenever I was batting, I could never eat at the lunch or tea breaks – maybe a banana and a sandwich but nothing more. The shakes made up these days and used by nearly all the players would have given me better sustenance and it would have been fascinating to have seen the results.

Mind you, saying that, I can only recall one innings when I really ran out of steam. It was when I made 259 not out against Nottinghamshire at Colwyn Bay in 1999, batting for 11½ hours, longer than required for a triple century the following season at the same ground.

I was pleading privately for captain Matthew Maynard to declare even though I was in sight of the Glamorgan record, set by Emrys Davies with his 287 not out in 1939. I was shot.

Was it a fitness issue? Or hydration? Or nutrition? I reckon it might have been fitness at that stage. For some reason I was not as fit then as I had been or would be in the future. As Kirk Russell says when assessing cramping and other related matters: 'I cannot stress enough how important fitness is.'

And it is so true. You want to score centuries, or make even bigger scores than that? Get yourself fit.

11

Daddy Hundreds

The nervous 290s. They really are a drag. Oh, please excuse the joke, and yet more noise from that little trumpet of mine. But to say that I was once in the 290s still seems rather odd.

It only happened once, of course. It was in 2000 at my favourite ground of Colwyn Bay in North Wales, and it was against Sussex. And there I was on 296 when something strange occurred.

I was not really nervous, if I'm honest. More excited. I hit a drive that for all money was going for four to bring up my triple century. But it was stopped quite brilliantly in the covers.

Suddenly there was a lot of noise from the Sussex fielders. I soon discovered why. I turned to look at the scoreboard and there was a man halfway up a ladder with a tin plate bearing the number three in his hands.

Talk about tempting fate. I laughed, but inside I was cursing a little. It did not matter, of course, because soon I was guiding a ball down to third man (where else?) off the left-arm spinner Umer Rashid, tragically no longer with us after drowning along with his brother during Sussex's pre-season tour of

Grenada in 2002, to reach my triple century, the first by a Glamorgan player.

And it is still the only one as I write, although my close friend Mike Powell agonizingly made 299 against Gloucestershire at Cheltenham College in 2006.

Anyway, the story of the man up the ladder has been one that I have always wanted to know more about, so it was a happy coincidence that a couple of years ago I met David Parry, the Colwyn Bay club's scorer and statistician.

He explained all. 'The gentleman who climbed the ladder was Tom Birchall, who was, at the time, the Chairman of our Cricket Committee,' he said. 'You presumably did not notice him when he put up the 200. As you are aware, our electronics can only display up to 199 for the individual batsmen, but a hook had been placed to hang 2 (and, as it happened, 3) in front of the 1. When you reached 200 early on the second morning Tom tried to put the 2 in place by leaning out of the upstairs window situated just below WKTS. However, he couldn't reach the hook, so the ladder was plan B. When you were in the 290s, he put the ladder in place in good time and stood beside it with the 3 in his hand, tempting fate somewhat, hence it was more noticeable.'

Tempting fate somewhat? You can say that again! Anyway, Parry described it as Colwyn Bay's 'most famous match'. That is very kind, because it was also most certainly my most famous day. To score a triple century truly is special.

They are relatively rare beasts, even if in first-class cricket Donald Bradman scored six of them, and Wally Hammond and Bill Ponsford four each. W. G. Grace, Graeme Hick, Brian Lara, Mike Hussey, Ravindra Jadeja and Cheteshwar Pujara all have three each.

As I write, there have only been 28 Test match triple centuries, with four players having scored two each – Bradman, Chris Gayle, Virender Sehwag and Lara.

Only five Test triple centuries have been scored by Englishmen – Len Hutton's 364, Hammond's 336, Graham Gooch's 333, Andy Sandham's 325 and John Edrich's 310 not out.

Sandham's innings was most remarkable. He became Test cricket's first triple centurion, and it was in his final Test, against West Indies in 1930 at Kingston. At 39 years and 272 days, he is, by almost five years, the oldest player to break the individual scoring record in Tests, beating R. E. Foster's 287. He also made the runs with a long-handled bat borrowed from his captain, Freddie Calthorpe, and wearing a pair of boots borrowed from Patsy Hendren that did not fit properly.

What's more, the Test was timeless. Seven days were played, before days eight and nine were washed out, and the England team then had to catch their boat home.

Next on the list after those five triples for England is Alastair Cook, who made 294 against India in 2011. Maybe those nervous 290s do exist after all. 'It's mad how you can be disappointed after scoring 294 – only cricket can do that,' Cook said. 'Yes, there was a tinge of disappointment at not making 300 but realistically I'm thrilled to have got a really big score. You have to look at it in terms of the 294 runs I did score rather than six I didn't get.'

And perhaps more importantly, coach Graham Gooch was pleased. 'He's quite happy, I think,' said Cook. That was because Cook had gone on from making a hundred. He had made, as the cliché dictated around that time, what was known as a 'daddy hundred'.

It is Gooch's phrase. Not that he can recall where it came from. 'It came from someone else but I can't remember who,' he says. 'But above 150 is a daddy hundred.'

So what was Cook's 294? David Hopps in the *Guardian* had the answer. 'This was no daddy hundred, this was a granddaddy hundred, not just because of its prodigious size, but because only your granddad could possibly remember when India had been made to look quite so ordinary,' he wrote with his typical humour.

But the source of Gooch's desire to get big scores is clear. It was Ken Barrington. '"Book in for bed and breakfast" was his term,' says Gooch. 'He said there was only one person that is going to get you out once you are past 100 and that is normally yourself. He used to say: "Just keep going, keep helping yourself. It is criminal to throw away a chance of a big score when the opportunity is there. One big score may easily be followed by a run of little ones and you'll be glad of that big score to fall back on. You never know what's going to happen next innings; you might get a good delivery, you might get a poor decision, you might get a ball that shoots along the deck. If you get a hundred, get a big one."'

So a score between, say, 100 and 110 was always the source of great disappointment?

'Absolutely, yes,' Gooch says. 'As Kenny used to tell me, the first 50 is the most difficult; you've got to get through that vulnerable period, you've got to get into your rhythm, you've got to get the pace of the wicket. The second 50 you should be "in your game": moving well, seeing it nicely, and just keeping your game going. From then on it should just get easier and generally the only one that gets you out at that stage is yourself.'

Viv Richards' father, Malcolm, was of a similar mind. 'If I scored a double hundred, he'd ask why I didn't make it a triple,' says Richards.

And Richards did make one triple century, for Somerset against Warwickshire in 1985, his 322 coming in a day at Taunton, off just 258 balls. He made nine other scores over 200, leaving him in equal 26th place in the list of highest scorers of double centuries (which, of course, means any score over 200, including triples).

Bradman is top of that roster with 37, with Wally Hammond second with 36. Patsy Hendren made 22 and next are Mark

Ramprakash and Herbert Sutcliffe with 17. Jack Hobbs made 16, along with C. B. Fry and Graeme Hick.

Me? I made six, a Glamorgan record of which I am very proud. Mind you, Javed Miandad is second with four and I think if he had played the 213 matches I did for the county, rather than the 83 he did, then the story might be rather different.

Hobbs may have made 16 double hundreds, but it appears that he was not always keen to adhere to the sort of advice Barrington was handing out years later. 'When I have made a hundred, I am not really anxious to add to my score,' Hobbs once said.

It might explain why, of his 197 centuries, 51 were scores between 100 and 110. Mind you, he liked entertaining, and in his career he made 20 centuries before lunch, 13 of them on the first day. No one has made more before lunch.

I did that once, in 1997 against Durham at Cardiff, and my team-mates were shocked to say the least. 'I've seen it all now,' laughed a disbelieving Tony Cottey.

As for Test double centuries, Bradman made 12, while next on the list at the time of writing is Kumar Sangakkara with 11. Brian Lara has nine. Wally Hammond made seven along with Mahela Jayawardene. The next Englishman is Len Hutton with four, while Kevin Pietersen made three.

'Daddy hundreds' do count more. 'I think "baby" hundreds are almost a waste of time,' says Matthew Maynard. 'Because you can still be bowled out as a team for 220. If you get a "daddy", the team is looking at 350 or 400.'

Murray Goodwin agrees. 'I don't want to sound arrogant,' he says. 'I know a hundred is great, but these days hundreds don't win games unless it is a dicey wicket or you've made it off 70 balls or something to change the game. I think 150 or 200 generally puts your team in a commanding position to win games. A hundred is great, but I think the guys who get picked in international teams are the ones who go on and get 150s and 200s. They are the guys who want to play Test cricket.'

In 1993 my good friend Adrian Dale scored a double century for Glamorgan against Middlesex. It was not any old double century either. He put on an unbeaten 425 with Viv Richards, the highest partnership for any wicket in Glamorgan's history.

Just imagine doing that with Richards. It has given Dale a smorgasbord of stories to cherish. One he tells at dinners is of how he hit a lovely stroke that was obviously going for four, but, still, out of habit, he ran down the pitch. 'Don't run, you'll spoil the shot,' bellowed Richards.

I ask Dale what he recalls of the way the partnership was constructed. 'I remember trying to go up in tens but don't really recall Viv being part of that,' he says. 'He was more concerned with telling me not to "slog out" otherwise I would have to answer to him! I used targets and he used threats!

'He never really seemed a technical person but I do remember him being enormously proud of the innings, mainly due to his age and the fact that many people had written him off.'

I remember thinking at the time: 'I could never imagine getting a double hundred.'

So it struck a chord when Andy Flower said to me: 'Scoring 200 wouldn't even have crossed my mind when I started playing first-class cricket.'

For Flower it was his Zimbabwe skipper, Dave Houghton, who convinced him that a double was possible. Houghton made 266 against Sri Lanka in Bulawayo in 1994. 'He always showed the way,' says Flower. 'I learnt a lot from watching him play that big 200 at Queen's against Sri Lanka. I remember getting out for 50 and I remember being horribly jealous of him going on to that score. I top-edged a sweep off [Kumar] Dharmasena when I was cruising. I hate to admit to the feeling of jealousy, but it hardened me up to making it count when I got in.'

And Flower did go on to make four double centuries, one of them in a Test against India (232 not out), two for Essex and one for Mashonaland.

Houghton had inspired him. Dale inspired me. It is rather like a young Ricky Ponting inspiring Adam Gilchrist. When Ponting scored his maiden first-class century in 1993, becoming the third youngest in the Sheffield Shield to do so, Gilchrist was making his Shield debut at 21 as a batsman. He had been Ponting's Academy captain and afterwards he simply thought to himself: 'If he can do it, so can I.'

What about 300s? Who ever thinks about them? Graham Gooch, of course, made 333 against India at Lord's in 1990. 'I had never really thought about getting 300,' he admits. 'Having the time to do it is unusual.'

And that is a key point about big scores. It is often not about your ability to make them, but rather being afforded the opportunity to make them.

Those opportunities are far more frequent these days, especially since four-day cricket was introduced to the county championship, first as a mix with three-day cricket in 1988 and then exclusively in 1993. When I was talking about that Glamorgan double-century record, I should perhaps have also mentioned that Alan Jones would probably hold the record had he played four-day cricket. As it was, he still managed to make one double century, 204 not out against Hampshire in 1980.

All my double centuries were made in four-day matches, although the first – against Leicestershire in 1995 – came after the first day of the match had been rained off and I then made 230 not out in a day.

Gooch recalls the opening game of that 1988 season, when he first encountered the county four-day stuff. It was against Kent at Chelmsford in late April. 'The Kent captain, Chris Cowdrey, won the toss and soon they were 200 for no wicket [through Mark Benson and Neil Taylor] and we were thinking: "We know what it's like to be Cambridge University now!"' he says. 'But they declared on 400-7 and we got 616. I got 275 and we won by eight wickets. The opportunity to get that sort of score doesn't come around very often.'

That score of 275 became an important driving force for Gooch. Indeed it occupied his mind when he made that 333 at Lord's.

'Micky Stewart [the England coach] gave me a bollocking when I got out for 333,' he says. 'I gave myself some room to try to drive, but I had run out of petrol. He said: "You should have got the record." I knew of [Garry] Sobers' 365 record but I can honestly say the only target I had was 300 because I'd scored that 275 against Kent at Chelmsford, when I had got myself out and kicked myself. I just wanted to get my 300. Afterwards, I have to say, I did wish I'd gone on – but it's not keeping me awake at night now!'

Although W. G. Grace can claim to being of granddaddy age (indeed he was opening the batting with his son W. G. Grace junior) when he made a triple century aged 48 years and 17 days (301 for Gloucestershire against Sussex at Bristol in 1896), some players start young in compiling their 'daddy hundreds', especially in India, where schools cricket is played over more than one day.

Take Sachin Tendulkar. He made his first century aged 12, but by the time he was 13 he had made a score of 276, and then aged 14 he made two 300s.

His appetite for runs was insatiable. It even got him in trouble on occasion. There is a famous story of the three-day Harris Shield semi-final in Mumbai in 1988 in which he was playing for Shardashram School against St Xavier's College.

In it Tendulkar put on 664 with Vinod Kambli, the left-hander who went on to play 17 Tests and 104 one-day internationals for India. But they were not supposed to have scored that many. Once the team total had passed 500 they had been urged to declare. Tendulkar was captain and had ignored the frantic arm-waving and shouting on the boundary's edge by assistant coach Laxman Chavan.

Tendulkar and Kambli just carried on batting. By lunch on the second day of the match Kambli was on 349 not out and Tendulkar 326 not out. But they knew they had disobeyed instructions. Their coach, Ramakant Achrekar, a man they both respected hugely, was not present, as he had to work that day.

At the interval Chavan told both of them that they should phone Achrekar. They did so and, upon answering, their coach asked the score. Over 700 was the reply. 'Declare!' screamed Achrekar, according to Vaibhav Purandare, an Indian author, in his book *Sachin Tendulkar: The Definitive Biography*.

'Sir, I'm batting on 349,' said Kambli, before the phone was passed to Tendulkar.

'Sir, Vinod needs one run to complete his 350, we'll declare as soon as he gets out,' Tendulkar said.

'Declare!' shouted Achrekar, and they did, but it was a rare example of Tendulkar, considered a cricketing deity long before the end of his career, upsetting anyone in India with his run-getting.

Later that year Tendulkar made his maiden first-class century, for Bombay against Gujarat. And the following year, at 16 years and 197 days, he became the youngest player to score a century in the Irani Trophy, when playing for the Rest of India against the Ranji Trophy champions, Delhi. It was during that game that Sunil Gavaskar gave him the famous Morrant fibreglass pads that became a trademark throughout his career.

And it was in that year that Tendulkar not only made his first 100 abroad, for Star Cricket club against Hayward's Heath in Sussex, but also made his Test debut, against Pakistan in Karachi, facing an attack of Imran Khan, Wasim Akram, Abdul Qadir and Waqar Younis, who was also making his debut.

'He took the elevator to the top,' said Kambli, 'whilst I took the stairs.'

But by 1993 they were on the top floor together in the

Indian Test team, with Kambli at No. 3 and Tendulkar at 4 in a series at home to England. In the third Test in Mumbai, Kambli made 224, still the highest Test score by an Indian against England.

In his next Test, against Zimbabwe, the left-handed Kambli made 227. Tendulkar was not to score his first Test double hundred for another six years, making 217 against New Zealand at Ahmedabad, having made his maiden first-class double century (204 not out) the previous year, for Mumbai against the touring Australians.

Tendulkar made eight double centuries in first-class cricket, the highest being his 248 not out in a Test against Bangladesh in 2004. But he did become the first batsman to score a double in a one-day international when making exactly 200 not out against South Africa in Gwalior in 2010.

Kambli's story is quite sad, with two very different paths being taken by the two schoolboy mates, emphasized sharply in late 2013 when Tendulkar announced his retirement amid an avalanche of paeans, while around the same time Kambli, at the age of just 41, was rushed to hospital in Mumbai having suffered a heart attack.

In his next two Tests after that Zimbabwe match, Kambli made two centuries against Sri Lanka. But after another 10 Tests he was dropped. That was in 1995, and he was aged just 23. Despite averaging 54.2, he never played another Test.

Cheteshwar Pujara has emerged as another Indian with a penchant for big scores. We have already mentioned his three first-class triple centuries, but at present he has made six in all, his first (306 not out) coming as a 12-year-old for Saurashtra Under 14s against Baroda Under 14s.

Murray Goodwin made two triple centuries, one of them famously when Sussex won their first county championship title against Leicestershire at Hove in 2003.

'I had never thought of getting 300,' he says. 'I had thought about double centuries [he has made nine including his two triples] but never 300.'

Sussex had begun the match needing just six points to secure the title. By the end of day one they had already secured three of them, having bowled out Leicestershire for just 179. Sussex were 137-1 with Goodwin 71 not out. The team needed to get to 300 to ensure that title.

'Before the day's play in the huddle I said: "Boys, I am going to have the attitude of being selfish today. I want to be the guy who scores the runs that win the championship,"' says Goodwin.

He did rather more than that. By the close of play Leicestershire were batting again and were two wickets down, with Sussex having declared on 614-4, with Goodwin having made 335 not out.

'I got 200,' he says. 'I was looking at 250, suddenly I start creeping up and eventually I make 300. "I can't believe I've just made 300," I thought. It didn't really sink in on the day.'

Goodwin's score was a club record, surpassing Duleepsinhji's 333 at Hove in 1930. 'I didn't know about the record,' he says. 'The crowd were clapping and I'm thinking: "What's going on?"'

I knew all about Emrys Davies' Glamorgan record of 287, though. When I had run out of steam in making 259, I had hoped that I would get another shot at Davies' record.

Luckily I did. I was pretty good at cashing in on the flatter pitches and the propitious circumstances of a match situation, but there was one occasion that I regret deeply: an occasion when I could have cashed in even more.

I could have scored 400 against Essex at Chelmsford in 2002, in the match mentioned earlier as regards my pusillanimity in facing one over at the end of day one.

We had bowled the home side out cheaply on the first day and by the end of the second day I was 235 not out. I could have batted until tea on the third day, but I made just 14 more and fell over to be lbw to the left-arm swing of Justin Bishop for 249.

My wonky knee was playing up by then, but still it was a huge opportunity missed.

On that second morning a young Essex batsman arrived at the ground and looked at the scoreboard. 'What a feeling that must be,' he thought as he looked at my score. I obviously did not know that at the time, but it was during the 2013/14 Ashes tour Down Under that a certain Alastair Cook told me that he had been to the Chelmsford ground that morning and those had been his thoughts.

It was some feeling too. To arrive at the ground with more than 100 to your name and plenty of time still to bat is truly heaven for any batsman. I was going to write 'stuff of dreams' there, but sleep and long innings do not always go well together.

It is always blithely assumed that a batsman sleeps like a baby after a long innings, but the truth is that the mind cannot rest after being so active for so long. You just end up playing the innings over and over in your mind. For those of us like myself who would get leg cramps at night, that would be another good reason why sleep was so elusive.

As Cook himself says: 'I always find it harder to sleep whenever I have scored runs. You just keep going through it in your head over and over again. For me, the buzz after a good innings makes sleep the last thing on my mind.'

His long-time partner for England, Andrew Strauss, certainly had problems the morning after the night before. He made 21 Test centuries, but on seven occasions he was not out overnight in a Test match with a century already to his name. On six of those occasions he did not score more than six runs the following morning.

When he made his highest score of 177 against New Zealand in Napier in 2008, an innings that basically saved his Test career after he had made a first-innings duck and looked set for the axe, he was 173 not out at the end of day three, but could only add another four runs the following morning.

In 2009 at Lord's he played one of his very best Test innings in making 161 against Australia to seize the advantage after Monty Panesar and James Anderson had somehow salvaged a draw in the first Test at Cardiff. But he was 161 not out at the end of the first day and was unable to go on the next day.

In Trinidad in 2009 against West Indies he was 139 not out at the end of day one, but could only add three more the next day to be out for 142.

In Durban in 2004 Strauss ended day three 132 not out but managed just four more on day four. On the same tour in Port Elizabeth he was 120 not out at the end of day two and only made six more.

And against West Indies at Lord's in 2012, he was 121 not out at the end of day two, and added just one more, but it was his first century after a worryingly barren spell that had lasted 25 innings without passing three figures.

The one exception to all this came just two innings later in 2012 at Trent Bridge, when he was 102 not out at the end of day two, and made a whopping 39 runs on day three, ending with 141.

I asked Strauss about this very obvious problem of not being able to kick on the day after, and he was admirably honest. 'The issues I had were really threefold,' he said. 'First there was the mental/physical tiredness after batting for the whole day before. Then there was the struggling to start again – I found that I was often fighting with myself to be patient, rather than going after the bowling. Finally there was the mental baggage of having done it a few times before. When these things become an issue, it becomes harder to overcome.

'I tried plenty of things to help overcome it – getting up early, having a long net session, getting up late, having no net session, having a few beers the night before, not having any beers the night before, lots of coffee, no coffee, etc., etc. . . . .

'Looking back, I just thought about it too much. One of the

great lessons in professional sport, I think, is not to try too hard. It never works!!'

Strauss has not been alone in that problem, though. It is interesting to look at some other top players in that regard. Strauss averaged just eight runs on those seven occasions when he was not out on a century overnight in Test cricket.

But, for instance, Jacques Kallis was in that position 14 times and only averaged 15 runs before being dismissed the next day. Shivnarine Chanderpaul was in that position five times, as was Mike Atherton, and they only averaged nine and seven runs before dismissal respectively.

If you look at the other end of the scale, you find that Brian Lara was not out on a century overnight 12 times and averaged 59 runs the next day. Mahela Jayawardene averaged 62 runs over 11 occasions, while Ricky Ponting averaged 62 as well, but on 12 occasions.

Strangely, I could never see why anyone could have a problem with this. For me the fear of failure was by far the worst part of batting: walking to the wicket without a run to your name and fearing that you might return quickly, still without a run to your name.

But in these situations there is no chance of that. You already have a century! The crowd will still applaud warmly even if you do not add many, or even any, to your overnight score. You can just play. It does not mean you can relax, but it just means that you can bat without the inevitable tension that the start of an innings brings.

But how do you carry on? How do you construct an innings that might go on for nearly two days? These are questions that I have often been asked, and, as with the conversion of fifties into hundreds, there is no secret formula.

In fact nothing changes. You just have to keep making good decisions for longer. That is what batting is essentially about.

As Graham Gooch says: 'It is not about going out on the

day playing your shots and it all fitting into place. It's about making tactical decisions in your jigsaw of a game on site, as it progresses.'

One of Gooch's most-heard mantras is that he coaches run-making not batting. 'Anyone can bat,' he says. 'It's about how you think about yourself, how you glean information about different conditions, how you concentrate for long periods. The important thing is knowing what you can do and knowing that method. That is one of Alastair Cook's greatest assets. He knew from the beginning. It took me a long while to work it out, for the penny to drop.'

Assessing the pitch, the bowler and the situation of the match, and then deciding how you are going to play, is key. 'All the little decisions are the difference between making runs and not – with planning beforehand,' he says.

Gooch cites the example of Cook's previously mentioned marvellous batting in the triumphant Test series in India in 2012, where Cook made three centuries – 176, 122 and 190 – and especially how he had decided to play the left-arm spin of Pragyan Ojha.

It sounds rather like the method employed by Gooch in the 1987 World Cup in India, where he made a match-winning 115 against the hosts in the semi-final by using the sweep shot continually against the spinners Maninder Singh and Ravi Shastri.

'As soon as Ojha tossed it up outside off stump Cook swept,' he says. 'He had worked out his way – that is the skill of run-making and making big scores.'

Indeed it is.

12

Nervous Nineties

I may have been flippant about being stuck on 296 at Colwyn Bay, but one should really treat the nervous nineties with more gravitas. They are an important and much-discussed part of the story of a century. There is a Wikipedia page all of its own about them, and there has even been a whole book on the subject, by Kersi Meher-Homji, with a foreword by Michael Slater, who, with nine, stands fourth in the list of those dismissed most times in the nineties in Test cricket.

The identities of the top three do rather indicate that we are dealing with a strange phenomenon here, though. All of them were dismissed on 10 occasions in the nineties, and they are Steve Waugh, Sachin Tendulkar and Rahul Dravid. They were three pretty decent players, and also three who possessed remarkable mental strength.

But Slater's record stands out because he only made 14 Test centuries. That is a poor conversion rate from nineties to hundreds. The West Indies' Alvin Kallicharran was not much better. He was dismissed in the nineties on eight occasions in Tests, and only went on to make 12 centuries.

Also in Tests Australia's Clem Hill was dismissed in the nineties six times and only made seven centuries (he scored 99, 98 and 97 in successive Test innings in 1902), Stephen Fleming floundered on the same number of occasions and only made nine centuries, while at the time of writing M. S. Dhoni has been out five times in the nineties and only made six centuries.

If you consider that Waugh, Tendulkar and Dravid made 32, 51 and 36 Test centuries respectively, then their failures in the nineties become more understandable.

But then Donald Bradman was not dismissed once in the nineties in Test cricket, going on to make a century on all 29 occasions on which he reached the nineties. His closest to this was his 89 against England at Lord's in 1948. He was, though, dismissed on six occasions in the nineties in first-class cricket, but never for 99. He made 98 against MCC at Lord's on that 1948 tour.

As mentioned earlier in the book, Bradman was also left stranded on 299 not out in a Test against South Africa, at Adelaide in 1932, when the No. 11 debutant Hugh 'Pud' Thurlow was run out as Bradman desperately tried to keep the strike. Interestingly, Thurlow never played another Test.

Bradman was also out for 191 against Hampshire in 1931 and for 192 playing for South Australia against Victoria in 1936/37.

Trying to get a batsman to admit to nerves in the nineties is difficult, however. You can even go back as far as Frank Woolley, who made 145 centuries between 1906 and 1938, but was also out 35 times in the nineties (as well as making 89 ducks) and have no joy in eliciting any sign of uneasiness at the approaching milestone. 'It was never a question of the nervous nineties, I was out many times forcing the game,' he said. 'We were never allowed to play for our averages in the Kent side or take half an hour to get the necessary runs.'

Take Andy Flower also, who was dismissed in the nineties five times in his first-class career, and, as we have already seen, only once in a Test match (when making 92 against India in 2002). 'I wouldn't admit to them because it never happened to me,' he says. 'Whenever I got near to 100 I disciplined myself to say: "Keep your processes exactly the same as they have been to get you into the nineties." It would be bloody stupid to change the processes that had been successful to that point. I wouldn't tighten up. I would just keep the same.

'Ideally I would always want to play in the way that suited the moment – either if the moment required a change of tempo or if it needed a certain momentum I tried to adapt to that. So adaptability and flexibility are so important. But taking it ball by ball is an absolutely vital skill if you want to make big scores. It is eminently achievable to do that, and your mind knows that and it can accept the setting of such small goals as managing one ball at a time and then slowly building towards something greater.'

Even Jason Gillespie, the former Australia fast bowler, who made an unlikely double century as nightwatchman against Bangladesh in Chittagong in 2006 when he had previously never made a hundred in any form of cricket, kept to a similarly simple plan in the nineties. 'If I've gotten 90 sticking to my game plan, why rush? Just keep batting as you have been and the runs will come,' he said to himself.

Gillespie described reaching the milestone, with a cover drive, as 'bizarre' and apparently was insufferable with his team-mates once he had reached his double.

'So, mate, tell me how you deal with the nerves when you're getting close to 200?' he would ask in jest. 'Oh, sorry, that's right, you've never been there before.' Bloody bowlers!

Flower and even Gillespie are right, though. The arrival of the nineties does usually bring with it the refrain of 'Keep playing as you were', which is clearly sound advice, but often I would just try to speed up, and get through them as quickly as possible. For someone so racked with the fear of failure at the start of an innings, I rarely experienced such a thing in the nineties.

I was dismissed five times in the nineties in first-class cricket. I can remember them all. I have already mentioned the first occasion. It was at Lord's when on 94 in 1992. I was brilliantly caught by Neil Williams out on the deep-square-leg boundary off John Emburey in a run chase. I never did score a century at the home of cricket. That still hurts.

The second was in the same season, 91 against Kent at Swansea. I was not bothered in the slightest. I played so poorly in that innings that I did not think I deserved a century. I was almost relieved to get out (I was stumped), it was that bad.

Next was 96 against Derbyshire in 1996. This was a killer. Derbyshire are the only county against whom I never scored a century. It was a wide half-volley from Phil de Freitas. I can still see it now. Why it ended up in wicketkeeper Karl Krikken's hands off an edge rather than at the cover boundary, I still do not know.

Then there was 90 against Warwickshire at Edgbaston the following season, again already mentioned. We followed on and I made 148 in the second innings. Shaun Pollock swore at me once. I must have played decently.

Finally there was 91 against Australia in Cardiff in 1997. I pulled a Michael Bevan long hop to mid-wicket purely because I could not read which way his chinamen were turning. This one turned away from me when I thought it would turn in.

My score left me 15 runs short of 1,000 for the season. Luckily I got them in the second innings, to become the first batsman to the milestone in the season (always a cherished honour), before succumbing again in exactly the same fashion to Bevan, this time for 79.

I never made 99. Not in professional cricket anyway. I did get dismissed twice for that figure, once playing for Welsh Schools against Ireland at Ynysygerwn (a game recalled recently by the Saracens rugby union club's director of rugby, Mark McCall, who was in the opposition that day) and secondly playing for Swansea University against Cardiff University on Llanrumney

Fields in Cardiff, where my excuse was that there was no scoreboard showing individual scores!

To be dismissed for 99 in a Test must be the most excruciating experience. Imagine if you did that and never went on to score a Test century, though.

Fate surely dealt its cruellest hand to England's Martyn Moxon in that regard. Early in his innings against New Zealand at Auckland in 1987/88 Moxon swept a three but the umpire gave them as leg byes. So when Ewen Chatfield dismissed him for 99, the feelings of regret ran deeper than for most.

In total, nine batsmen have made 99 in a Test but never gone on to make a century later in their careers, with Australia's Mitchell Starc the latest to do so, in 2013 against India in Mohali. He may yet make a century.

The others will not, though, even if Pakistan's Asim Kamal was still playing first-class cricket in 2014, having played his last Test in 2005. Along with Moxon and Kamal are Shane Warne, John Beck (New Zealand), Maqsood Ahmed (Pakistan), Dipak Patel (New Zealand), Rusi Surti (India) and England's Norman Yardley.

Only five players have been left 99 not out in Tests, but four of them made centuries at other points of their careers. Andrew Hall only made one Test hundred and Shaun Pollock made two, but Geoffrey Boycott and Steve Waugh made considerably more.

So the most unlucky was probably England's Alex Tudor, whose only Test fifty was a 99 not out as nightwatchman against New Zealand in 1999.

Mind you, Waugh's was an interesting tale. It came in the fifth Ashes Test in Perth in 1995 and he was left stranded when his brother Mark, who was acting as a runner for Craig McDermott, was run out. Steve sent Mark back but it soon became obvious that he was not going to make it. 'Watching the scene unfold was harder to take than being told that Santa Claus wasn't real,' said Steve.

In a rage, he stormed into the dressing room and screamed: 'Look out, the helmet's coming!' It hit a door frame and rolled into the shower room.

He couldn't sleep that night. 'Why didn't I take that easy single to wide mid-off?' he was asking himself, or 'How come I smashed that long hop straight to point? Why didn't I just go over the infield on 99?'

In Tests only two players have made 199 not out – Andy Flower and Kumar Sangakkara. Flower's came against South Africa in Harare in 2011, and he had already made 142 in Zimbabwe's first innings before they followed on.

He was left with last man Doug Hondo. Nursing a tail-ender through is always a tricky business. How much strike do you allow him? How much do you think you can allow him? Do you just play normally and take every run on offer, with fields inevitably set back to give you an easy single in order to get at the tail-ender? For instance, Steve Waugh simply took every run on offer.

Here Flower took a single off the fourth ball of Andre Nel's over. Mind you, Hondo had just faced the whole of the previous over from Jacques Kallis and had indeed hit the fifth ball for four. Should he have played some bigger shots or manipulated the strike better before that? There are clearly a few moments that still stick with Flower, and you can understand why. Test match double centuries do not grow on trees.

'I left him two balls to face,' says Flower somewhat ruefully. 'I thought he could do it. But I had the opportunity to get to that 200 if I had milked the strike better and played a few bigger shots. It was a pity. I would have loved a 200 there.'

Only one batsman has made 299 not out in Tests, as mentioned before: Donald Bradman. Seven batsmen have been dismissed for 199 – Mudassar Nazar, Mohammad Azharuddin, Matthew Elliott, Sanath Jayasuriya, Steve Waugh, Younis Khan and Ian Bell – but only one has been out for 299: New Zealand's Martin

Crowe against Sri Lanka in 1991. 'It's a bit like climbing Everest and pulling a hamstring in the last stride,' he memorably said.

Mike Powell is the only other batsman to have been out for 299 in first-class cricket, although Worcestershire's Daryl Mitchell was out for 298 against Somerset in 2009.

As previously mentioned, Powell scored 299 for Glamorgan against Gloucestershire at Cheltenham in 2006, out pushing forward at left-arm spinner Ian Fisher and edging behind. Powell is a good friend of mine, and it looked as if that day he was going to break my Glamorgan record of 309 not out. I was covering an England Test at Old Trafford that day, and the ribbing in the press box began early, as it was decided that my record was about to go.

If the truth be told I had given it up when I received a text message from a friend at the ground to say that Powell had been dismissed for 299. My feelings? Mixed, if I am totally truthful. I said to him afterwards that if anyone was going to beat my record, then I would have been happy for it to have been him, but I am also very proud of my record and would obviously like to keep it for as long as possible.

Powell was actually out to a good delivery from Fisher that turned and bounced. He admits that he was probably thinking more about my record than the passing of 300. 'The field was in and I always thought that I would get a bad ball to put away to get 300,' he says.

Does he have any regrets? 'Yes, it would have been nice to get it,' he says.

The triple hundred or my record? 'The triple hundred,' he says. 'It would have been nice to have been out for 302. You were a better player than me so it is right that you have the record.'

That is very kind, but there have also been a lot of better players than me who have batted for Glamorgan.

Nobody has been dismissed for 399 in first-class cricket, although Naved Latif made 394 in a first-class match in Pakistan in 2000, and Stephen Cook, son of Jimmy, did make 390 for the Lions against the Warriors in a South African domestic match in 2009.

But how about being out for 499? That is what happened to Hanif Mohammad, of course, in 1959 for Karachi against Bahawalpur in the Quaid-e-Azam Trophy semi-final, still the second-highest first-class score, behind Brian Lara's 501 not out.

In 2009, fifty years after the innings, the *Guardian* published a fascinating first-person account of it by Hanif.

'By the end of the second day I was nearing a triple and we had a rest day,' he said. 'In the evening Wazir, the captain [and Hanif's brother], told me I was in sight of Don Bradman's first-class record. We used to call Wazir "Wisden" because he knew all records. I had no idea what the record was and when he told me it was 452 [Bradman made 452 not out for New South Wales against Queensland in 1930], I just laughed and said it's too far away. I was really tired but both Wazir and my mother insisted I push for it. Wazir had my body massaged with olive oil that night, ensured I got proper rest and basically ordered me to go for the record.

'Concentration had never been a problem – it came naturally. I played only one lofted shot in the innings, a straight drive for four – and I broke Bradman's record with an on-driven boundary, a small, appreciative crowd there to cheer it.

'The end was unfortunate because it came from a scoreboard error. There were two balls left of the third day and the manually operated scoreboard showed I was on 496. I wanted to get to 500 so Wazir could declare. I played a ball out to point where there was a misfield so I thought I'd chance the second, which would leave me needing two off the day's last ball to get 500.

'But the fielder gathered it, threw back to the keeper's end, and I was short by a yard and a half. I thought I was gone for 497, but as I walked back the scoreboard showed 499. They had been a little slow and hadn't updated my score when I looked initially! I would never have pushed so hard if I knew I was on 498 and not 496. It was hugely irritating for a while but when telegrams and messages came from all over the world, including one from Sir Bradman, I got over it – 499 is better than most scores!'

Goodness, that must be frustrating. It is little surprise that when Lara made his 501 not out in 1994, Hanif, despite calling Lara to extend his congratulations and make sure there was no ill feeling towards the first man to 500, declared: 'Those damn fool scorers got it wrong.'

The saddest near-miss I have seen was Mike Atherton's 99 against Australia at Lord's in 1993 when he was run out. Atherton never did score a century at Lord's, and, even if he has some illustrious company in his absence from the honours board there, including four of the leading run scorers in Test cricket in Sachin Tendulkar, Ricky Ponting, Jacques Kallis and Brian Lara (Rahul Dravid is the other in the top five, but he scored 103 not out at Lord's in 2011), this was a horrible cock-up. Allan Border was bowling his very friendly left-arm spin, for goodness' sake!

The sight of Atherton, having slipped, crawling down the pitch as wicketkeeper Ian Healy took the bails off was a study in cruelty. Little surprise that that photograph adorns the front of Meher-Homji's book. Nothing like it quite captures the anguish of a batsman denied the thrill of a century.

I can recall watching it on television and the words of the commentator. 'Oh tragedy, tragedy!' said Tony Lewis. Atherton had been on 97 when he hit the ball from Border towards deep mid-wicket. His partner was Mike Gatting, who immediately presumed the ball had gone for four.

Let us allow Atherton to take up the story in his auto-biography, written in 2002. 'Mike Gatting was jogging the runs but I knew I had not timed the flick perfectly,' he said. '"You'll have to run hard Gatt," I hissed as we crossed. As Merv Hughes gathered the ball under the grandstand Gatting called me for the third run that would have brought up my 100, and then he sent me back. I was batting in half rubbers and slipped on the lush grass next to the cut strip. I tried to make my ground and slipped again and was still grovelling yards short when Ian Healy gathered in the throw and broke the stumps. Run out on 99, England v Australia at Lord's – a nightmare.'

Atherton stormed off and smashed his bat against the dressing-room door. 'I was inconsolable,' he wrote.

This is his take now. 'Gatt thought it was going to go for four,' he told me. 'I was aware that I hadn't quite middled it so we had to run hard. I turned and got sent back wearing half spikes and half rubbers. I don't think about it now, though. I never think about my career actually, but in a Lord's Test against Australia I suppose it would have been nice to have got a hundred.'

Atherton has mellowed, unsurprisingly given that he has been so successful in his second career in journalism, where he has won award after award.

He was out five times in the nineties in Test cricket, including another 99, against South Africa at Headingley a year later in 1994. But that came just after the famous 'dirt-in-the-pocket' affair, during which he came under intense pressure as England captain. To score 99 after that was a triumph.

He was caught-and-bowled by Brian McMillan. 'Maybe I took the ball a bit early,' he says. 'I was probably a bit too keen to put bat on ball, and maybe it was an example of thinking ahead and not just focusing on the ball, doing something you might not normally do. Normally I played the ball quite late.'

Notice that there is no mention of nerves. 'At Lord's I slipped, it was not nerves,' he says. 'I had played quite easily through the nineties, if I remember. I don't know about nervous but the hard thing is to stay in the moment and not think ahead about getting the hundred and how nice it would be. The key thing for a batsman is to stay in the moment – not worry about what's gone on and what's coming. It is not necessarily about being nervous but the mind can drift, and you can lose focus on just the ball coming down. It is not nerves but it can have the same effect.'

If one player has confessed to the nervous nineties, it is Graham Gooch, who was run out on 99 from the last ball before tea against Australia in Melbourne in 1980.

'I was well aware what my score was,' he has written. 'Yes, that time I must admit to the nervous nineties. I pushed it towards mid-on. Kim Hughes came round and fielded it, and I know I'm struggling. I was out by about six inches. I glumly led them all into tea. Back in, I just said to [Mike] Brearley [captain] "Spot the deliberate mistake?" Ian Chappell, the Australian captain, looked at me as though I had a screw loose. "What, don't you like scoring centuries or something?"'

Gooch was actually out in the nineties 19 times in his first-class career, but only once more in a Test (93 versus Pakistan in 1987). He had learnt a lesson.

'The skill is just to let it come,' he says to me now. 'But ninety is a watershed and you are within grasping distance. Players do get nervous and try to force it. Ninety-nine is only one short of the magical figure with which records are logged, so really it should be no big deal, for you've obviously batted well.'

And so that was his mantra. 'As I grew older and wiser down the years any actual nervousness in the nineties was not a factor at all,' he says. 'Even if I was on 89, I would not have given a century a thought or consideration. I would just say: "Steady, boy, don't cock it up now, don't do anything silly or hasty, just let it come, let it come."'

If only it was as simple as the advice once offered to Sachin Tendulkar by his son. In 2007 Tendulkar had been out six times in the nineties in one-day internationals, and so his son Arjun said to him: 'Next time you are on 94, just hit a six.'

Ah, the 'grand manner', as we have mentioned before. I reached a century once with a six, off a good friend of mine, the

Surrey and Durham off-spinner James Boiling. It was at Neath (when Boiling was playing for Surrey) and the ball hit the wall of the swimming pool behind the bowler's arm. It never happened again, nor was it likely to.

That 'grand manner' is fairly common actually, with Gary Ballance reaching his maiden Test century for England in that way during the 2014 summer against Sri Lanka, but some obviously stand out more than others. As a personal favourite I would pick Viv Richards reaching his 100th hundred with a six, hitting Greg Matthews over long-on at the Sydney Cricket Ground against New South Wales in 1988.

Steve Waugh also became the first man to get to a Test century with back-to-back sixes against Pakistan in 2002. That was his 28th Test century; the first, though, had been anything but as straightforward. 'It's amazing how that elusive first Test hundred somehow equates to a graduation,' he has said. 'Until it is achieved a batsman can't quite be deemed the "genuine article". It's why you see extreme emotions from players when they complete their "rite of passage". I would come to know all this only too well.'

Indeed he did. He made his Test debut in 1985, but did not make his first Test century until 1989 in his 27th Test. Of the English batsmen considered to have taken an awfully long time to register their first Test century, Mark Ramprakash made his debut in 1991 and made his first century in his 22nd Test, in 1998, and Mike Gatting debuted in 1978 and made his first century in 1984 in his 31st Test.

That is nothing, though, compared to India's Anil Kumble, whose first Test century came in his 118th Test. Granted, his forte was leg-spin bowling, but still that is some wait.

Next on the list is Sri Lanka's Chaminda Vaas, whose first century came in his 97th Test. He is followed by other bowlers, Harbhajan Singh, Jason Gillespie, Heath Streak, Shaun Pollock and Daniel Vettori. Then comes a wicketkeeper, Ian Healy, before the first specialist batsman, Zimbabwe's Alistair Campbell, who scored his first century in his 47th Test.

There was a time when Waugh thought he would never get a Test century. He told team-mate Graeme Wood in Pakistan in 1988: 'I'm not sure I'm ever going to score a Test hundred. I just can't seem to make the breakthrough with the bat.'

'You'll get there one day,' said Wood. 'You'll get a hundred and it will all seem worthwhile. You'll look back on this time and wonder why you were worrying so much.'

It was sage advice. Waugh's first hundred did indeed come, at Headingley in 1989. He reached 99. 'I was so dry in the mouth my breathing was shallow, and all I could think of was: *"don't stuff it up now! Just get bat on ball"*. If I'd got out then I may never have got a Test hundred, because the insecurity and self-doubt I was carrying had accumulated to such an extent that getting a century wasn't a target but a barrier.

'The shot that finally got me there was one I played on automatic pilot, a back-foot push out to the deep-cover fieldsman, who for some unknown reason wasn't in the circle sweating on a single. Absolute joy and relief swept over me. I was so glad I had the baggy green on and not a helmet.'

It is good evidence of how the nineties can become a mental barrier. 'I went through a period in club cricket in Perth where I got out in the nineties three times,' says Murray Goodwin. 'You don't get a huge amount of bats out there, so I made a bit of an issue of it. "Why am I getting out?" I kept asking myself. I had two stages in my career, one where I was getting past 50 and then not getting past 70, then stage two where I was getting nineties. It was not nerves. I was trying to be too careful, putting myself under pressure. Sometimes you relax too much then you go the other way and tighten up too much and end up trying too hard.'

The mindset of Andrew Strauss when nearing a Test century on debut at Lord's against New Zealand also tells a good story. 'It takes me 10 overs to get from 80 to 90 and I am getting edgy,' he wrote in his autobiography. 'I am frustrated about scoring slowly and the thought of getting a hundred on debut is starting to consume me. I am thinking too much about the final result, getting a hundred, and not enough about the process, getting 10 runs. I resolve to play every ball on its merits, but the adrenalin is flowing.'

Then there is the lucky four mentioned earlier in the book off Chris Martin.

'I am now on 96,' wrote Strauss. 'It has taken an age to get the last six runs and I can feel the anticipation in the crowd. Everyone seems to know that I am going through a difficult patch and is willing me to get through it. I, on the other hand, am hating the pressure. The emphasis has changed from he could get a hundred to he should get a hundred, and that makes things more difficult. It is now a battle with myself and my emotions.'

Mark Butcher was his partner. 'Keep watching the ball, Straussy,' he said. 'In a minute he is going to bowl you a wide one, and you are going to smack it through the covers for four. Be patient.'

Martin runs in, it is wide and Strauss smacks it through the covers. 'In one moment, all the tension, adrenalin, fear and nerves leave my body, to be replaced by pure unadulterated joy,' he wrote. 'I raise my bat to my team-mates, all of whom are on the balcony cheering me on. I look around the ground. Everyone is on their feet cheering. The giant scoreboard displays a message: "Congratulations Andrew Strauss on scoring 100 on debut." I cannot believe this is happening to me.'

That didn't actually sound like much fun until the moment of exhilaration, but the nineties can be fun. When England played West Indies at Sabina Park in 1990 Allan Lamb received applause for his century, but then the scoreboard operators suddenly changed his score back to 99. 'No problem,' said Lamb to himself. The next ball he hit for four. 'Jeez, that's two centuries in one day, the last one the fastest in Test history,' he said to his partner, Robin Smith.

Be careful about taking the mick out of the subject of the nineties, however. It once got very nasty between Michael Slater and Ricky Ponting on this very matter. Inevitably drink was involved, even though it was in Pakistan, at the American Club in Karachi.

More in jest than anything Ponting started by saying that Slater would always get out in the nineties because he started slogging when he got there. That did not go down well with Slater, who could be very highly strung at times. Then it all got a bit serious, with Steve Waugh trying to intervene before a fight could break out and being called a 'coward' by Slater for his troubles. It was deemed so serious in the end that Slater wrote a letter of apology the next day.

The best story I have heard about the nineties, nervous or otherwise? Not my own of being stranded for three nights on 99 not out at Liverpool in 1997 while the rain abated (I did get the century, and then some 'throw-ups' as a game was contrived), but that of Gerald Crutchley in the 1912 Varsity Match.

The Oxford University batsman made 99 not out on the first day before running out of partners and then discovering that he had been batting with measles. The story goes that his temperature rose by at least two degrees during the innings.

Now if a man ever deserved a century, it was Crutchley. And that is coming from a Cambridge man too. Mind you, Cambridge did win the match by three wickets, so all ended well.

13

Celebration Time

I shouldn't say this really, but I found it quite funny. In the summer of 2011 India came to England. At every Test match some poor sod was briefed to write the Tendulkar piece. That was the piece glorifying Sachin Tendulkar's century that would take him to 100 centuries in international cricket.

But it did not happen. He made 91 in the final Test at the Oval, but that was it. He made 94 that November in a Test against West Indies in Mumbai, but it was not until the following March that he finally made the 100th century, against Bangladesh in Dhaka, just over a year after his previous hundred, against South Africa in the World Cup in Nagpur. And that was it. He finished his magnificent career with 51 Test centuries and 49 in one-day internationals.

It always seemed a rather contrived statistic to me. Where else are first-class and one-day centuries combined? But it also served as a pointed reminder of how important centuries are and how we so like to celebrate them.

There was nothing wrong with venerating Tendulkar. Indeed

he was constantly deified in his own country. 'Countdown to God's 100 hundreds' was one of the typical banners paraded at games until he did achieve the feat.

He was simply the greatest batsman I have seen. Little wonder, as mentioned earlier, that Sir Donald Bradman once famously observed that, of all modern batsmen, Tendulkar reminded him most of himself. 'He plays much the same as I played,' he said.

I only played against Tendulkar once. It was the week after he had scored his maiden Test century in 1990. We were playing a three-day match against the tourists at Swansea.

And to stare greatness, if only nascent greatness at the time, straight in the eye for the first time was an unforgettable experience. It took me only one small incident to realize that was the case.

It became the subject of one of my Final Whistle columns for the *Daily Telegraph*. 'At the fall of their fourth wicket a tiny, impossibly young-looking fellow with a curly mop of hair poking out of his helmet had come to the crease,' I wrote. 'So this was the kid they had all been talking about; the kid who had scored his first Test century at Old Trafford barely a week before.

'Being a sad devotee of the game and especially its technical nuances, I studied him closely. He was remarkably small, smaller even than our own Tony Cottey. He carried his bat as if it were a railway sleeper. It was clearly too heavy. It also looked too tall, given that he gripped it at the lowest point of its handle. And he wore those tightly rounded, ultra-soft polythene pads that were considered highly untrendy at the time.

'But within minutes he had played one of the greatest shots I had ever seen. Bowling for us was a chap called Hamish Anthony, an Antiguan of dubious ability to be a high-class overseas player, but of no little pace. He bowled a decent good-length ball on about middle and off stumps. It should have been defended back down the pitch. Instead the little fellow was up on his toes on the back foot and punching the ball, with an impossibly high elbow and no follow through, back past Anthony for four. Standing in the gully, I gasped audibly, to some of my team-mates' chagrin, it must be said. Sachin Tendulkar had announced himself.'

He certainly had. Sadly, he only made 68 that day at Swansea, so I never did get to be on the field for one of his 81 first-class centuries (the same number as Sunil Gavaskar, the man who gave him those pads).

So what was the best century I have seen? It is a ridiculous question really, but I am pretty certain that the finest century in any match in which I played was made by Matthew Maynard at Taunton in 1997 in the match in which Glamorgan clinched the county championship title.

Maynard made 142 and there was not one single in passing his century off just 89 balls. The stakes were high – Glamorgan had not won a championship for 28 years – rain had already taken time out of the game and the light was poor.

These were the days when there was a five-light system attached to each county scoreboard. One light meant that the light was deteriorating, three probably meant that it was time to go off. Five was simply Stygian.

There were five lights on for most of Maynard's innings, and Somerset's Andy Caddick was in fine form, with his outswinger arcing menacingly. Maynard's riposte? He kept hitting Caddick through mid-on for four. It was a quite remarkable innings in the circumstances.

Maynard admits that it was his best innings. 'It was,' he says. 'One because of the conditions and, two, the need to make a big score – the weather was closing in, Kent [who finished second, only four points behind Glamorgan] were on the way to beating Surrey. It was one of the few instances in your career when you are in that bubble and everything happens slowly. By the bubble I mean that your concentration is 100 per cent pure. You are so focused that it does not matter what else is going on.'

Interestingly given his comments earlier in this book about the importance, or relative lack of it, of one-day centuries, Maynard rates a one-day century by our colleague Hugh Morris as one of the finest he has seen.

Morris made 136 not out against Kent in 1996 in a Benson & Hedges Cup match, hitting his 100 off just 68 balls. It was the final group game and we not only needed to win but win quickly. In fact we needed to make 209 in 38.4 overs. As it was, we got there in 32.4 for the loss of just two wickets (I made a sedate 60).

If you think that South Africa's AB de Villiers hit a one-day international century off just 31 balls against West Indies shortly before this book went to print, breaking Corey Anderson's record (36 balls for New Zealand against the same opponents the previous year), then it may not sound that spectacular, but Maynard says: 'It is still the best innings I have ever seen in one-day cricket.'

That is some praise, and it was some display of clean hitting from the left-handed Morris, who, at earlier times in his career, could get a little bogged down at the start of a one-day innings (not that I was any better, mind!). Here he was magnificently positive from the off, and the result was quite stunning.

As I put the finishing touches to this book, in November 2014, Viv Richards' long-standing record of fastest Test century, 56 balls against England in Antigua in 1986, was equalled by Misbah-ul-Haq of Pakistan, against Australia in Abu Dhabi. Like Azhar Ali, he had also scored a century in the first innings, making it only the second time two team-mates had each scored centuries in both innings of a Test, Ian and Greg Chappell having achieved that feat 40 years previously.

Recently a book called *Masterly Batting* was published by Patrick Ferriday and Dave Wilson. It attempted to unearth the 100 greatest Test centuries, another almost impossible task. They used 10 key measuring sticks: size of innings, conditions, bowling strength, percentage of team total, chances, speed, series impact, match impact, intangibles (such as injury to the batsman) and compatibility (of, say, the bowling attack to the conditions). They then weighted those factors and determined that conditions and bowling strength should be given the most weight.

And the result? It was calculated that Graham Gooch's 154 not out against West Indies at Headingley in 1991 was the No. 1 Test century. I have no quibble with that, as I revealed earlier in this tome. It was against an attack of Curtly Ambrose, Patrick Patterson, Courtney Walsh and Malcolm Marshall, a truly fearsome foursome, on a pitch that was offering plenty of assistance to them. And England won, as Gooch made his second-innings undefeated 154 out of a total of just 252. Even he says: 'It was my best innings in the context of the game and the opposition.'

But I am sure that there will be plenty who do quibble about that conclusion. In second place was Brian Lara's 153 not out against Australia in Barbados in 1999. And in third was Graeme Smith's 154 not out against England in Birmingham in 2008. As I said much earlier, that is the finest innings I have reported upon, I think, even if it is a Test that has probably become better known for precipitating the resignation of Michael Vaughan as England captain.

When I talk to him about great centuries, Gooch mentions an innings played away from the international game, but one that I have heard much about. It was by Javed Miandad for Glamorgan against Essex at Colchester in 1981. 'It is probably the most brilliant innings I have ever witnessed,' says Gooch.

Miandad scored an unbeaten 200 out of Glamorgan's 311 in a tense run chase, with only three other players getting to double figures. The ball was turning square with David Acfield and Ray East bowling.

But Miandad used his wristy strokes (with hands always well apart on the bat) and superb running between the wickets to farm the strike so successfully that No. 9 batsman Robin Hobbs was out first ball, but 43 had been added before he was. Agonizingly, last man Simon Daniels was lbw to John Lever and Glamorgan lost by 13 runs.

For sheer drama nothing can surely beat Steve Waugh's last-ball-of-the-second-day Ashes century at Sydney in 2002/03. It was an electric moment. Little wonder that Waugh entitled the chapter about it in his autobiography 'The Perfect Day'.

Up until that Test it had actually been a strange time for Waugh. Even though he had made 77 in the previous Test, and indeed only seven innings had passed since a century against Pakistan, there were still calls for his head: for him to be sacked as captain and dropped from the side. But this was a Test on his home ground, his 156th, equalling Allan Border's record. He went on to play another 12, his 168 the same number as Ricky Ponting. Only Sachin Tendulkar, with 200, has played more.

As he waited to bat just before tea Waugh admitted that he had 'a million thoughts racing around in my head'. But when Justin Langer was out to Andrew Caddick, Waugh arrived at the crease to huge applause.

He was nine not out at tea, and by the time the last over of the day was to be bowled by off-spinner Richard Dawson, he was on 95. Already an hour earlier there had been much celebration from the full house of 42,000 when he had reached 69, passing 10,000 runs in Tests, only the third player after Border and Sunil Gavaskar to have done so.

Eight others – Kumar Sangakkara, Shivnarine Chanderpaul, Mahela Jayawardene, Brian Lara, Rahul Dravid, Jacques Kallis, Ponting and Tendulkar – have since passed that mark.

In the previous over Waugh had very nearly been run out. Many players might have shut up shop for the evening and come back the next morning to reach the milestone. But not Waugh. He was intent on ensuring that there was an ending to the day that nobody would ever forget.

From the first three balls he did not score. Then to the fourth he improvised a shot through the off side that squirted off the outside edge out towards the boundary. He ran three.

Two balls remaining and, with Waugh on 98, his partner, Adam

Gilchrist, was facing. He simply had to get a single. Thankfully he did, with the crowd roaring their appreciation.

This was it. One ball. Two runs required. 'Do you write your own scripts these days?' asked wicketkeeper Alec Stewart from behind the stumps.

The England captain, Nasser Hussain, did nothing to diffuse the tension. He made Waugh wait and wait, talking to his bowler, Dawson, while carefully moving his field. All the while Waugh wiped his face with his famous red cloth.

Hussain and Dawson thought that Waugh would attempt a sweep/slog over the leg side. The plan was for Dawson to bowl the ball straight and quick.

That was what he did. Well, actually, he gave Waugh about two inches of width outside off stump. It was barely any width at all if the truth be told. Most batsmen would have defended it.

Not Waugh. He was on to it like a flash. 'I just released the arms and locked in the wrists,' he said. And the ball sped to the cover boundary amid a cacophony of noise and elation. Waugh had made his 29th Test century, equalling Donald Bradman's number. It was pure theatre.

Sometimes the equalling of a record can be deemed more important than its passing. That was certainly the case with Jack Hobbs during the summer of 1925, as he strove to equal W. G. Grace's record of 126 centuries. Even though he was 42 years old then and had begun the season on 113 centuries, and had never previously made more than 11 in one season, the scrutiny was intense. 'I felt that every eye in England was on me,' Hobbs said. 'I began to get harassed.'

But for him it was beating the record that counted more. 'To me the 127th was – and is – the more important,' he said.

One short, having made 12 centuries that season, the runs dried up. Well, actually he went nearly a month without a century, which was nine innings in those days.

But eventually, as mentioned previously when talking about

luck and superstition, Hobbs went to Somerset and equalled Grace's record. And guess what? He passed the record in the second innings of the match there. London buses and all that.

He ended up with 16 centuries that season, his best, and only two short of Denis Compton's record of 18 in a season in 1947. Wally Hammond made 15 in 1938 and Herbert Sutcliffe 14 in 1932, but 13 in a season has been achieved on 12 occasions, including by Geoffrey Boycott in 1971.

Graham Gooch made 12 in 1990, the year in which my Glamorgan colleague Hugh Morris also made 10. Mark Ramprakash made 10 in two separate seasons – 1995 and 2007. Me? Seven was my best, in two successive seasons, 1996 and 1997. Small fry.

After that Sydney epic, Steve Waugh made eight more first-class centuries in his career, including three more in Tests, ending his career with a tally of 79. But that was two behind his brother, Mark. Like Sachin Tendulkar and Sunil Gavaskar, Mark made 81 centuries in first-class cricket. Above those three on 81, there are 41 players with more centuries.

And there are 25 players who have made 100 hundreds, the ultimate achievement in century-making. They are:

W. G. Grace, Tom Hayward, Jack Hobbs, Philip Mead, Patsy Hendren, Frank Woolley, Herbert Sutcliffe, Ernest Tyldesley, Wally Hammond, Andrew Sandham, Donald Bradman, Les Ames (the only wicketkeeper to have done so), Len Hutton, Denis Compton, Tom Graveney, Colin Cowdrey, John Edrich, Geoffrey Boycott, Glenn Turner, Zaheer Abbas, Dennis Amiss, Viv Richards, Graham Gooch, Graeme Hick and Mark Ramprakash.

Grace was the first to 100 hundreds in 1895 at the age of 47, and Ramprakash will surely be the last to reach that remarkable milestone. You look on Cricinfo for the list of century-makers in first-class cricket and they stop the names at 75. There is no current cricketer on there.

The players of today simply do not have enough innings. For instance, in 2008 Ramprakash played just 23 first-class innings. In 1907 Hobbs had 63.

In 1965 David Green also had 63 first-class innings, and made over 2,000 runs without making a century. And between 1961 and 1968 my hero, Alan Jones, never had fewer than 50 first-class innings a season. And, of course, he passed 1,000 runs on all those occasions. Indeed Jones passed 1,000 runs for 23 consecutive English (and Welsh!) seasons between 1961 and 1983 before his retirement. Only 10 players have made 1,000 runs in more seasons, with Grace and Woolley topping the list with 28.

So maybe this was why there was so much fuss in 2008 about Ramprakash's ascent to the 100 summit. At the time it did seem as if it took him an awfully long time making the leap from 99 to 100. There was some talk of an England recall, even though he had not played Test cricket since 2002, and that resurfaced again in 2009 when England realized they needed to drop Ravi Bopara for the final Test at the Oval (Jonathan Trott came in and did rather well instead).

As Kevin Pietersen said in an interview on 23 July that year: 'It's interesting that Ramprakash scored his 99th first-class hundred in early May and he's still waiting. Since then I've seen him abuse the television camera when he's walked off in a game and there are reports that he's lost the plot big style. People have always said he's had a problem dealing with pressure. The England set-up were very interested to see how quickly he was going to get to 100 hundreds. All of the pressure and media were on him and that's almost the same kind of spotlight you get in international cricket. You have a look at his results since the media descended and it shows the character, doesn't it? I don't know him at all, but it's very interesting to see how people handle the pressure when it's on.'

Pretty scathing stuff. Ramps was bottling it, apparently. And I will admit that I was of that mind as well at the time. But the truth is that the wait was not that long. It took three months, but those three months were not taken up exclusively by first-class cricket. There was a lot of Twenty20 in that period.

As Ramprakash pointed out, probably with just a little too much self-justification to be honest, in the introduction to his book *Strictly Me*, he usually had seven innings between hundreds. Here it was 10. Wally Hammond had 27 for his 100th, Ramprakash says.

Ramprakash's 99th was in early May and his 100th in early August against Yorkshire at Headingley (his first had also been against Yorkshire in 1989), but the whole of June had indeed been taken up by Twenty20 and in July he missed one match because of food poisoning.

Ramprakash's wait was certainly nothing compared with Surrey's Hayward, who took 47 innings to go from 99 to 100 over the 1912 and 1913 seasons. It is a huge thing, as even Jack Hobbs showed.

Hobbs made his 100th hundred at Bath in 1923. But he had made a duck in the first innings, and then been involved in two run-outs in the morning – he was usually a good runner apparently – but he was then further hampered by the fact that the scoreboard was not showing individual scores.

So when he was on 94 his colleague Herbert Strudwick, the Surrey wicketkeeper, signalled his score from alongside the scorers' tent by putting up six fingers. 'Then I suddenly grasped the astonishing situation,' Hobbs said. 'I became anxious, desperately anxious. It is not just six runs between 94 and 100. It is a terribly long journey, believe me.'

For Ramprakash there was the added problem of a broken bat. He had passed 2,000 runs in successive seasons with a bat given to him by Shane Warne. But it broke after he got his 99th century, against Sussex at Hove in May. Being very particular about his bats, Ramprakash tried five different bats after that but never felt totally comfortable with any of them.

On the morning of the match against Yorkshire, he was having throw-downs with his team-mate Scott Newman. He picked up one of Newman's bats, and although it was lighter than the ones he was used to, he quite liked it. Newman suggested he use it. Ramprakash did, and the century that he so craved arrived.

Ramprakash's 100th hundred at Headingley was, of course, not quite the most momentous passing of that milestone on that ground. That belongs to Geoffrey Boycott and his century there in August 1977 in an Ashes Test. His on-driven four off the medium pace of Greg Chappell, with non-striker Graham Roope leaping out of the way to avoid the ball, is an image that has endured and will surely continue to do so.

'I can see it now in slow motion,' wrote Boycott. 'I saw it then with an amazing amount of clarity and something approaching elation. As soon as it left his hand I knew I was going to hit it and I knew where I was going to hit it. Long before it pitched I knew exactly what I was going to do, as though I was standing outside myself, watching myself play the shot. It was a fantastic feeling. As soon as I struck it I lifted the bat high in the air. In the millisecond that followed I realised what it all meant and my arms folded over my head.

'Somehow, I was destined to get a century that day. It was my karma. It must have been written by someone, somewhere before I went in to bat. There is no other explanation for the memory and magic of it.'

Boycott was the 18th batsman to pass the milestone and the first to do so in a Test match. On his home ground too!

Zaheer Abbas is the only other player to have made his 100th hundred in a Test match, when making 215 against India in Lahore in 1982.

When Boycott struck that four, the whole of Yorkshire seemed to appear on the field to congratulate him. He was enveloped, and when the crowd dispersed back to the boundary's edge, it was revealed that Boycott's cap had been stolen.

On a much smaller scale, I have a similar story of having my bat stolen when Glamorgan won the county championship at Taunton in 1997. With a large crowd having swarmed on and first having lifted me on their shoulders and then dropped me unceremoniously, I was also relieved of a stump that I had grabbed for my team-mate Adrian Dale.

So I was left with only the one stump I had taken for myself as a souvenir as I made my way back to the changing rooms. Standing there at the bottom of the Taunton stairs when I arrived, though, was Dale, with a stump in his hand! His brother, a policeman, had taken it from a fleeing fan!

He had not got my bat for me, however, and I had to wait until a plea in the local Cardiff newspaper reaped reward with a sheepish individual appearing at Sophia Gardens one day to return it.

Boycott did not have to wait so long. He refused to continue his innings until his cap was returned. Joe Lister, the Yorkshire secretary, asked for its return over the loudspeaker and it was duly handed over to a policeman. Boycott had his cap back and the show could go on.

Nowadays pitch invasions are simply not permitted. Even at sparsely attended county matches, stewards lurk at the boundary's edge to prevent anyone putting a foot on the hallowed outfield. But that in turn has led to some extravagant individual celebrations of centuries.

Indeed at times it has appeared that the celebration has become every bit as important as the century itself. Some cricketers have become peacocks, fluttering their feathers upon reaching their milestone. And we are not just talking about Kevin Pietersen here, even if he is the obvious example of how the century has become an exultant exhibition of self-glorification, rather than the acknowledgement of the crowd's applause, as it was once merely was.

Goodness, when Patsy Hendren made a century for

Middlesex in his last match in 1937, the crowd sang 'For He's a Jolly Good Fellow'!

It is probably all Michael Slater's fault. When he made an Ashes century at Lord's in 1993, his first Test century in only his third innings, he ran, leapt wildly and punched the air, and then took off his helmet to kiss his Australia badge.

'I was pretty out of control,' Slater said. 'After that it became my thing – the emotion I always played with. I'm glad I did it. If I started a trend it is a good one. People have said, "Were you always going to do that if you got 100?" And it was "no". It was very instinctual. It was the only way I could express what it meant to me at the time.'

As a youngster Michael Clarke had a poster of that celebration on his bedroom wall, and he vowed that he would kiss the Australia badge too when he made his maiden Test century.

But he wanted to kiss the badge on his baggy green cap rather than a helmet, so in October 2004 in Bangalore when he was on 97 he stopped the bowler, the left-arm seamer Zaheer Khan, and called for his baggy green. It was a hugely brave move, tempting fate, as well as enraging the bowler, because all fast bowlers see it as an affront these days if a batsman does not don a helmet.

But, no matter, soon afterwards Clarke was clipping Irfan Pathan through mid-wicket and beginning his own frenzied celebrations: running, jumping, waving at his parents, maybe even crying a little, before planting that kiss on the badge of his cap.

'I remember calling for my baggy green on 97 because when I was a young kid sitting in the car with my dad, I said to him "If I ever get the chance to play cricket for Australia and if I score a hundred, I want to do it wearing that baggy green cap,"' says Clarke.

When Ricky Ponting made his first Test hundred, in his seventh Test, against England at Headingley in 1997, he admits that 'I nearly pulled my right arm [the one holding his bat] out of its socket as I punched the air in delight.'

For Michael Vaughan his first Test century did not quite go to plan. He was on 84 not out overnight against Pakistan at Old Trafford in 2001. 'Try as I might to avoid it,' he says, 'I could not get out of my head how I was going to celebrate three figures and where I was going to raise my bat to. Was I going to be superficially cool or let my emotions all hang out?'

As it happened he got to his hundred when Wasim Akram hurled the ball for four overthrows. He had actually hit a six to reach his maiden Test century, but it was hardly in the 'grand manner'. There was an awkward pause until the crowd realized. 'So much for the classic celebration!' said Vaughan.

By contrast West Indian wicketkeeper Denesh Ramdin had his celebratory intentions well planned, should he get a century at Edgbaston against England in 2012. Remarkably he had written a note to Sir Vivian Richards that he wanted to show in response to criticism from the great Antiguan batsman. And this was even though he had made just one century from 44 previous Tests.

He made the century and duly showed the note to the world. 'Yeah Viv, talk nah,' it said. But it was silly in so many ways. As Nasser Hussain said: 'My first thought when I saw Denesh Ramdin wave his bit of paper was: "Crikey, I hope he doesn't mean that Viv!" Because, let's face it, Sir Isaac Vivian Richards is not the first bloke you'd pick a fight with.'

Exactly. I would wager that Richards learnt a bit over the years from his love of proper pugilism in the ring. He is not a man with whom to mess. And Ramdin's gesture was made to look even sillier when he was fined 20 per cent of his match fee.

As match referee Roshan Mahanama said: 'We all understand the importance of celebrating a milestone; however, one should not use that time as an opportunity to hit out at one's critic or send messages to the world.

'I hope Mr Ramdin has learnt his lesson from this incident and that we will not see such behaviour by him or any player in the future when celebrating an achievement within a game of international cricket.'

There can be fun in century (or double-century) celebrations, though. When Steve Waugh made 200 against West Indies in Kingston in 1995, his highest Test score, his former team-mate Greg Ritchie, who was leading a tour group, came onto the field.

'The fumes of the Cockspur had the same effect on me as smelling salts on a knocked-out boxer,' said Waugh. 'I sprang to life, catching the comments of Richie Richardson: "Hello, 'Fat Cat', what are you doing here? You should know better."'

It was rather like when Wales rugby union winger George North's father ran onto the field after North scored against France in Paris in 2013.

When Murray Goodwin made a century against England at Trent Bridge in 2000 he tried to kiss his bat, but then realized that he was still wearing his helmet. 'Yes, the grille was in the way!' he laughs.

For many, though, the celebrations are still understated, old-school even. Take Peter Fulton when he made his twin centuries (his only two in Test cricket) against England in Auckland in 2013. He merely raised his bat undemonstratively and carried on almost regardless.

So too Australia's Chris Rogers. Such was his struggle to make his maiden Test century against England at Durham in 2013 that he almost seemed embarrassed. As I wrote at the time: 'He removed his helmet and raised his bat in the air. It was the most old-fashioned of celebrations from a very old-fashioned and, in modern cricketing terms, a very old Test cricketer. Rogers will be 36 at the end of the month.'

Graham Gooch would have approved. 'I'm one of those guys – pretty boring and miserable – for whom there is not a lot of difference between getting nought and 100,' he says. 'There was no kissing of the badge, although if I'd thought about that at the time I would have done that. Kissing the wicket [as Brian Lara did when twice breaking the world record] is a good idea!'

So too Andy Flower. 'My celebration was always fairly muted,' he says. 'The reason for that was the crowd applauds you when you get 100 and the raising of the bat is in acknowledgement of their applause. I would imagine that is done in a reasonably dignified manner. You are saying thank you. It is not a raising of the bat saying: "Wow, look at me, this is how great I am." I think that maybe that is missed by some players – each to his own. I am overjoyed for people who score hundreds and if they want to celebrate in their own way that is their right. I never pointed at the number on my back.'

Flower tails off with a mischievous smile. It is a little dig aimed at his former Essex team-mate Nasser Hussain (and the 'Wow, look at me' reference may just have been to Kevin Pietersen), who in 2002 at Lord's scored his only one-day international century and gave a three-fingered salute to the media centre before pointing to the number on his back. He had been heavily criticized about his role at No. 3 in the one-day side by the likes of Jonathan Agnew, Ian Botham and Bob Willis, and this was his response.

'I had decided to use the criticism I'd received as a motivational factor,' Hussain says. 'When I reached three figures, I felt I would not have been true to myself had I not carried through with the promise I'd made to myself – so I ended up doing my mad gesticulation. I can barely go a session in the commentary box these days without some comedian bringing it up!'

Yes, we all do things we regret. It will be of no surprise to you to learn that I was not an ostentatious celebrator. A quick raise of the bat to the dressing room and to the crowd, and that was it. But on one occasion I did go a little further.

It was upon making a Sunday League hundred at Hartlepool in 1994. I was not in the county championship side at the time and my jumping up and down and fist pumping was directed at captain Hugh Morris.

It was puerile, and served no purpose whatsoever. That night I had to drive to Sittingbourne in Kent to play a second-team match. I made 37 in the first innings, but in the second I was out first ball. The lesson was clear: do not mess with the game.

And do not take it for granted either.

Upon retiring in 2004, I said I would miss two things from playing professional cricket. One was, slightly light-heartedly, playing touch rugby with the boys in the morning and the other was the thrill of scoring a century.

For the first I have found a replacement in that, although I could never play touch rugby these days because of my dodgy knee, my love of rugby union has been sated by my recent appointment as the *Sunday Telegraph*'s rugby union correspondent.

For the second? Sadly, there is no replacement. I have actually scored one century since retirement, for Lydney in a midweek match against a touring side. But I doubt I will ever score another, because the body is no longer willing.

It is a feeling you simply cannot replicate, but, goodness, I miss it.

Bibliography

Arnot, Chris, *Britain's Lost Cricket Festivals: The Idyllic Club Grounds That Will Never Again Host the World's Best Players* (Aurum Press, 2014)

Atherton, Mike, *Opening Up: My Autobiography* (Hodder & Stoughton, 2002)

Boycott, Geoffrey, *Boycott: The Autobiography* (Macmillan, 1987)

Bradman, Sir Donald, *The Art of Cricket* (Hodder & Stoughton, 1974)

Cook, Alastair, *Starting Out: My Story So Far* (Hodder & Stoughton, 2008)

Ezekiel, Gulu, *Sachin: The Story of the World's Greatest Batsman* (Penguin India, 2002)

Fletcher, Duncan, *Behind the Shades: The Autobiography* (Simon & Schuster, 2007)

Gatting, Mike, *Limited Overs* (Macdonald: Queen Anne Press, 1986)

Gladwell, Malcolm, *Outliers: The Story of Success* (Allen Lane, 2008)

Gooch, Graham, *Gooch: My Autobiography* (CollinsWillow, 1995)

Gower, David, *An Endangered Species: The Autobiography* (Simon & Schuster, 2013)

Hayden, Matthew, *Standing My Ground* (Aurum Press, 2011)

Hick, Graeme, *My Early Life* (Macmillan, 1991)

Hignell, Alastair, *Higgy: Matches, Microphones and MS* (A. & C. Black, 2011)

Hussain, Nasser, *Playing With Fire: The Autobiography* (Michael Joseph, 2004)

Hussey, Michael, *Mr Cricket: Driven to Succeed* (Hardie Grant, 2007)

Jones, Alan, *Hooked on Opening* (Gomer Press, 1984)

Langer, Justin, *Seeing the Sunrise* (Allen & Unwin, 2008)

Lara, Brian, *Beating the Field: My Own Story* (Partridge Press, 1995)

McKinstry, Leo, *Jack Hobbs: England's Greatest Cricketer* (Yellow Jersey, 2011)

Meher-Homji, Kersi, *The Nervous Nineties* (Kangaroo Press, 1994)

Murphy, Patrick, *The Centurions from Grace to Ramprakash* (Fairfield Books, 2009)

Peel, Mark, *England Expects: A Biography of Ken Barrington* (Kingswood Press, 1992)

Ponting, Ricky, *Ponting: At the Close of Play: My Autobiography* (HarperSport, 2013)

Prior, Matt, *The Gloves Are Off: My Life in Cricket* (Simon & Schuster, 2013)

Purandare, Vaibhav, *Sachin Tendulkar: The Definitive Biography* (The History Press, 2008)

Ramprakash, Mark, *Strictly Me: My Life under the Spotlight* (Mainstream, 2009)

Richards, Viv, *Sir Vivian: The Definitive Autobiography* (Michael Joseph, 2000)

Smith, Ed, *Luck: What It Means and Why It Matters* (Bloomsbury, 2012)

Strauss, Andrew, *Driving Ambition: My Autobiography* (Hodder & Stoughton, 2013)

Syed, Matthew, *Bounce: How Champions Are Made* (Fourth Estate, 2010)

BIBLIOGRAPHY

Vaughan, Michael, *Time to Declare: My Autobiography* (Hodder & Stoughton, 2009)

Waugh, Steve, *Out of My Comfort Zone: The Autobiography* (Michael Joseph, 2006)

Index

INDEX

The Plan
How Fletcher and Flower Transformed English Cricket
Steve James

CRICKET WRITERS' CLUB BOOK OF THE YEAR 2012

In the summer of 2011, England demolished India to become the number one Test team in the world. It was a stunning achievement, following back-to-back Ashes victories, marked by devastating bowling, ruthless batting and all-round excellence on and off the field. Yet twelve years earlier, England could not have stooped lower. Defeat by New Zealand saw the nation that invented the game hit rock bottom, below even Zimbabwe. Just how did this remarkable transformation happen?

In *The Plan*, Steve James recounts how Duncan Fletcher and Andy Flower were at the heart of the renaissance. With unprecedented inside access to key figures in the sport, astute tactical analysis and entertaining anecdotes, it is the authoritative account of a brilliant, and very deliberate, overhaul of English cricket.

> 'Rich in unfamiliar detail . . . The cricket points are well made, the personal judgements astute. Like his subjects, James has made a good plan and stuck to it'
> Gideon Haigh, *The Cricketer*

> 'The most insightful cricket book of the year'
> *Daily Mail*

> 'Excellent'
> *The Times*